Econometrics

FOR

DUMMIES®

A Wiley Brand

by Roberto Pedace

FOR

DUMMIES®

A Wiley Brand

Econometrics For Dummies®

Published by
John Wiley & Sons, Inc.
111 River St.
Hoboken, NJ 07030-5774
www.wiley.com

Copyright © 2013 by John Wiley & Sons, Inc., Hoboken, New Jersey

Published by John Wiley & Sons, Inc., Hoboken, New Jersey

Published simultaneously in Canada

For general information on our other products and services, please contact our Customer Care Department within the U.S. at 877-762-2974, outside the U.S. at 317-572-3993, or fax 317-572-4002.

For technical support, please visit www.wiley.com/techsupport.

Wiley publishes in a variety of print and electronic formats and by print-on-demand. Some material included with standard print versions of this book may not be included in e-books or in print-on-demand. If this book refers to media such as a CD or DVD that is not included in the version you purchased, you may download this material at http://booksupport.wiley.com. For more information about Wiley products, visit www.wiley.com.

Library of Congress Control Number: 2013934761

ISBN 978-1-118-53384-0 (pbk); ISBN 978-1-118-53387-1 (ebk); ISBN 978-1-118-53388-8 (ebk); ISBN 978-1-118-53391-8 (ebk)

Manufactured in the United States of America

10 9 8 7 6 5 4 3 2 1

About the Author

Roberto Pedace is an associate professor of economics at Scripps College in Claremont, California. Prior to joining the faculty at Scripps College, he held positions at Claremont Graduate University, the University of Redlands, Claremont McKenna College, and the U.S. Census Bureau. He holds a PhD in economics from the University of California, Riverside.

Roberto regularly teaches courses in the areas of statistics, microeconomics, labor economics, and econometrics. While at the University of Redlands, he was nominated for both the Innovative Teaching Award and the Outstanding Teaching Award. At Scripps College, he was recognized for his scholarly achievements by winning the Mary W. Johnson Faculty Achievement Award in Scholarship.

Roberto's academic research interests are in the area of labor and personnel economics. His work addresses a variety of important public policy issues, including the effects of immigration on domestic labor markets and the impact of minimum wages on job training and unemployment. He also examines salary determination and personnel decisions in markets for professional athletes. His published work appears in the *Southern Economic Journal,* the *Journal of Sports Economics, Contemporary Economic Policy, Industrial Relations,* and other outlets.

Roberto is also a soccer fanatic. He's been playing soccer since the age of 5, paid for most of his undergraduate education with a soccer scholarship, and had a short semi-professional stint in the USISL (now known as the United Soccer League). He continues to participate in leagues and tournaments but now mostly enjoys sitting on the sidelines watching his children play soccer.

Dedication

To my wife, Cynthia, for supporting me emotionally and being a wonderful mother to our children. To my children, Vincent and Emily, for brightening up my days.

Author's Acknowledgments

None of this would have been possible if my professors hadn't motivated me and given me a solid foundation in economics. My undergraduate adviser at California State University, San Bernardino, Thomas Pierce, opened my eyes to the world of economics and gave me wonderful advice in preparation for graduate school. I was fortunate to have taken several courses from Nancy Rose and Mayo Toruño, who helped me see economics in a different light when standard theory just wasn't helping me understand certain aspects of the world. Kazim Konyar was the first to introduce me to the realm of econometrics and helped me understand how it could be a powerful complement to economic theory. At the University of California, Riverside, Aman Ullah's uncanny ability to make advanced econometric theory comprehensible to a first-year graduate student solidified my interest in the topic. Finally, in his labor economics course and as my dissertation adviser, David Fairris taught me the art of using econometrics to address important economic policy issues.

Many of my econometrics students deserve special gratitude. Several of them stand out: Lora Brill, Megan Cornell, Guadalupe De La Cruz, Matthew Lang, Chandler Lutz, India Mullady, and Stephanie Rohn. Some became friends, a few colleagues, and a couple coauthors, but all inspired me to think of effective approaches to making econometrics accessible, useful, and interesting.

I thank Sean Flynn, my friend and colleague, for believing that I'd be the best person to write this book and Linda Roghaar, my literary agent, for listening to Sean and having faith in my ability to complete the project.

The folks at Wiley have also been incredibly supportive. In particular, I'd like to thank Jennifer Tebbe, my project editor, for working with me every step of the way and keeping me motivated to stay on track with my deadlines. No matter how long the tunnel, she always helped me see the light at the end. Erin Calligan Mooney, my acquisitions editor at Wiley, also helped me get through my sample chapter and ensured that it would meet the standards of others on the editorial team. My copy editor, Caitie Copple, and technical reviewers, Ariel Belasen and Nicole Bissessar, were ideal for this project. Their "eagle eyes" were instrumental in finding my mistakes and improving the finished product.

My research assistant, Anne Miles, gathered data for some of the examples I use in the book and assisted with the imaging of figures and graphs. Her turnaround time was amazing, and I'll be forever grateful for all the hard work she provided on this project. I also want to thank my friend and colleague, Latika Chaudhary, for responding immediately to an urgent request for a sample of panel data.

Last, but not least, I'd like to thank my family and friends for being patient with me while I wrote this book. I know that sometimes I wasn't myself and that I'll need to make up for lost time.

Publisher's Acknowledgments

We're proud of this book; please send us your comments at http://dummies.custhelp.com. For other comments, please contact our Customer Care Department within the U.S. at 877-762-2974, outside the U.S. at 317-572-3993, or fax 317-572-4002.

Some of the people who helped bring this book to market include the following:

Acquisitions, Editorial, and Vertical Websites

Project Editor: Jennifer Tebbe

Acquisitions Editor: Erin Calligan Mooney

Copy Editor: Caitlin Copple

Assistant Editor: David Lutton

Editorial Program Coordinator: Joe Niesen

Technical Editors: Ariel Belasen, Nicole Bissessar

Editorial Manager: Christine Meloy Beck

Editorial Assistants: Rachelle S. Amick, Alexa Koschier

Cover Photo: © iStockphoto.com/studiocasper

Composition Services

Project Coordinator: Sheree Montgomery

Layout and Graphics: Carrie A. Cesavice, Christin Swinford

Proofreader: Melissa Cossell

Indexer: Riverside Indexes, Inc.

Publishing and Editorial for Consumer Dummies

Kathleen Nebenhaus, Vice President and Executive Publisher

David Palmer, Associate Publisher

Kristin Ferguson-Wagstaffe, Product Development Director

Publishing for Technology Dummies

Andy Cummings, Vice President and Publisher

Composition Services

Debbie Stailey, Director of Composition Services

Contents at a Glance

Table of Contents

Introduction

・・・

*M*y appreciation for econometrics grew out of my interest in trying to figure out how the world works. I discovered that empirical techniques tailored to specific circumstances could help explain all sorts of economic outcomes. As I came to understand how the theoretical structure of economics combines with information contained in real-world data, I began to see observed phenomena in a different light. I'd often ask myself questions about my observations. Could I determine whether the outcomes were random and simply appeared to be related? If I believed that two or more things I observed had a logical connection, could I use data to test my assertions? Increasingly, I found myself relying on the tools of econometrics to answer these types of questions.

I've written *Econometrics For Dummies* to help you get the most out of your economics education. By now, your classes have taught you some economic theory, but you're craving more precision in the predicted outcomes of those theories. Perhaps you're even questioning whether the theories are consistent with what you observe in the real world. I find that one of the most attractive characteristics of properly applied econometrics is that it's "school of thought neutral." In other words, you can adapt an econometric approach to a variety of initial assumptions and check the results for consistency. By using econometrics carefully and conscientiously, you can get the data to speak. But you better learn the language if you hope to understand what it's saying!

About This Book

Econometrics For Dummies provides you with a short and simple version of a first-semester course in econometrics. I don't cite the seminal work or anything from the large collection of econometric theory papers published in scholarly journals. The organization of topics may have some resemblance to traditional econometrics textbooks, but my goal is to present the material in a more straightforward manner. Even if you're taking a second-semester (advanced) econometrics course or a graduate course, you may find this book to be a useful, one-stop, nuts-and-bolts resource.

Of course, some technical sophistication is essential in econometrics. Besides, you've taken introductory economics, statistics, and maybe even intermediate economic theory, so now you're ready to show off your technical prowess. But wait a minute! Sometimes, with all the technical skills being mastered in learning econometrics, students fail to appreciate the insights from the simplicity. In fact, you may even forget why you're approaching a problem with a particular technique. That's where this book can help.

Please note that I have tried to remain consistent with my terminology throughout the book, but econometricians sometimes have several different words for the same thing. Also, note that I use the statistical software STATA 12.1 throughout, but sometimes I refer to it simply as *econometrics software* or just *STATA*.

Foolish Assumptions

If you're following the normal course of action, you take an econometrics course after you complete courses on principles of microeconomics, principles of macroeconomics, and statistics. In some cases, depending on the school, you may also be required to complete intermediate economic theory courses before taking econometrics. I cover the topics in a way that accommodates some variation in preexisting knowledge, but I've had to make the following assumptions about you:

- You're a college student taking your first econometrics class taught in a traditional manner — emphasizing a combination of theoretical proofs and practical applications.

- Or you're a graduate student (or are taking an advanced undergraduate econometrics class) and would like to refresh your memory of basic econometric concepts so you can feel more comfortable with the transition into advanced material.

- You remember basic algebra, principles of economics, and statistics. I review the concepts from your statistics course that are most important for econometrics, but I also assume that a quick overview is all you need to get up to speed (and you can skip it if you're ready to dig right in).

- Numbers, equations, and Greek letters don't intimidate you. I know that on the surface using the so-called dismal science with quantitative methods isn't exactly the most attractive combination of topics. By this point in your studies, however, I'm sure you're over the fear people often have at the mere mention of these subjects.

- You'll be using some econometrics software in your class and are willing to adapt my examples in STATA to the software you're using (although chances are high you're using STATA in your class anyway).

Icons Used in This Book

Throughout the book, you may notice several different icons along the left margin. I use them to grab your attention and make the book easier to read. Each icon has an important function.

If you see this icon, it means I'm applying the techniques of a particular chapter or section with STATA. I briefly summarize the data I'm using to produce the output, show you how to format the data or create the variables required for the analysis, and point you to the most important components of the output.

I use this icon to signal that the information that follows is essential for your success in applying econometric analysis. To the extent possible, I explain these important, big-picture ideas in a nontechnical manner. However, keep in mind that this book is about econometrics, and therefore some technical sophistication may be required for even the most basic principles.

This icon appears next to information that's interesting but not essential for your understanding of the main ideas. You're welcome to skip these paragraphs, but if your econometrics class is more theory based (something that usually depends on the professor's preferences), you may need to spend more time with this material.

I use this icon to indicate shortcuts that can save you time or provide alternative ways of thinking about a concept.

This icon flags information that helps you steer away from misconceptions, common pitfalls, and inappropriate applications of a particular econometric technique.

Beyond the Book

You may not always have your e-reader or a copy of this book handy, but I'm guessing you have almost constant access to the Internet courtesy of a smartphone or tablet. That's why I include a wealth of accessible-from-anywhere additional information at www.dummies.com.

In need of some of the most useful formulas in econometrics? Looking for a breakdown of how you can give your econometric model some flexibility? Head to www.dummies.com/cheatsheet/econometrics to access this book's helpful e-Cheat Sheet, which covers these topics and more.

But that's not all. Because *econometrics* is synonymous with *forecasting* in some fields, I've put a bonus chapter online at www.dummies.com/extras/econometrics. It's all about helping you hone your forecasting skills so you can select the right method to predict an outcome based on the information you have and later vet the accuracy of your forecast.

Where to Go from Here

Unlike most books, you don't need to start at the beginning and read through to the end in order to gain an understanding of fundamental econometric concepts. Simply turn to the topic that most interests you. Are you struggling with the intuition or justification for a particular type of econometric model? Do you think that a specific econometric tool will help you reveal more insights from your data? You can find that topic in the table of contents or the index and then jump right to it.

Maybe you're not puzzled and are simply curious about the various tools econometrics has to offer for data analysis. Feel free to browse through the chapters. Maybe an interesting paragraph or a fascinating equation will catch your eye and give you ideas about approaching a problem — hey, it's possible!

If your statistics knowledge is rusty, I recommend you begin with the first couple chapters. On the other hand, if your experience with statistics wasn't a good one, you'd like to avoid disturbing flashbacks, and you're confident in your ability to catch on quickly, then by all means start at any other point. No matter where you start, you'll never look at data the same way after learning econometrics (for better or for worse!).

Part I
Getting Started with Econometrics

In this part . . .

✔ Get familiar with the approach economists use when investigating empirical issues — not controlled experiments that never seem to contradict standard statistical assumptions.

✔ Find out the basic commands you need to work with data files in STATA 12.1, a popular form of econometric software, and discover the syntax structure for executing estimation commands.

✔ Review the probability concepts that are most relevant for your study of econometrics: topics that focus on the properties of probability distributions and their use in calculating descriptive statistics of random variables.

✔ Reinforce your knowledge of statistical inference so you can be better equipped to use surveys and other forms of sample data to test your hypotheses and draw conclusions.

Chapter 1

Econometrics: The Economist's Approach to Statistical Analysis

- -

In This Chapter

▶ Discovering the goals of econometric analysis

▶ Understanding the approach and methodology of econometrics

▶ Getting familiar with econometrics software

- -

*W*elcome to the study of econometrics! The Econometric Society, founded in 1930, defines econometrics as a field based on a "theoretical-quantitative and empirical-quantitative approach to economic problems." This mouthful means that, at times, econometricians are mathematicians and use complex algorithms and analytical tools to derive various estimation and testing procedures. At other times, econometricians are applied economists using the tools developed by theoretical econometricians to examine economic phenomena.

In this chapter, you see that a distinguishing feature of econometrics is its development of techniques designed to deal with data that aren't derived from controlled experiments and, therefore, situations that violate many of the standard statistical assumptions. You also begin to understand that, under these circumstances, obtaining good quantitative results depends on using reliable and adequate data as well as sound economic theory.

And because computers and econometric software are now commonly used in introductory econometrics courses, I also devote a section of this chapter to introducing basic commands in STATA (version 12.1), a popular econometrics software program. This software allows you to immediately apply theoretical concepts and enhance your understanding of the material.

Evaluating Economic Relationships

Economics provides the theoretical tools you use to evaluate economic relationships and make qualitative predictions of economic phenomena using the *ceteris paribus* assumption. You may recall from your previous courses that the *ceteris paribus* assumption means that you're keeping everything else constant. Two examples among numerous possibilities are:

- ✔ In microeconomic theory, you'd expect economic profits in a competitive market to induce more firms to enter that market, *ceteris paribus*.

- ✔ In macroeconomic theory, you'd expect higher interest rates to reduce investment spending, *ceteris paribus*.

Econometrics ties into economic theory by providing the tools necessary to quantify the qualitative statements you (or others) make using theory. Unknown or assumed relationships from abstract theory can be quantified using real-world data and the techniques developed by econometricians.

The following section explains how econometrics helps characterize the future and describe economic phenomena quantitatively, and then I clarify why an econometrician must always make sensible assumptions.

Using economic theory to describe outcomes and make predictions

One of the characteristics that differentiate applied research in econometrics from other applications of statistical analysis is a theoretical structure supporting the empirical work.

Econometrics is typically used to explain how factors affect some outcome of interest or to predict future events. Regardless of the primary objective, your econometric study should be linked to an economic model. Your model should consist of an outcome of interest (dependent variable, Y) and causal factors (independent variables, Xs) that are theoretically or logically connected to the outcome.

Relying on sensible assumptions

A variation of a famous joke about economists goes as follows: A physicist, a chemist, and an economist are stranded on an island with nothing to eat.

A can of soup washes ashore. The physicist says, "Let's smash the can open with a rock." The chemist says, "Let's build a fire and heat the can first." The economist says, "Let's assume that we have a can opener. . . ." Despite the joke, making assumptions about reality can help you construct logical arguments and predict outcomes when specific preexisting conditions apply. In econometrics, however, making assumptions without checking the feasibility of their reality can be dangerous.

Making too many assumptions about preexisting conditions, functional form, and statistical properties can lead to biased results and can undermine the estimation accuracy you're trying to accomplish. Although you have to make some assumptions to perform your econometric work, you should test most of them and be honest about any potential effects on your results from those you can't test.

Testing predictions from economic theory or logical reasoning is rarely a straightforward procedure. Observed data don't tend to be generated from a controlled experiment, so testing economic theory is challenging in econometric work because of the difficulty in ensuring that the *ceteris paribus* (all else constant) assumption holds. Consequently, in applying econometrics, you need to give considerable attention to the control (independent) variables you include in the analysis to simulate (as closely as possible) the *ceteris paribus* situation.

Applying Statistical Methods to Economic Problems

Most econometrics textbooks assume you've learned all the statistics necessary to begin building econometric models, estimating, and testing hypotheses. However, I've discovered that my students always appreciate a review of the statistical concepts that are most important to succeeding with econometrics. Specifically, you need to be comfortable with probability distributions, the calculation of descriptive statistics, and hypothesis tests. (If your skills are rusty in these areas, make sure you read the material in Chapters 2 and 3.)

Your ability to accurately quantify economic relationships depends not only on your econometric model-building skills but also on the quality of the data you're using for analysis and your capacity to adopt the appropriate strategies for estimating models that are likely to violate a statistical assumption. The data must be derived from a reliable collection process, but you should also be aware of any additional limitations or challenges. They may include, but aren't limited to

- **Aggregation of data:** Information that may have originated at a household, individual, or firm level is being measured at a city, county, state, or country level in your data.

- **Statistically correlated but economically irrelevant variables:** Some datasets contain an abundance of information, but many of the variables may have nothing to do with the economic question you're hoping to address.

- **Qualitative data:** Rich datasets typically include qualitative variables (geographic information, race, and so on), but this information requires special treatment before you can use it in an econometric model.

- **Classical linear regression model (CLRM) assumption failure:** The legitimacy of your econometric approach always rests on a set of statistical assumptions, but you're likely to find that at least one of these assumptions doesn't hold (meaning it isn't true for your data).

Econometricians differentiate themselves from statisticians by emphasizing violations of statistical assumptions that are often taken for granted. The most common technique for estimating an econometric model is ordinary least squares (OLS), which I cover in Chapter 5. However, as I explain in Chapters 6 and 7, a number of CLRM assumptions must hold in order for the OLS technique to provide reliable estimates. In practice, the assumptions that are most likely to fail depend on your data and specific application. (In Chapters 10, 11, and 12, you see how to identify and deal with the most common assumption violations.)

In the following sections, I describe how familiarity with certain characteristics of your data can help you build better econometric models. In particular, you should pay attention to the structure of your data, the way in which variables are measured, and how quantitative data can be complemented with qualitative information.

Recognizing the importance of data type, frequency, and aggregation

The data that you use to estimate and test your econometric model is typically classified into one of three possible types (for further details on each type, see Chapter 4):

- **Cross sectional:** This type of data consists of measurements for individual observations (persons, households, firms, counties, states, countries, or whatever) at a given point in time.

✔ **Time series:** This type of data consists of measurements on one or more variables (such as gross domestic product, interest rates, or unemployment rates) over time in a given space (like a specific country or state).

✔ **Panel or longitudinal:** This type of data consists of a time series for each cross-sectional unit in the sample. The data contains measurements for individual observations (persons, households, firms, counties, states, countries, and so on) over a period of time (days, months, quarters, or years).

The type of data you're using may influence how you estimate your econometric model. In particular, specialized techniques are usually required to deal with time-series and panel data. I cover time-series techniques in Chapter 12, and I discuss panel techniques in Chapters 16 and 17.

You can anticipate common econometric problems because certain CLRM assumption failures are more likely with particular types of data. Two typical cases of CLRM assumption failures involve heteroskedasticity (which occurs frequently in models using cross-sectional data) and autocorrelation (which tends to be present in models using time-series data). For the full scoop on heteroskedasticity and autocorrelation, turn to Chapters 11 and 12, respectively.

In addition to knowing the type of data you're working with, make sure you're always aware of the following information:

✔ **The level of *aggregation* used in measuring the variables:** The level of aggregation refers to the unit of analysis when information is acquired for the data. In other words, the variable measurements may originate at a lower level of aggregation (like an individual, household, or firm) or at a higher level of aggregation (like a city, county, or state).

✔ **The *frequency* with which the data is captured:** The frequency refers to the rate at which measurements are obtained. Time-series data may be captured at a higher frequency (like hourly, daily, or weekly) or at lower frequency (like monthly, quarterly, or yearly).

All the data in the world won't allow you to produce convincing results if the level of aggregation or frequency isn't appropriate for your problem. For example, if you're interested in determining how spending per pupil affects academic achievement, state-level data probably won't be appropriate because spending and pupil characteristics have so much variation across cities within states that your results are likely to be misleading.

Avoiding the data-mining trap

As you acquire more data-analysis tools, you may be inclined to search the data for relationships between variables. You can use your knowledge of statistics to find models that fit your data quite well. However, this practice is known as *data mining,* and you don't want to be seduced by it!

Although data mining can be useful in fields where the underlying mechanism generating the outcomes isn't important, most economists don't view this approach favorably. In econometrics, building a model that makes sense and is reproducible by others is far more important than searching for a model that has a perfect fit. I reinforce the importance of building sensible models in Chapter 4 and provide some specific examples of common economic models in Chapter 8.

Incorporating quantitative and qualitative information

Economic outcomes can be affected by both quantitative (numeric) and qualitative (non-numeric) factors. Generally, quantitative information has a straightforward application and interpretation in econometric models.

Qualitative variables are associated with characteristics that have no natural numeric representation, although your raw data may code qualitative characteristics with a numeric value. For example, a U.S. region may be coded with a 1 for West, 2 for South, 3 for Midwest, and 4 for Northeast. However, the assignment of the specific values is arbitrary and carries no special significance. In order to utilize the information contained in qualitative variables, you'll usually convert them into *dummy variables* — dichotomous variables that take on a value of 1 if a particular characteristic is present and 0 otherwise. I illustrate the use of dummy variables as independent variables in an econometric model in Chapter 9.

Sometimes the economic outcome itself is qualitative or contains restricted values. For example, your dependent variable could measure whether or not a firm fails (goes bankrupt) in a given year using various firm characteristics as independent variables. Although standard techniques are sometimes acceptable with qualitative and noncontinuous dependent variables, usually they result in assumption violations and require an alternative econometric approach. Flip to Chapters 13 and 14 to discover the appropriate techniques for situations when your dependent variable isn't continuous.

Using Econometric Software: An Introduction to STATA

Specialized software makes the application of econometric techniques possible for anyone who's not a computer programming genius. Keep in mind that several good software options are available to you and that, as a good economist, you should weigh the cost and benefits of each. Of course, the type of software you ultimately end up working with in your introductory econometrics course depends on what your professor uses for his research or finds to be the easiest to integrate into the course. I rely on STATA extensively in my academic research and use it exclusively in my econometrics courses, but your professor may employ EVIEWS, SAS, or some other program.

Because I find STATA to be the best software, it's what I use exclusively in this book. It provides an excellent combination of a user-friendly interface, consistent structure in syntax, and simple commands to implement all the techniques you learn about in econometrics, and it's available for a variety of platforms or operating systems.

STATA can be used as a *point-and-click* software (like you would use Excel or most other software these days). With point-and-click, you can use the icons and menu bar at the top to execute tasks. However, over time, you're likely to prefer using STATA as a *command-driven* program because it's faster and easier. When used in this manner, you perform tasks by providing STATA with specific syntax on the command line (using lowercase letters for the commands). In this chapter, I explain both methods, but in the later chapters, I rely almost exclusively on the command-driven approach.

The following sections show you some STATA commands that allow you to get started with the software. (Note that I introduce STATA commands as needed in other chapters.)

My coverage of STATA is not exhaustive. The supporting documentation consists of a User's Guide and several Reference manuals (thousands of pages), so clearly I can't cover every facet of STATA that you may use in econometrics. However, if you run into an obstacle, the manuals are easy to use and provide good examples. With STATA running on your computer, you also have access to the Help menu and online documentation.

Getting acquainted with STATA

In this section of the chapter, I show you how to open data files, log your modifications to data, and save your data files.

Creating and saving STATA datasets

In order to begin doing any exploratory data analysis or econometric work, you need a dataset that's in STATA format (*.dta). If you're downloading data from an online source, you may be able to obtain the data in STATA format. Many econometrics textbooks also give you access to data files in STATA format. In addition, the STATA program is preloaded with examples that you can use to familiarize yourself with the basic commands.

After opening STATA, you can access the sample datasets by selecting **File** ⇨ **Example Datasets...** If you want to open any other dataset that's already in STATA format, select **File** ⇨ **Open** and then choose the file you want to work with. On the command line, you can open a STATA dataset by typing "use *filename*" and hitting return.

If you're inputting data manually or downloading it in a non-STATA format, then you can use one of two methods to read it into STATA:

✔ Select **File** ⇨ **Import:** This option can be used if the data is in Excel, SAS XPORT, or Text format. You select the appropriate format of your raw data, and then you're prompted to select the file you'd like to import into STATA.

✔ Select **Data** ⇨ **Data Editor:** This option opens an editor that resembles a spreadsheet. You can paste columns of data into the editor or input data manually.

If you import a dataset that wasn't originally in STATA format, you need to save the dataset in STATA format in order to use it again, particularly if you inputted data through the editor and want to avoid replicating all your efforts. Also, if you made any changes to an existing STATA dataset and want to retain those changes, you need to save the revised dataset. I recommend you select **File** ⇨ **Save As** (or type "save *new filename*" on the command line) and choose a new name for the modified file. That way if you accidentally delete a variable or drop observations, you can always go back to the original data file.

Viewing data

Before you begin doing econometric analysis, make sure you're familiar with your data. After all, you don't want to estimate an econometric model with data that's mostly incomplete or full of errors.

In version 12.1 of STATA, the default setting allows you to open a dataset as large as 64 megabytes (MB) and containing up to 5,000 variables. If your dataset is larger than 64MB, you need to increase the memory allocated to STATA by typing "set memory #m" on the command line, where # is the size of your dataset in MB. Similarly, if your dataset contains more than 5,000 variables, you need to type "set maxvar #" on the command line, with # being the number of variables in your dataset.

The **Data** tab in the menu bar contains most of the elements you need in order to get acquainted with your data. After opening a STATA dataset, you'll regularly use the following commands:

✔ Select **Data** ⇨ **Describe data** ⇨ **Describe data in memory** or type "describe" on the command line and hit return: STATA shows you how many observations and variables are contained in the dataset. In addition, it lists the names and types (numeric or string) of all the variables.

✔ Select **Data** ⇨ **Describe data** ⇨ **Summary statistics** or type "summarize" on the command line and hit return: With this command, STATA provides you with basic descriptive measures for all the numeric variables in your dataset. Specifically, you get the number of observations with nonmissing values, mean, standard deviation, minimum value, and maximum value for each variable. *Note:* The string variables contain letters, names, or phrases, so no mean or standard deviation can be calculated for them.

In Figure 1-1, I use the "describe" and "summarize" commands to view the fundamental characteristics of my dataset.

The **Data** tab or "describe" and "summarize" commands provide the basic information you use for your econometric analysis. Examine the tables containing the descriptive information and make sure that all the values are sensible. In other words, make sure that the minimum, maximum, and mean values are feasible for each variable in your dataset.

You can also use the "list" command on occasion, but be careful with it because it displays the value for every variable and every observation. In other words, it displays the entire dataset. With a large dataset (thousands of observations and dozens of variables), this list isn't likely to help you find errors unless you refine the list to a specific observation using an "if" statement or by subscripting (I discuss this in the later "Creating new variables" section).

```
. describe

Contains data from /Applications/Stata/ado/base/c/census.dta
  obs:            50                          1980 Census data by state
 vars:            13                          6 Apr 2011 15:43
 size:         2,900

              storage  display    value
variable name   type   format     label      variable label

state          str14   %-14s                 State
state2         str2    %-2s                  Two-letter state abbreviation
region         int     %-8.0g     cenreg     Census region
pop            long    %12.0gc              Population
poplt5         long    %12.0gc              Pop, < 5 year
pop5_17        long    %12.0gc              Pop, 5 to 17 years
pop18p         long    %12.0gc              Pop, 18 and older
pop65p         long    %12.0gc              Pop, 65 and older
popurban       long    %12.0gc              Urban population
medage         float   %9.2f                Median age
death          long    %12.0gc              Number of deaths
marriage       long    %12.0gc              Number of marriages
divorce        long    %12.0gc              Number of divorces

Sorted by:

. summarize

    Variable |     Obs        Mean    Std. Dev.       Min        Max

       state |       0
      state2 |       0
      region |      50        2.66     1.061574         1          4
         pop |      50     4518149      4715038    401851   2.37e+07
      poplt5 |      50    326277.8     331585.1     35998    1708400

     pop5_17 |      50    945951.6     959372.8     91796    4680558
      pop18p |      50     3245920      3430531    271106   1.73e+07
      pop65p |      50    509502.8     538932.4     11547    2414250
    popurban |      50     3328253      4090178    172735   2.16e+07
      medage |      50       29.54     1.693445      24.2       34.7

       death |      50    39474.26     41742.35      1604     186428
    marriage |      50     47701.4     45130.42      4437     210864
     divorce |      50    23679.44     25094.01      2142     133541
```

Figure 1-1:
Examining
data two
ways in
STATA.

Keep in mind that the results section of STATA, by default, displays approximately one page of output. STATA then prompts you with the "-more-" message. Hitting the return key allows you to see an additional line of output, and hitting the spacebar shows another page of output. If you don't want STATA to pause for "-more-" messages, type "set more off" on the command line. Subsequent output is then displayed in its entirety.

Interpreting error messages

If you make a mistake with a command, STATA responds with an error message and code. The error message contains a brief description of the mistake, and the code has the format r(#), where # represents some number. Reading the error message and carefully examining the command that resulted in the error usually helps you arrive at a solution. If not, the codes, known as a return codes, are stored in STATA, and clicking on the code allows you to obtain a more detailed description of the error.

The outcome of a command can be identified quickly by looking at the colors of the text in the results area (the middle portion of STATA's interface). If you see the color red, it means something has gone wrong and you should correct your mistake before moving on.

Stopping STATA

When you occasionally want to terminate a process in STATA, you can just click the **Break** button on the toolbar (right below the menu bar). Stopping STATA may be appropriate if an estimation procedure doesn't converge to a result or you change your mind about the command you'd like to execute and don't want to wait until the process is complete. After you stop STATA, your data remains in memory, and you can continue with any command.

In Figure 1-2, I use the "list" command to see each observation in the dataset. However, after I see a few of the observations, I decide that I don't need to see more observations one by one. I click the **Break** button to stop the command.

Preserving your work

Saving your commands and resulting output in a log file is one of the most essential things you can get into the habit of doing while using STATA. You can do it by selecting **File ⇨ Log ⇨ Begin...** from the menu bar and then assigning the file a name or by typing "log using *filename*" on the command line and hitting return. After you complete the work you want to save, select **File ⇨ Log ⇨ Close** or type "log close" on the command line and hit return. Your log files are given a .smcl file extension.

```
. list
```

1.	state	state2	region	pop	poplt5	pop5_17	pop18p	pop65p	popurban	medage
	Alabama	AL	South	3,893,888	296,412	865,836	2,731,640	440,015	2,337,713	29.30

death		marriage		divorce	
35,305		49,018		26,745	

2.	state	state2	region	pop	poplt5	pop5_17	pop18p	pop65p	popurban	medage
	Alaska	AK	West	401,851	38,949	91,796	271,106	11,547	258,567	26.10

death		marriage		divorce	
1,604		5,361		3,517	

3.	state	state2	region	pop	poplt5	pop5_17	pop18p	pop65p	popurban	medage
	Arizona	AZ	West	2,718,215	213,883	577,604	1,926,728	307,362	2,278,728	29.20

death		marriage		divorce	
21,226		30,223		19,908	

```
4. ┌──────Break──────
   r(1);
```

Figure 1-2:
The break action in STATA.

In Figure 1-3, I open a log file, execute a "summarize" command, and close the log file. I can examine the contents of the log file by selecting **File ➪ View...** from the menu bar and then choosing my log file.

```
. log using "/Research/Econometrics for Dummies/ExampleData/Chapter1.smcl"

      name:  <unnamed>
       log:  /Research/Econometrics for Dummies/ExampleData/Chapter1.smcl
  log type:  smcl
 opened on:  29 Dec 2012, 19:04:55

. summarize
```

Variable	Obs	Mean	Std. Dev.	Min	Max
state	0				
state2	0				
region	50	2.66	1.061574	1	4
pop	50	4518149	4715038	401851	2.37e+07
poplt5	50	326277.8	331585.1	35998	1708400
pop5_17	50	945951.6	959372.8	91796	4680558
pop18p	50	3245920	3430531	271106	1.73e+07
pop65p	50	509502.8	538932.4	11547	2414250
popurban	50	3328253	4090178	172735	2.16e+07
medage	50	29.54	1.693445	24.2	34.7
death	50	39474.26	41742.35	1604	186428
marriage	50	47701.4	45130.42	4437	210864
divorce	50	23679.44	25094.01	2142	133541

Figure 1-3:
Saving
log files in
STATA.

```
. log close
      name:  <unnamed>
       log:  /Research/Econometrics for Dummies/ExampleData/Chapter1.smcl
  log type:  smcl
 closed on:  29 Dec 2012, 19:05:21
```

Using STATA's viewer, you can always go back to your log file to see how you modified the data or any statistical estimates you may have previously calculated. You can also copy and paste from your log file to any other file, or you can simply print your log file.

Don't forget to close your log file when you're done with the work you want to retain. Otherwise, everything you do in STATA continues to be written to the log file you opened, which may create an unnecessarily huge file.

Creating new variables

After you compile your data, you'll likely want to create new variables for the analysis. Your econometric model may specify that a variable should be measured in logs, or you may need to use a squared term for a quadratic function

(I cover these types of econometric models in Chapter 8). Your data may also contain qualitative variables that you want to convert into dummy variables (turn to Chapter 9 for guidance on using dummy variables). These examples are just a couple of the many instances in which creating a new variable is in your best interest.

You can create new variables in STATA by selecting **Data ⇨ Create or change data ⇨ Create new variable** from the menu bar or by typing "generate *new variable = exp* [*if*] [*in*]" on the command line, where *new variable* is the name you choose to assign the new variable, *exp* specifies how the new variable is created, and the terms in brackets are optional expressions that can be used to restrict the subsample over which you'd like to define the new variable.

A number of arithmetic, relational, and logical operators have been programmed into STATA and can be used to create new variables. You can browse through them in the STATA manuals or the electronic documentation.

I recommend using the "summarize" command after you create new variables. Doing so allows you to confirm that your new variable doesn't contain errors and that its values are in line with what you intended.

Estimating, testing, and predicting

After you collect your data and create any additional variables necessary for analysis, you're ready to estimate your econometric model and perform hypothesis tests.

The appropriate estimation technique depends on the nature of your econometric model. All the model estimation commands can be found by selecting **Statistics** from the menu bar. If you use the command line, you use similar syntax for all estimation techniques; the syntax is "command variable1 variable2 . . . [*if*] [*in*] [*weight*] [, *options*]" followed by hitting return, where variable1 is the dependent variable in your model.

In Figure 1-4, I estimate a multiple regression model using a sample of workers. The natural log of the hourly wage *(lnwage)* is my dependent variable, and I use years of work experience *(ttl_exp),* years with the same employer *(tenure),* and a dummy variable indicating whether the individual graduated from college *(collgrad)* as my independent variables. I also estimate the same model using the subsample of nonunionized workers.

```
. regress lnwage ttl_exp tenure collgrad
```

Source	SS	df	MS
Model	170.188489	3	56.7294962
Residual	562.028579	2227	.252370265
Total	732.217068	2230	.328348461

```
                                            Number of obs =   2231
                                            F(  3,  2227) = 224.79
                                            Prob > F      = 0.0000
                                            R-squared     = 0.2324
                                            Adj R-squared = 0.2314
                                            Root MSE      = .50236
```

lnwage	Coef.	Std. Err.	t	P>|t|	[95% Conf. Interval]	
ttl_exp	.0356556	.0028345	12.58	0.000	.030097	.0412142
tenure	.0114908	.0023639	4.86	0.000	.0068551	.0161265
collgrad	.3772924	.0251529	15.00	0.000	.3279667	.4266181
_cons	1.266701	.031668	40.00	0.000	1.204599	1.328803

```
. regress lnwage ttl_exp tenure collgrad if union==0
```

Source	SS	df	MS
Model	112.636632	3	37.545544
Residual	273.242718	1404	.19461732
Total	385.87935	1407	.274256823

```
                                            Number of obs =   1408
                                            F(  3,  1404) = 192.92
                                            Prob > F      = 0.0000
                                            R-squared     = 0.2919
                                            Adj R-squared = 0.2904
                                            Root MSE      = .44115
```

lnwage	Coef.	Std. Err.	t	P>|t|	[95% Conf. Interval]	
ttl_exp	.039485	.0031004	12.74	0.000	.033403	.045567
tenure	.008717	.0026303	3.31	0.001	.0035573	.0138768
collgrad	.3984273	.0283724	14.04	0.000	.3427703	.4540842
_cons	1.194306	.0351505	33.98	0.000	1.125353	1.263259

Figure 1-4:
A STATA
regression
estimation.

STATA also has a number of postestimation commands for hypothesis testing, obtaining residuals, and predicting the dependent variable. You can explore them in the STATA manuals or electronic documentation. However, throughout the book, I also provide several examples of postestimation commands alongside the relevant econometric model estimates.

Chapter 2

Getting the Hang of Probability

● ●

In This Chapter

▶ Reviewing the basics of probability theory

▶ Understanding probability density functions for discrete and continuous random variables

▶ Finding the relationship between two random variables

● ●

*T*he purpose of this chapter is to review some fundamental concepts of probability theory that are essential to moving forward with your understanding of econometrics. These topics center on the properties of probability distributions and their use in calculating descriptive measures of random variables. Other topics are either less important for econometrics or are covered as necessary in the relevant chapters of this book. (If you find that your probability skills are rustier than you expected, consult *Statistics For Dummies* [by Deborah J. Rumsey; John Wiley & Sons, Inc.] and a good statistics or probability textbook.)

In this chapter you get a refresher on the properties of probability distributions for both discrete and continuous random variables. Then you find out how you can use information from probability distributions to calculate measures of central tendency, dispersion, and correlation.

Reviewing Random Variables and Probability Distributions

Because one of the objectives of econometrics is to explain seemingly random events, the building blocks naturally rely on some probability theory.

Random events are uncertain outcomes from an experiment. When you take those outcomes and describe them numerically, you create *random variables*. So a random variable measures something that has an uncertain value.

In economics, you're typically concerned with outcomes that have uncertain values. These random variables include things like output, demand, profit, wages, and so on. The precise random variable you're interested in depends on your problem or research question.

Random variables can be discrete or continuous. A *discrete* random variable is one that can be described by integers (whole numbers), so the outcomes are countable. A *continuous* random variable, on the other hand, can have any real value, so the outcomes are infinite and not countable.

Suppose I'm interested in the number of jobs (full time or part time) individuals held over the past year, and I obtain this information for all potential workers. The outcome for each worker is an integer value, like 0, 1, 2, and so on. Individuals either had one or more jobs or they had no jobs; no one had a fraction of a job. Because the outcomes are countable whole numbers, this problem uses a discrete random variable. If, however, I was interested in the wages earned by these individuals, then I'd be talking about a continuous random variable. Possible wages can be zero and whole numbers but also fractions (like $9.42 per hour).

In the following sections, I introduce various functions that describe probability for discrete and continuous random variables.

Looking at all possibilities: Probability density function (PDF)

A *probability density function* (PDF) shows the probabilities of a random variable for all its possible values. The probabilities associated with specific values (or events) from a random variable must adhere to the properties $0 \leq f(X) \leq 1$ and $\sum f(X_j) = 1$, where X_j represents the possible values (outcomes) of random variable X. In other words, the chances of any random event occurring must be anywhere from impossible (probability of 0) to certain (probability of 1), and the sum of the probabilities for all events must be 1 (or 100 percent).

The PDF for discrete random variables

If you're observing a discrete random variable, the PDF can be described in a table or graph. To construct a table, you set up one column with the possible values of your random variable and one column with the probability that they'll occur. In a graphical depiction of the PDF (a bar graph), you'd place the possible values of the random variable on the horizontal axis, and the height of the vertical bars at each value show the probability that they occur.

Suppose I perform an experiment that consists of tossing three coins at the same time. I'm interested in the number of times they land heads up, so I call the number of heads observed random variable X. In Table 2-1, I list the possible outcomes for this experiment and the values for X generated from the process.

Table 2-1   **Outcomes from Tossing Three Coins**

Outcome	First Coin	Second Coin	Third Coin	Number of Heads, X
1	T	T	T	0
2	T	T	H	1
3	T	H	T	1
4	H	T	T	1
5	T	H	H	2
6	H	H	T	2
7	H	T	H	2
8	H	H	H	3

Out of eight possible outcomes, you get 0 heads in one outcome, 1 head in three outcomes, 2 heads in three outcomes, and 3 heads in one outcome. You can summarize the information in Table 2-1 with a tabular or graphical depiction of the PDF for X. In Table 2-1, you see 8 total outcomes and four possible values for X: 0, 1, 2, and 3. This information allows you to calculate the probability associated with each X value. For example, $X = 0$ occurs only once, so $f(X = 0) = ⅛ = 0.125$. In Table 2-2, I calculate the probabilities for the other X values and show a tabular form of the PDF. In Figure 2-1, I show a graphical version.

Table 2-2   **Probability Density Function, 3-Coin-Toss Experiment**

X	f(X)
0	$\frac{1}{8} = 0.125$
1	$\frac{3}{8} = 0.375$
2	$\frac{3}{8} = 0.375$
3	$\frac{1}{8} = 0.125$

Note that the probabilities in the right-hand column add up to 1. The total probabilities for any experiment must always equal 1.

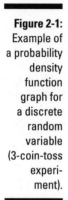

Figure 2-1:
Example of a probability density function graph for a discrete random variable (3-coin-toss experiment).

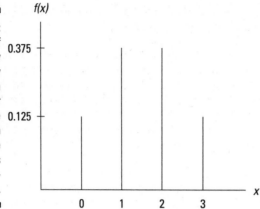

The PDF for continuous random variables

If you're observing a continuous random variable, the PDF can be described in a function or graph. The function shows how the random variable behaves over any possible range of values. In a graphical depiction of the PDF, the possible values of the random variable are on the horizontal axis, and a curve (without any bars or breaks) is somewhere above the axis.

The most common continuous PDF is that of a normally distributed random variable. The graphical depiction of this PDF is shown in Figure 2-2.

Figure 2-2:
A graphical depiction of a probability density function for a normally distributed random variable.

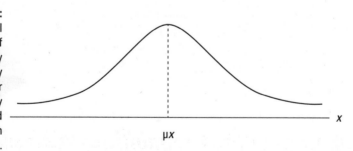

Regardless of the values of the mean (μ_x) and standard deviation (σ_x), the total density (area) under the curve is equal to 1. In addition, about 68 percent of the density is within one standard deviation, about 95 percent of the density is within two standard deviations, and about 99.7 percent of the density is within three standard deviations.

Because a continuous random variable can take on infinitely many values, the probability that a specific value occurs is zero!

An example can help illustrate this point. Suppose I randomly choose one of my econometrics students. What is the probability that the student will be *exactly* 21 years of age? Answer: essentially zero. The reason is that student would have to be randomly selected at the precise day, hour, minute, second, and fraction of a second that he or she was born 21 years ago. That would be virtually impossible. There would, however, be some chance of randomly selecting a student who's between the ages of 20 and 22.

Probabilities with continuous random variables are measured over intervals. Mathematically, this probability measurement is expressed as $f(X_a \leq X \leq X_b)$, where X_a and X_b are possible values that can be taken by the random variable X. I illustrate this graphically in Figure 2-3.

Figure 2-3:
A continuous probability density function where the shaded area represents the probability of observing a value between X_a and X_b.

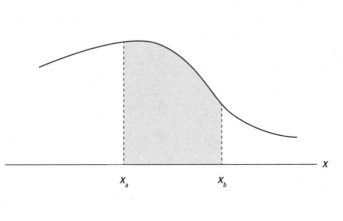

Summing up the probabilities: Cumulative density function (CDF)

The *cumulative density function* (CDF) of a random variable X is the *sum* or *accrual* of probabilities up to some value. It shows how the sum of the probabilities approaches 1, which sometimes occurs at a constant rate and sometimes occurs at a changing rate. In the following sections, I tell you how to find the CDF for discrete and random variables, and I show you how to describe it using a table, function, or graph.

The CDF for discrete random variables

For a discrete random variable, the CDF is equivalent to $F(X_j) = f(X \leq X_j)$, where $f(X)$ is the probability density function (see the preceding section for details).

If you're observing a discrete random variable, the CDF can be described in a table or graph. To construct a table, put the possible values of your random variable in one column, the probability that they will occur in another column, and the sums of the probabilities up to any given value in a third column. In a graphical depiction of the CDF, you place the possible values of the random variable on the horizontal axis, and the height of a horizontal line at each value shows the probability of that value summed with the probabilities of all smaller values.

Suppose I perform an experiment that consists of tossing two coins at the same time. I'm interested in the number of times the coin lands heads up, so I designate the number of heads observed as my random variable X. In Table 2-3, I illustrate the possible outcomes for this experiment and the values for X generated from the process.

Table 2-3	Outcomes from Tossing Two Coins		
Outcome	*First Coin*	*Second Coin*	*Number of Heads, X*
1	T	T	0
2	T	H	1
3	H	T	1
4	H	H	2

You can summarize the information in Table 2-3 with a table or graph of the CDF for X. In Table 2-4, I show a tabular form of the CDF. Recall that the PDF, $f(X)$, represents the probability of a given random event, and the CDF, $F(X)$, is the sum of the probabilities up to any random value. For example, $f(X = 1) = \frac{1}{2} = 0.50$ and $F(X = 1) = \frac{1}{4} + \frac{1}{2} = \frac{3}{4} = 0.75$. In Figure 2-4, I show the same information graphically.

Table 2-4	Cumulative Density Function Table, Two-Coin-Toss Experiment	
X	f(X)	F(X)
0	0.25	0.25
1	0.50	0.75
2	0.25	1

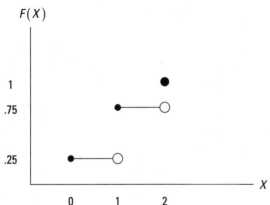

Figure 2-4:
An example of a cumulative density function graph for a discrete random variable (two-coin-toss experiment).

The CDF for continuous random variables

Get ready for some calculus! (I can hear the cheers from here.) The CDF is a sum of probabilities, and for a continuous function, finding a sum means integration. *Integration* is a calculus procedure that allows you to find densities under nonlinear functions. For a continuous random variable, the CDF is

$$F(X) = \int_{-\infty}^{X_j} f(X)$$ where f(X) is the probability density function (see the earlier

section "Looking at all possibilities: Probability density function [PDF]" for details).

If you're observing a continuous random variable, the CDF can be described in a function or graph. The function shows how the random variable behaves over any possible range of values. In Figure 2-5, I display the CDF for a normally distributed random variable.

The precise shape of the CDF depends on the mean and variance (the square of the standard deviation) of your random variable. A smaller mean shifts the curve to the left, and a larger mean shifts the curve to the right. A smaller variance makes the curve steeper, whereas a larger variance makes the curve flatter.

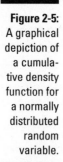

Figure 2-5:
A graphical
depiction of
a cumula-
tive density
function for
a normally
distributed
random
variable.

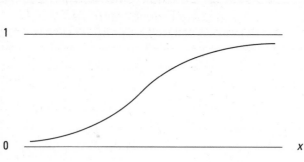

Putting variable information together: Bivariate or joint probability density

Because one primary objective of econometrics is to examine relationships between variables, you need to be familiar with probabilities that combine information on two variables.

A *bivariate* or *joint probability density* provides the relative frequencies (or chances) that events with more than one random variable will occur. Generally, this information is shown in a table.

For two random variables, X and Y, you're already familiar with the notation for joint probabilities from your statistics class, which uses the intersection term, $\cap$, like this: $P(X = a \cap Y = b)$.

The variables a and b are possible values for the random variable. However, in econometrics, you likely need to become familiar with this mathematical notation for joint probabilities: $f(X, Y)$. In this notation, the comma is used instead of the intersection operator.

In Table 2-5, I provide an example of a *joint probability table* for random variables X and Y. The column headings in the middle of the first row list the X values (1, 2, and 3), and the first column lists the Y values (1, 2, 3, and 4). The values contained in the middle of Table 2-5 represent the *joint* or *intersection probabilities*. For example, the probability X equals 3 (see column 3) and Y equals 2 (row 2) is 0.10. In your econometrics class, the mathematical notation used to express this is likely to look like $f(X = 3, Y = 2) = 0.10$.

Table 2-5	Joint Probability Table			
Y	X			f (Y)
	1	2	3	
1	0.25	0	0.10	0.35
2	0.05	0.05	**0.10**	0.20
3	0	0.05	0.20	0.25
4	0	0	0.20	0.20
f(X)	0.30	0.10	0.60	1.00

You can also see that the column sums, f(X), contain the *marginal* or *unconditional* probabilities for random variable X and the row sums, f(Y), contain the same information for random variable Y. For example, f(Y = 3) = 0.25; that is, the probability that Y equals 3 is 0.25.

Predicting the future using what you know: Conditional probability density

Prediction in econometrics involves some prior knowledge. For example, you may attempt to predict how many "likes" your status update will get on Facebook given the number of "friends" you have and time of day you posted. In order to do so, you'll want to be familiar with conditional probabilities.

Conditional probabilities calculate the chance that a specific value for a random variable will occur *given* that another random variable has already taken a value.

Calculating conditional probability density

Conditional probabilities use two variables, so you'll need the *joint* and *marginal* probabilities (see the preceding section). Typically, this information is displayed in a table. The joint probabilities for random variables X and Y are shown in the middle rows and columns of Table 2-5, and the marginal probabilities are on the outside row for variable X and outside column for variable Y.

You can calculate conditional probabilities using the following formula:

$$f(Y \mid X) = \frac{f(X,Y)}{f(X)}$$

It reads, the *probability of Y given X* equals the *probability of Y and X* divided by the *probability of X*.

Suppose you're interested in calculating a specific conditional probability using Table 2-5; the probability that *Y* equals 1 given that *X* equals 3. Using this formula and plugging in the probabilities from Table 2-5, your answer would be

$$f(Y=1 \mid X=3) = \frac{f(Y=1, X=3)}{f(X=3)} = \frac{0.10}{0.60} = \frac{1}{6} \approx 0.17$$

The numerator in your calculation of a conditional probability is a joint probability, so it doesn't matter if you write it as *Y* and *X* or *X* and *Y*.

Checking for statistical independence

Regardless of the strength of your theory and the appeal of your common sense, in econometrics you'll ultimately want to examine the statistical relationship between variables. You may first want to determine if any relationship exists at all.

Events are said to be *independent* if one event has no statistical relationship with the other event. One way you can determine statistical independence is by observing that the probability of one event is unaffected by the occurrence of another event.

If $f(Y \mid X) = f(Y)$, then the events are statistically independent; that is, the events are independent if the conditional and unconditional probabilities are equal. If $f(Y \mid X) \neq f(Y)$ (meaning the conditional and unconditional probabilities are not equal), then they are dependent.

Using Table 2-5, I can calculate the probability that *Y* equals 4 given that *X* equals 3, as follows:

$$f(Y=4 \mid X=3) = \frac{f(Y=4, X=3)}{f(X=3)} = \frac{0.20}{0.60} = \frac{1}{3} \approx 0.33$$

I can also calculate the probability that *Y* equals 4 by summing the values in row 4: $f(Y=4) = 0 + 0 + 0.20 = 0.20$.

Because the values (the conditional and unconditional probabilities) are unequal, I conclude that *X* and *Y* are *dependent*.

Understanding Summary Characteristics of Random Variables

When you want to describe the distribution of a random variable with numbers, you need to calculate the *summary measures* (or *moments*). The two most commonly reported measures are the *expected value* (or mean) and the variance. When you're examining two random variables simultaneously, the *covariance* or *correlation* is frequently reported.

Making generalizations with expected value or mean

The expected value (or mean) of a random variable provides a measure of central tendency, which means that it provides one measurement of where the data tends to cluster.

The expected value is the average of a random variable. If you have a discrete random variable, you can calculate the expected value with the equation $E(X) = \sum_X X \cdot f(X)$, where X represents the different possible values for the random variable, and $f(X)$ is the probability that each value will occur.

Expected value is like the mean, so you can use μ_X instead of $E(X)$ to symbolize it.

If you have a continuous random variable, then you calculate the expected value with this equation:

$$E(X) = \int_{-\infty}^{\infty} X \cdot f(X) dX$$

Although you may need to recognize the difference between discrete and continuous random variables, you probably won't need to perform manual calculations of expected value for continuous random variables. You should, however, know how to perform manual calculations for a discrete random variable.

Suppose I'm examining random variable X with the probability distribution shown in the first two columns of Table 2-6. I can find the expected value by multiplying each possible value for X by its probability of occurring and then adding those values. I show this operation in the third column, which gives me $E(X) = 1.5$.

Table 2-6	Expected Value of a Random Variable	
X	*Probability (f(X))*	*X · f(X)*
0	0.125	0
1	0.375	0.375
2	0.375	0.750
3	0.125	0.375
Total:	1	1.5

If you're manipulating equations containing an expected value operator, you'll find the following five properties useful:

✔ The expected value of a constant is just the constant itself: $E(a) = a$

✔ The expected value of two random variables added together is equal to the sum of each of their expected values: $E(X + Y) = E(X) + E(Y)$

✔ The expected value of a random variable multiplied by a constant is equal to the constant multiplied by the expected value of the random variable: $E(aX) = aE(X)$

✔ If X and Y are independent random variables, then the expected value of their product is equal to the product of their expected values: $E(XY) = E(X)E(Y)$

✔ If X and Y are independent random variables, then the expected value of their ratio is equal to the ratio of their expected values: $E\left(\frac{X}{Y}\right) = \frac{E(X)}{E(Y)}$

Suppose I create a random variable W defined by $W = 5 + 2X + XY$, where the random variable X has an expected value equal to 3, the random variable Y has an expected value equal to 10, and they're independent random variables. Using the expected-value properties, I calculate the expected value of W as

$$E(W) = E(5 + 2X + XY)$$
$$= E(5) + E(2X) + E(XY)$$
$$= 5 + 2E(X) + E(X)E(Y)$$
$$= 5 + (2)(3) + (3)(10)$$
$$= 41$$

Measuring variance and standard deviation

The variance of a random variable provides a measure of dispersion. Measures of dispersion offer a quantitative value of the diversity in the data. The variance increases the value of dispersion exponentially as measurements deviate from the mean. The variance is used to produce other summary measures, including the standard deviation, which is the square root of the variance. The standard deviation is a commonly quoted measure of dispersion because its values are on the same scale as the variable being measured.

The *variance* is the average squared difference between the value of a random variable and its mean. If your random variable is discrete, you can calculate the variance as $Var(X) = \sum_X (X - E(X))^2 f(X)$, where X represents the different possible values for your random variable, $E(X)$ is the mean of your random variable, and $f(X)$ is the probability that each value will occur.

You can also write the variance formula this way: $\sigma_X^2 = \sum_X (X - \mu_X)^2 f(X)$.

If your random variable is continuous, then you calculate the variance with $Var(X) = \int_{-\infty}^{\infty} (X - \mu_X)^2 f(X) dX$.

You'll probably be required to recognize the difference between discrete and continuous random variables, but you'll probably only need to perform manual calculations for discrete random variables.

Suppose I'm examining random variable X with the probability distribution shown in the first two columns of Table 2-7. First, I calculate the mean by taking each possible value for X, multiplying them by their probability of occurring (shown in column 2), and then adding these values. I show this operation in the third column, which gives me $E(X) = \mu_X = 1.5$. Second, I square the difference between each value of X and its mean, multiply by the probability the X value occurs, and add those numbers. I show this final step in the fourth column, which gives me $Var(X) = 0.75$.

Table 2-7		Variance of a Random Variable	
X	**f(X)**	**X · f(X)**	**(X − μ_X)²f(X)**
0	0.125	0	$(0 - 1.5)^2(0.125) = 0.281$
1	0.375	0.375	$(1 - 1.5)^2(0.375) = 0.094$
2	0.375	0.750	$(2 - 1.5)^2(0.375) = 0.094$
3	0.125	0.375	$(3 - 1.5)^2(0.125) = 0.281$
Total:	1	1.5	0.75

The following properties are helpful if you're manipulating equations containing a variance operator:

- The variance of a constant is zero: $Var(a) = 0$
- The variance of a constant added to a random variable is equal to the variance of the random variable: $Var(a + X) = Var(X)$
- The variance of a random variable multiplied by a constant is equal to the constant squared multiplied by the variance of the random variable: $Var(aX) = a^2Var(X)$
- The variance of two random variables added together is equal to the variance of one plus the variance of the other plus two times the covariance of the two variables: $Var(X + Y) = Var(X) + Var(Y) + 2Cov(X, Y)$
- The variance of one random variable subtracted from another random variable is equal to the variance of one plus the variance of the other minus two times the covariance of the two variables: $Var(X - Y) = Var(X) + Var(Y) - 2Cov(X, Y)$

If two random variables are independent, then their covariance is zero. Covariance measures how two variables are related, so three outcomes are possible: The covariance is positive if the two variables have a direct relationship, the covariance is negative if the two variables have an inverse relationship, and the covariance is zero (or close to it) if there's no clear relationship between the two variables (see the following section "Looking at relationships with covariance and correlation" for a discussion of this topic).

Suppose I create a random variable W defined by $W = 3 + X - Y$, where the random variable X has a variance equal to 16, the random variable Y has a variance equal to 25, and the covariance of variables X and Y is –4. Using the variance properties, I calculate the variance of W as

$$
\begin{aligned}
Var(W) &= Var(3 + X - Y) \\
&= Var(X - Y) \\
&= Var(X) + Var(Y) - 2Cov(X,Y) \\
&= 16 + 25 - (2)(-4) \\
&= 49
\end{aligned}
$$

You can calculate the standard deviation by taking the square root of the variance. The calculation can be described by $sd(X) = \sqrt{Var(X)}$ or $\sigma_X = \sqrt{\sigma_X^2}$. Although mathematical manipulations and distributions are usually based on the variance measure, the standard deviation is commonly reported in statistics and econometrics because it's measured in the same units as the random variable. In the previous example, the $Var(W) = 49$, so the $sd(W) = 7$.

Looking at relationships with covariance and correlation

When you start considering two random variables at the same time, you want to be able to summarize their relationship. *Covariance* and *correlation* are the most common measures used to summarize how two random variables are related.

Figuring out which way they're going: Covariance

Covariance uses the difference between the value of each random variable and its mean to determine how they vary with one another. You can calculate the covariance of two random variables, *X* and *Y*, as

$$Cov(X,Y) = \sum_X \sum_Y (X - E(X))(Y - E(Y))f(X,Y)$$

where *X* and *Y* represent the different possible values for your two discrete random variables, $E(X)$ is the mean of random variable *X*, $E(Y)$ is the mean of random variable *Y*, and $f(X, Y)$ is the joint probability that each value will occur (see the earlier section "Putting variable information together: Bivariate or joint probability density" if you need a refresher on these types of probabilities).

You can also write the covariance formula as $\sigma_{XY} = \sum_X \sum_Y (X - \mu_X)(Y - \mu_Y)f(X,Y)$
or $\sigma_{XY} = \sum_X \sum_Y (XY)f(X,Y) - \mu_X\mu_Y$. If the random variables are continuous, the covariance is calculated using the formula

$$\sigma_{XY} = \int_{-\infty}^{\infty}\int_{-\infty}^{\infty} XY \cdot f(X,Y)dY\,dX - \left(\int_{-\infty}^{\infty} X \cdot f(X)dX\right)\left(\int_{-\infty}^{\infty} Y \cdot f(Y)dY\right)$$

In Table 2-8, I provide an example of a *joint probability table* for random variables *X* and *Y*.

Table 2-8		Joint Probability Table		f(Y)
Y		X		
	1	2	3	
1	0.25	0	0.10	0.35
2	0.05	0.05	0.10	0.20
3	0	0.05	0.20	0.25
4	0	0	0.20	0.20
f(X)	0.30	0.10	0.60	1.00

Using the information in Table 2-8 for random variables X and Y, you can calculate their covariance with the following steps:

1. **Calculate the expected value or mean, μ_x, of X.** In this step, you multiply each X value in the column headings by its respective probability ($f(X)$) in the last row and sum the values.

$$\mu_X = (1)(0.30) + (2)(0.10) + (3)(0.60) = 2.3$$

2. **Calculate the expected value or mean, μ_y, of Y.** In this step, you multiply each Y value in the first column by its respective probability ($f(Y)$) in the last column and sum the values.

$$\mu_Y = (1)(0.35) + (2)(0.20) + (3)(0.25) + (4)(0.20) = 2.3$$

3. **Calculate the covariance of X and Y.** In this step, you multiply each X and Y value by its respective joint probability ($f(X,Y)$) in the inner cells of the table and sum the values. Then you subtract the product of the means of X and Y calculated in Steps 1 and 2.

$$\sigma_{XY} = \sum_X \sum_Y (XY) f(X,Y) - \mu_X \mu_Y$$

$$\sigma_{XY} = (1 \cdot 1)(0.25) + (2 \cdot 1)(0) + (3 \cdot 1)(0.10)$$
$$+ (1 \cdot 2)(0.05) + (2 \cdot 2)(0.05) + (3 \cdot 2)(0.10)$$
$$+ (1 \cdot 3)(0) + (2 \cdot 3)(0.05) + (3 \cdot 3)(0.20)$$
$$+ (1 \cdot 4)(0) + (2 \cdot 4)(0) + (3 \cdot 4)(0.20)$$
$$- (2.3)(2.3)$$

$$\sigma_{XY} = 0.66$$

Unlike variance (which can only be a positive number), covariance can be positive or negative. A positive value indicates that the two variables tend to move in the same direction; when one goes up, the other one goes up. A negative value indicates that the two variables tend to move in opposite directions; when one goes up, the other goes down.

If you're manipulating equations containing a covariance operator, the following properties help you:

✔ The covariance of two independent random variables is zero: $Cov(X, Y) = 0$ if $f(X|Y) = f(X)$ or $f(X, Y) = f(X)f(Y)$

✔ The covariance of two random variables multiplied by a constant is equal to the product of the constant times the covariance of the random variables: $Cov(aX, bY) = abCov(X, Y)$

✔ The covariance of a random variable times itself is equal to the variance of the random variable: $Cov(X, X) = Var(X)$

The magnitude of the covariance is influenced greatly by the units of measurement. Therefore, you can use covariance to determine the *direction* of the relationship between two variables (positive or negative), but you shouldn't use covariance to determine the *strength* of the relationship.

Gauging just how strong the relationship is: Correlation

A measure related to covariance known as the *correlation coefficient* can be used to measure the strength of the relationship between two variables.

The correlation between two random variables is the ratio between their variance and the product of their standard deviations (see the previous section "Measuring variance and standard deviation" if you need to review these calculations). The correlation coefficient, therefore, is defined as

$$Corr(X,Y) = \frac{Cov(X,Y)}{sd(X)sd(Y)} \text{ or } \rho_{XY} = \frac{\sigma_{XY}}{\sigma_X \sigma_Y}$$

The sign of the resulting value is the same as the covariance (positive or negative) and must be between −1 and +1.

A value of −1 indicates a perfectly negative relationship, and a value of +1 implies a perfectly positive relationship. In Figure 2-6, I show one graph with a perfect negative relationship and one graph with a perfect positive relationship.

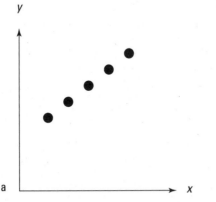
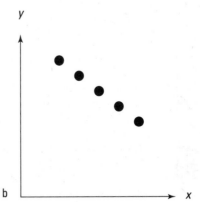

Figure 2-6:
Two random
variables
with a
perfect pos-
itive (a) and
negative (b)
relationship.

You're unlikely to encounter situations where a perfect relationship exists between two variables. Typically, the relationships you see will look like those in Figure 2-7.

The more difficult identifying a clear positive or negative relationship becomes, the closer the correlation coefficient gets to zero. In Figure 2-8, I show a random dispersion of values for *X* and *Y*. When you see something like this, your correlation coefficient is zero (or very close to zero).

Figure 2-7:
Two random
variables
with an
imperfect
positive (a)
and nega-
tive (b)
relationship.

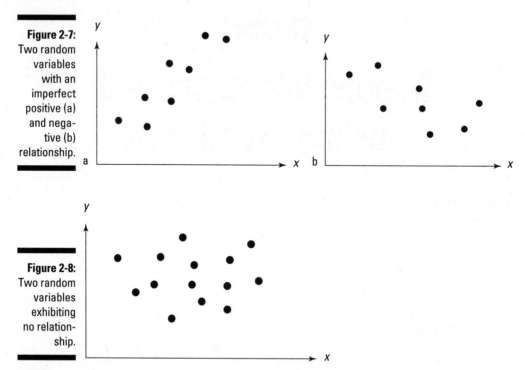

Figure 2-8:
Two random
variables
exhibiting
no relation-
ship.

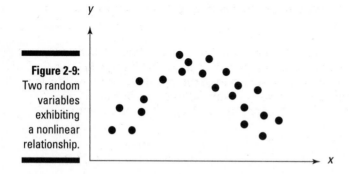

WARNING!

Correlation coefficients identify *linear* relationships, but they can be misleading if the relationship between two variables is *nonlinear.*

In Figure 2-9, I show two variables that clearly have a nonlinear relationship.

Figure 2-9:
Two random
variables
exhibiting
a nonlinear
relationship.

If you calculate the correlation coefficient in a situation like this, you get a
value of zero (or close to zero). However, you shouldn't ignore relationships
simply because they aren't linear. Instead, use other techniques to identify
relationships like the one in Figure 2-9 (which I cover in Chapter 8).

Chapter 3

Making Inferences and Testing Hypotheses

*O*ne goal of both statistics and econometrics is to develop concepts that can be used to make predictions and forecasts with data. As a student, you typically use surveys and other forms of sample data to test your hypotheses and draw conclusions, and to do so, you need to understand how statistical inference works.

Statistical inference and hypothesis testing focus on the process of making generalizations for a population from sample information. Although econometrics courses cover inference procedures, you need to understand the foundational concepts covered in this chapter to fully grasp and appreciate those techniques.

This chapter reviews characteristics of well-known probability distributions and some fundamental concepts of statistical inference. If you find your statistics background isn't strong enough to go through this chapter relatively quickly, then I recommend that you consult *Statistics For Dummies* (by Deborah Rumsey; John Wiley & Sons, Inc.) and a good statistics textbook.

Getting to Know Your Data with Descriptive Statistics

Descriptive statistics are measurements that can be used to summarize your sample data and, subsequently, make predictions about your population of interest.

When descriptive measures are calculated using population data, those values are called *parameters.* When you calculate descriptive measures using sample data, the values are called *estimators* (or *statistics*).

In the following sections, I tell you how to calculate the most common descriptive measures used in econometrics. (The calculation of population parameters using probability density information is explained in Chapter 2.) I also help you determine whether a particular estimator is good.

Calculating parameters and estimators

When you collect a random sample of data and calculate a statistic with that data, you're producing a *point estimate,* which is a single estimate of a population parameter.

You could estimate many population parameters with sample data, but here I show you how to calculate the most popular statistics: mean, variance, standard deviation, covariance, and correlation. The following list indicates how each parameter and its corresponding estimator is calculated. (If you're having trouble remembering what each of these is designed to measure, flip to Chapter 2.)

- **Mean (average):** The *mean* is the simple average of the random variable, *X.* The population mean for *X* is

$$\mu_X = \frac{\sum_{i=1}^{N} X_i}{N}$$

where X_i represents the individual measurements and N is the size of the population. The sample mean is

$$\bar{X} = \frac{\sum_{i=1}^{n} X_i}{n}$$

The difference between the sample and population mean is that that the sample mean uses the sample size n instead of the population size N.

✔ **Variance:** The *variance* is the average of the squared differences from the mean. The population variance for a random variable X is

$$\sigma_X^2 = \frac{\sum_{i=1}^{N}(X_i - \mu_X)^2}{N}$$

where X_i represents the individual measurements, μ_x is the population mean, and N is the size of the population. The sample variance is

$$s_X^2 = \frac{\sum_{i=1}^{n}(X_i - \bar{X})^2}{n-1}$$

Note that the denominator for the sample variance not only uses the sample size n but also subtracts 1 from that number. This change is known as a *degrees of freedom* adjustment. Degrees of freedom adjustments are usually important in proving that estimators are unbiased. This concept is discussed in the following section, "Determining whether an estimator is good."

✔ **Standard deviation:** The *standard deviation* measures how spread out the random variable is, on average, from the mean. The standard deviation is the square root of the variance, so the population standard deviation for random variable X is

$$\sigma_X = \sqrt{\sigma_X^2} = \sqrt{\frac{\sum_{i=1}^{N}(X_i - \mu_X)^2}{N}}$$

and the sample standard deviation is

$$s_X = \sqrt{s_X^2} = \sqrt{\frac{\sum_{i=1}^{n}(X_i - \bar{X})^2}{n-1}}$$

✔ **Covariance:** The *covariance* measures how much two random variables change together. The population covariance between two random variables X and Y is

$$\sigma_{XY} = \frac{\sum_{i=1}^{N}(X_i - \mu_X)(Y_i - \mu_Y)}{N}$$

where X_i represents the individual X values, Y_i represents the individual Y values, and N is the total number of measurements in the population. The sample covariance is

$$s_{XY} = \frac{\sum_{i=1}^{n}(X_i - \bar{X})(Y_i - \bar{Y})}{n-1} = \frac{1}{n-1}\sum_{i=1}^{n}(X_i - \bar{X})(Y_i - \bar{Y})$$

where $\bar{X}$ is the sample mean of X, $\bar{Y}$ is the sample mean of Y, and n is the sample size.

✔ **Correlation:** The *correlation* refers to the relationship between two random variables or sets of data. The population correlation coefficient between two random variables X and Y is

$$\rho_{XY} = \frac{\sigma_{XY}}{\sigma_X \sigma_Y}$$

where σ_{XY} is the population covariance, σ_X is the population standard deviation of X, and σ_Y is the population standard deviation of Y. The sample correlation coefficient is

$$r_{XY} = \frac{s_{XY}}{s_X s_Y}$$

where s_{XY} is the sample covariance, s_X is the sample standard deviation of X, and s_Y is the sample standard deviation of Y.

Now, try working with some numbers. In Table 3-1, I show five observations of hamburger sales and prices. Use the formulas to calculate the mean, variance, standard deviation, covariance, and correlation.

Table 3-1	Hamburger Prices and Sales
Hamburger Sales (in units), Y	**Hamburger Price (in $), X**
100	1
80	2
63	3
45	4
21	5

You can use computer software, such as STATA, to calculate descriptive statistics from the data in Table 3-1. By typing "sum" on the command line, you get the descriptive statistics for all the variables in your dataset. If you want the correlation between two variables, select **Statistics ⇨ Summaries, tables, and tests ⇨ Summary and descriptive statistics ⇨ Correlations and covariances** from the menu bar. Or you can enter "corr *variable1 variable2*" on the command line. In your command, replace *variable1* and *variable2* with the actual names you've given the variables in your dataset. You can get covariance by adding an option to the correlation command; type "corr *variable1 variable2*, cov" on the command line. I execute these commands and show you STATA's output in Figure 3-1.

```
. sum

    Variable |     Obs       Mean    Std. Dev.      Min       Max
           y |       5       61.8     30.57286       21       100
           x |       5          3     1.581139        1         5

. corr y x
(obs=5)
```

```
            |        y            x
          y |   1.0000
          x |  -0.9981       1.0000

. corr y x, cov
(obs=5)

            |        y            x
          y |    934.7
          x |   -48.25          2.5
```

You should verify that your manual calculations of these measures are consistent with STATA's output.

Summarizing data with descriptive statistics is a relatively simple procedure, but make sure you examine the values carefully. You can use descriptive measures to ensure that your sample contains measurements that are realistic. For example, if your population of interest is college graduates, you wouldn't expect your random sample from that group to have an average age of 21. Careful attention to these details provides more credibility in your data and the subsequent inferences you make.

Determining whether an estimator is good

Statisticians and econometricians typically require the estimators they use for inference and prediction to have certain desirable properties.

For statisticians, unbiasedness and efficiency are the two most-desirable properties an estimator can have. An estimator is *unbiased* if, in repeated estimations using the method, the mean value of the estimator coincides with the true parameter value. An estimator is *efficient* if it achieves the smallest variance among estimators of its kind. In some instances, statisticians and econometricians spend a considerable amount of time proving that a particular estimator is unbiased and efficient.

The estimator linearity property

Besides unbiasedness and efficiency, an additional desirable property for some estimators is *linearity*. An estimator has this property if a statistic is a linear function of the sample observations.

This property isn't present for all estimators, and certainly some estimators are desirable (efficient and either unbiased or consistent) without being linear. The linearity property, however, can be convenient when you're using algebraic manipulations to create new variables or prove other estimator properties.

Sometimes statisticians and econometricians are unable to prove that an estimator is unbiased. In that case, they usually settle for consistency. An estimator is *consistent* if it approaches the true parameter value as the sample size gets larger and larger. For this reason, consistency is known as an *asymptotic property* for an estimator; that is, it gradually approaches the true parameter value as the sample size approaches infinity.

In practical situations (that is, when you're working with data and not just doing a theoretical exercise), knowing when an estimator has these desirable properties is good, but you don't need to prove them on your own. You simply want to know the result of the proof (if it exists) and the assumptions needed to carry it out.

Laying the Groundwork of Prediction with the Normal and Standard Normal Distributions

To fully grasp prediction and hypothesis testing in econometrics, you need to know the properties of the normal distribution and remember how to work with normally distributed random variables.

Recognizing usual variables: Normal distribution

A random variable with a normal distribution has a probability density function that is *continuous, symmetrical,* and *bell-shaped.* Although many random variables can have a bell-shaped distribution, the density function of a normal distribution is precisely

$$f(X) = \left(\frac{1}{\sigma_X \sqrt{2\pi}}\right) \exp\left(\frac{-(X - \mu_X)^2}{2\sigma_X^2}\right) = \left(\frac{1}{\sigma_X \sqrt{2\pi}}\right) e^{\left(\frac{-(X - \mu_X)^2}{2\sigma_X^2}\right)}$$

where μ_X represents the mean of the normally distributed random variable X, σ_X is the standard deviation, and σ_X^2 represents the variance of the normally distributed random variable.

TIP

A shorthand way of indicating that a random variable, X, has a normal distribution is to write $X \sim N(\mu_X, \sigma_X^2)$.

I show a generic normal distribution in Figure 3-2. A distinctive feature of a normal distribution is the probability (or density) associated with specific segments of the distribution. I divide the normal distribution in Figure 3-2 into the most common intervals (or segments): one, two, and three standard deviations from the mean.

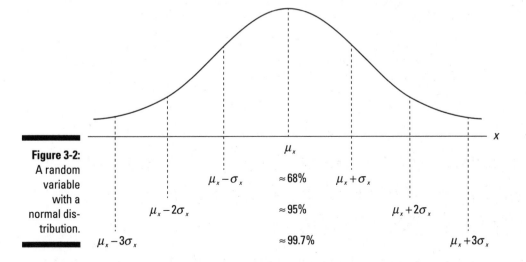

Figure 3-2:
A random variable with a normal distribution.

μ_x

$\mu_x - \sigma_x$ $\approx 68\%$ $\mu_x + \sigma_x$

$\mu_x - 2\sigma_x$ $\approx 95\%$ $\mu_x + 2\sigma_x$

$\mu_x - 3\sigma_x$ $\approx 99.7\%$ $\mu_x + 3\sigma_x$

As I illustrate in Figure 3-2, with a normally distributed random variable, approximately 68 percent of the measurements are within one standard deviation of the mean, 95 percent are within two standard deviations, and 99.7 percent are within three standard deviations.

Suppose you have data for the entire population of individuals living in retirement homes. You discover that the average age of these individuals is 70, the variance is 9 (standard deviation, $\sigma_X = \sqrt{9} = 3$), and the distribution of their age is normal. Using shorthand, you could simply write this information as $X \sim N(70, 9)$. If you randomly select one person from this population, what are the chances that he or she is more than 76 years of age?

Using the density from a normal distribution, you know that approximately 95 percent of the measurements are between 64 and 76 ($70 - 2\sigma_X < X < 70 + 2\sigma_X$) (notice that 6 is equal to two standard deviations). The remaining 5 percent are individuals who are less than 64 years of age or more than 76. Because a normal distribution is symmetrical, you can conclude that you have about a 2.5 percent ($5\% \div 2 = 2.5\%$) chance that you randomly select somebody who is more than 76 years of age.

If a random variable is a linear combination of another normally distributed random variable(s), it also has a normal distribution.

Suppose I have two random variables described by these terms:

$$X \sim N\left(\mu_X, \sigma_X^2\right)$$

$$Y \sim N\left(\mu_Y, \sigma_Y^2\right)$$

In other words, random variable X has a normal distribution with a mean of μ_X and variance of σ_X^2, and random variable Y has a normal distribution with a mean of μ_Y and a variance of σ_Y^2. If I create a new random variable, W, as the following linear combination of X and Y, $W = aX + bY$, then W also has a normal distribution. Additionally, using expected value and variance properties (I discuss these in Chapter 2), I can describe my new random variable with this shorthand notation: $W \sim N\left(a\mu_X + b\mu_Y, a^2\sigma_X^2 + b^2\sigma_Y^2 + 2ab\sigma_{XY}\right)$.

Putting variables on the same scale: Standard normal distribution (Z)

A specific version of a normally distributed random variable is the standard normal.

A *standard normal distribution* is a normal distribution with a mean of 0 and a variance of 1. It's useful because you can convert any normally distributed random variable to the same scale, which allows you to easily and quickly calculate and compare probabilities.

Typically, the letter Z is used to denote a standard normal, so the standard normal distribution is usually shown in shorthand as $Z \sim N(0, 1)$.

You can obtain a standard normal random variable by applying the following linear transformation to any normally distributed random variable:

$$Z = \frac{X - \mu_X}{\sigma_X}$$

where X is a normally distributed random variable with mean μ_X and standard deviation σ_X.

Suppose you're working with population data for individuals living in retirement homes. The average age of these individuals is 70, the variance is 9, and the distribution of their age is normal; that is, $X \sim N(70, 9)$. If you randomly select one person from this population, what are the chances that he or she is more than 75 years of age? You can figure out this probability by using the normal probability density function (see Chapter 2) and applying integral calculus, but fortunately the standard normal distribution simplifies the problem. Instead, you simply convert the X value of 75 to a Z value and use the standard normal probability table (Table A-1 in the appendix) to look up the density in that part of the distribution. Using the formula for Z and the standard normal probability table, you get

$$f(X > 75) = f\left(Z > \frac{X - \mu_X}{\sigma_X}\right) = f\left(Z > \frac{75 - 70}{3}\right) = f(Z > 1.67) = 0.0475$$

This answer tells you that you have a 4.75 percent chance of selecting somebody from the population who's more than 75 years of age.

 The other popular continuous probability distributions — chi-squared (χ^2), t, and F — are based on the normal or standard normal distributions. I discuss those distributions in the later section "Defining the chi-squared (χ^2), t, and F distributions."

Working with Parts of the Population: Sampling Distributions

Many random variables don't have a normal distribution. So why is the normal distribution so popular? The answer has to do with sampling distributions.

 A *sampling distribution* is a probability distribution (or density) of a statistic when random samples of size n are repeatedly drawn from a population. It is *not* the distribution of your sample measurements.

A population parameter can be estimated with a statistic using sample data. For example, if you calculate a mean, median, variance, and so on using a random sample from your population, presumably you are using those figures as estimates of their population (true) or parameter values. Now imagine that you sample your population numerous times and calculate these statistics for every sample that you draw. The values of these statistics change because the measurements in your sample change. The probability distribution of these values is a sampling distribution.

In the following sections, I explain how the sampling distribution of the mean is used to derive the properties of the central limit theorem and how this ends up forming the foundation for probability distributions commonly used in statistics and econometrics.

Simulating and using the central limit theorem

One sampling distribution with very desirable characteristics is the distribution of sample means.

One of the most important concepts in statistics, the *central limit theorem* (CLT) utilizes the distribution of sample means. The CLT states that if random samples of *n* observations are drawn from a population with mean μ_X and variance σ_X^2, then when *n* is large, the distribution of the sample mean $\bar{X}$ is approximately normally distributed with mean $\mu_{\bar{X}} = \mu_X$ and variance $\sigma_{\bar{X}}^2 = \dfrac{\sigma_X^2}{n}$.

I can write it more simply as $\bar{X} \sim N\left(\mu_X, \dfrac{\sigma_X^2}{n}\right)$.

You may be wondering how big exactly *n* must be in order to be considered large. How many observations are required to obtain a normal distribution for the sample mean? The answer depends on the shape of the source population distribution. Figure 3-3 shows you a graphical illustration of the CLT's result, which the following points summarize:

- ✔ When the probability distribution of *X* is normal, the distribution of $\bar{X}$ is exactly normally distributed regardless of sample size.

- ✔ When the probability distribution of *X* is symmetrical, the CLT applies very well to small sample sizes (often as small as $10 \leq n \leq 25$).

- ✔ When the distribution of *X* is asymmetrical, the approximation to a normal distribution becomes more accurate as *n* becomes large.

You're not likely to know exactly how your population data is distributed. Consequently, bigger is better, because it ensures a more accurate approximation to the normal distribution. With a large sample size, you don't need a population with a normal distribution for your sample means to have a normal distribution.

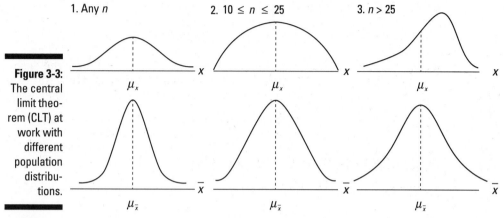

Figure 3-3:
The central limit theorem (CLT) at work with different population distributions.

With the result of the CLT, you can convert the distribution of a sample mean to a standard normal. Because the CLT tells you that

$$\bar{X} \sim N\left(\mu_X, \frac{\sigma_X^2}{n}\right)$$

and any normally distributed variable can be converted to a standard normal, then Z is defined as

$$Z = \frac{\bar{X} - \mu_X}{\frac{\sigma_X}{\sqrt{n}}}$$

Generally, a good convergence of the sample mean distribution to a normal distribution can be achieved with a sample size of 25 or more. If you're planning to simultaneously analyze numerous variables, as is typical in econometrics, you want to use many more observations.

Defining the chi-squared (χ^2), t, and F distributions

In econometrics, you use the chi-squared (χ^2), t, and F distributions extensively. The following sections review the logic of their derivation and their basic characteristics to help you understand when and how to use them.

The chi-squared distribution

The chi-squared distribution is useful for comparing estimated variance values from a sample to those values based on theoretical assumptions. Therefore, it's typically used to develop confidence intervals and hypothesis tests for population variance. First, however, you should familiarize yourself with the characteristics of a chi-squared distribution.

The χ^2 distribution is a *squared standard normal* random variable, so it takes only nonnegative values and tends to be right-skewed. The extent of its *skewness* depends on the degrees of freedom or number of observations. The higher the degrees of freedom (more observations), the less skewed (more symmetrical) the chi-squared distribution.

I illustrate a few chi-squared distributions in Figure 3-4, where df1, df2, and df3 indicate increasing degrees of freedom.

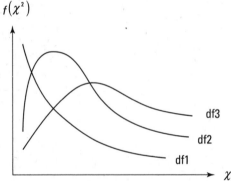

Figure 3-4: Chi-squared distributions with various degrees of freedom.

The chi-squared distribution is typically used with *variance* estimates and rests on the idea that you begin with a normally distributed random variable, such as $X \sim N(\mu_X, \sigma_X^2)$. With sample data, you estimate the variance of this random variable with

$$s_X^2 = \frac{\sum_{i=1}^{n}\left(X_i - \bar{X}\right)^2}{n-1}$$

where $\bar{X}$ is the sample mean and n is the sample size. If you algebraically manipulate this formula, you arrive at the chi-squared distribution:

$$(n-1)s_X^2 = \sum_{i=1}^{n}\left(X_i - \bar{X}\right)^2$$

$$\frac{(n-1)s_X^2}{\sigma_X^2} = \frac{\sum_{i=1}^{n}\left(X_i - \bar{X}\right)^2}{\sigma_X^2} \sim \chi_{n-1}^2$$

The last step, in which you divide both sides by the known (or assumed) population variance, is what standardizes your sample variance to a common scale known as chi-squared.

You can find the densities for various parts of the chi-squared distribution in Table A-3 of the appendix.

The t distribution

You probably used the *t* distribution extensively when dealing with means in your statistics class, but in econometrics you also use it for regression coefficients. Before you find out how that works, you should know how the *t* distribution is derived and its basic properties.

The *t* distribution is derived from a ratio of a standard normal random variable and the square root of a χ^2 random variable. It's bell-shaped, symmetrical around zero, and approaches a normal distribution, as the degrees of freedom (number of observations) increases.

I show how the *t* distribution changes with degrees of freedom in Figure 3-5. The df1, df2, and df3 indicate increasing degrees of freedom (or observations). As the sample size approaches the population size, the *t* distribution approaches the standard normal.

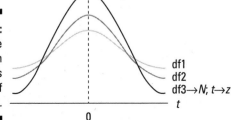

Figure 3-5:
The
t distribution
with various
degrees of
freedom.

If you have a normally distributed sample mean, such as

$$\bar{X} \sim N\left(\mu_X, \frac{\sigma_X^2}{n}\right)$$

then you can convert it to a standard normal by

$$Z = \frac{\bar{X} - \mu_X}{\frac{\sigma_X}{\sqrt{n}}}$$

Similarly, if you have a squared normal, such as the sample variance s_X^2, you can convert it to a chi-squared by

$$\frac{s_X^2}{\sigma_X^2} \sim \chi_{n-1}^2$$

When you take the ratio of the standard normal to the square root of your chi-squared distribution, you end up with a t distribution:

$$\frac{\dfrac{\bar{X} - \mu_X}{\dfrac{\sigma_X}{\sqrt{n}}}}{\sqrt{\dfrac{s_X^2}{\sigma_X^2}}} = \frac{\bar{X} - \mu_X}{\sigma_X} \cdot \frac{\sigma_X}{s_X} = \frac{\bar{X} - \mu_X}{\dfrac{s_X}{\sqrt{n}}} \sim t_{n-1}$$

You can find the densities for various parts of the t distribution in Table A-2 of the appendix.

The F distribution

You probably used the F distribution in your statistics class to compare variances of two different normal distributions. In econometrics, you have a similar use for the F distribution. You'll find that the F distribution is easier to use if you're familiar with some of its characteristics, so I discuss those in this section.

The F distribution is derived from a *ratio* of a *two* χ^2 distributions divided by their respective degrees of freedom. The F distribution tends to be right-skewed, with the amount of skewness depending on the degrees of freedom. As the degrees of freedom in the numerator and denominator increase, the F distribution approaches a normal distribution.

I show how the F distribution changes with your degrees of freedom in Figure 3-6. The df1df1, df2df2, and df3df3 indicate increasing degrees of freedom (or observations) in both the numerator and denominator. Although the skewness of the F distribution decreases when either the numerator or denominator degrees of freedom increase, it approaches a normal distribution when both become large.

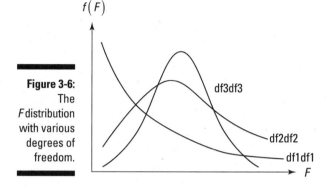

Figure 3-6:
The
F distribution
with various
degrees of
freedom.

If X and Y are two normally distributed random variables, then the squared deviations of the X and Y values from their mean have a chi-squared distribution ($\sum_{i=1}^{n}\left(X_i - \bar{X}\right)^2 \sim \chi_{n-1}^2$ and $\sum_{i=1}^{m}\left(Y_i - \bar{Y}\right)^2 \sim \chi_{m-1}^2$). When you take the ratio of the chi-squared distributions and divide each by its degrees of freedom, you end up with an F distribution:

$$\frac{\dfrac{\sum_{i=1}^{n}\left(X_i - \bar{X}\right)^2}{n-1}}{\dfrac{\sum_{i=1}^{m}\left(Y_i - \bar{Y}\right)^2}{m-1}} = \frac{s_X^2}{s_Y^2} \sim F_{(n-1),(m-1)}$$

You can find the densities for various parts of the F distribution in Table A-4 of the appendix.

Making Inferences and Testing Hypotheses with Probability Distributions

When you want to test a theory (or an assumption) about the value of a population parameter, you perform some type of hypothesis test. In most cases, you use one of the four most common probability distributions to perform your test: the Z (standard normal), t, χ^2, or F distributions.

Performing a hypothesis test

When you test an assumption or prior belief about a population parameter (such as a mean, variance, or regression coefficient), the assumption is typically labeled your *null hypothesis* (H_0). You test it against an *alternative hypothesis* (H_1). Hypothesis tests can be either *one-tailed* (right or left) or *two-tailed* (both left and right). At the conclusion of your hypothesis test, you either *reject* the null hypothesis or *fail to reject* the null hypothesis. (You rarely hear an econometrician or statistician refer to "accepting" a hypothesis.)

To perform a hypothesis test, follow these steps:

1. **Estimate the population parameter using your sample data.**

   This step can be accomplished with *point estimation*. A point estimate is a single estimate of your parameter of interest.

2. **Determine the appropriate distribution.**

   Estimators usually follow one of the well-known continuous probability distributions (the Z, t, chi-squared, or F). In Table 3-2, I summarize how you choose the appropriate distribution.

3. **Calculate an interval estimate or test statistic.**

   If you decide to use the *confidence interval approach* to test your hypothesis, then you need to calculate an interval estimate of your population parameter (I provide more details and an example of interval estimation in the section "The confidence interval approach").

   If you use the *test of significance approach* to test your hypothesis, then you calculate the appropriate test statistic (I review the formulas for common test statistics in the section "The test of significance approach"). Regardless of whether you decide to use the confidence interval or test of significance, you need your point estimate from Step 1 and the distribution you chose in Step 2.

4. **Determine the hypothesis test outcome.**

   After you complete Step 3, you determine whether you reject or fail to reject the null hypothesis based on some predetermined level of significance (α) or confidence ($1 - \alpha$). The most common values for α are 0.01, 0.05, and 0.10 (or 1 percent, 5 percent, and 10 percent). See the sidebar "A note on levels of significance and p-values" for more detail.

Table 3-2	Probability Distributions for Various Hypothesis Tests		
Purpose of Test	**Sample Type**	**Typical Null Hypothesis, H_0**	**Appropriate Distribution**
Value of one mean	One random sample with known population variance	$H_0: \mu_X = c$	Z
Value of one mean	One random sample with unknown population variance	$H_0: \mu_X = c$	t
Value of one variance	One random sample	$H_0: \sigma_X^2 = c$	χ^2
Comparing two means	Two random and independent samples with unknown population variances	$H_0: \mu_X - \mu_Y = 0$	t
Comparing two means	One paired sample with unknown population variances	$H_0: \mu_X - \mu_Y = 0$	t
Comparing two variances	Two random and independent samples drawn from a normal population	$H_0: \sigma_X^2 = \sigma_Y^2$ or $H_0: \dfrac{\sigma_X^2}{\sigma_Y^2} = 1$	F

In Table 3-2, treat c as a number representing a hypothesized value. The list of hypotheses in Table 3-2 isn't exhaustive, but it should remind you of the types of tests encountered in your statistics course. If you're comfortable with these scenarios, then you're well prepared for other tests that you'll encounter in econometrics.

The confidence interval approach

When you use the confidence interval approach to hypothesis testing, you calculate a *lower limit* and an *upper limit* for a *random interval* and attach some likelihood that the interval contains the true parameter value. If you're testing a hypothesis, the values of your estimated interval relative to the assumed value of the parameter determine whether you reject the null hypothesis or do not reject the null hypothesis.

In your statistics class, you likely saw a number of different formulas for confidence intervals. The formula you choose depends on the purpose of the hypothesis test (testing a population mean, a population variance, and so on). Figure 3-7 illustrates the general concept of using confidence intervals for hypothesis testing.

Figure 3-7:
Confidence interval used for hypothesis testing.

Critical region	Confidence interval	Critical region
$\alpha/2$	$1-\alpha$	$\alpha/2$

Lower limit   Upper limit

If the hypothesized value for your parameter of interest is in the critical region, you reject the null hypothesis. If it's in the confidence interval, you fail to reject the null hypothesis.

You should feel comfortable using confidence intervals before moving forward with other material in econometrics, so be sure to review that material in your statistics text if necessary.

You can say that your confidence interval has a $1 - \alpha$ probability of containing the true parameter value. However, you shouldn't say that the parameter value has a $1 - \alpha$ probability of being contained within the interval. The interval is random because it depends on random estimators, but the parameter (even though not known) is fixed and nonrandom.

The test of significance approach

With the test of significance approach, you calculate a test statistic and then compare that calculated value to the critical value from one of the probability distributions (Z, t, χ^2, or F) to determine the outcome of your hypothesis test.

Which formula you choose for your test (and you should know a few from statistics) depends on the purpose of the hypothesis test (such as testing a population mean or a population variance). Figure 3-8 illustrates the general concept of using a test statistic for hypothesis testing.

Figure 3-8: Test statistic used for hypothesis testing in one-tailed and two-tailed tests.

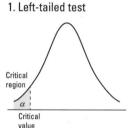
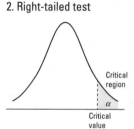
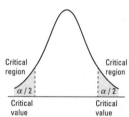

If your calculated test statistic is in the critical region, you reject the null hypothesis, and you can also say that your test is *statistically significant*. If your calculated test statistic is not in the critical region, you fail to reject the null hypothesis, and you say that your test is *statistically insignificant*.

Be sure to review test statistics and the test of significance approach to hypothesis testing more before moving forward if you're not comfortable with it.

A note on levels of significance and *p*-values

In some cases, you perform a hypothesis test with a predetermined level of significance (α) or confidence ($1 - \alpha$). In other cases, you report the *p*-value of your test and allow whoever's examining your output to determine the outcome of the test.

If you don't feel that setting a predetermined level of significance is appropriate, you should report the *p*-value of the test instead. The *p-value* is the lowest level of significance at which you could reject the null hypothesis given your calculated test statistic. Your econometrics software typically calculates these values for you when you do any type of hypothesis test. I show a graphical depiction of a *p*-value in the following figure.

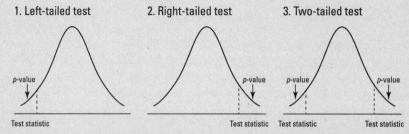

1. Left-tailed test   2. Right-tailed test   3. Two-tailed test

The most common predetermined levels of significance are 1 percent, 5 percent, and 10 percent (or $\alpha = 0.01$, $\alpha = 0.05$, and $\alpha = 0.10$), but there's nothing sacred about these values.

Any value for α leaves you susceptible to type I and type II errors. A *type I error* occurs when you reject a null hypothesis that is in fact true. A *type II error* results when you fail to reject a null hypothesis that is in fact false. The table summarizes these types of errors:

	H_0 *True*	H_0 *False*
Reject H_0	Type I error	Correct
Do not reject	Correct	Type II error

When you increase the value of α, then you increase the chance of rejecting your null hypothesis. Because you don't know whether that hypothesis is true or false, you're increasing the chance of committing a type I error.

When you reduce the value of α, you increase the chance of failing to reject your null hypothesis. You don't know whether that hypothesis is true or false, so you're increasing the chance of committing a type II error.

One reason for reporting *p*-values is to allow people examining your output to apply their own tolerance for committing type I and type II errors. This divulgence relieves you from criticism of applying some arbitrary value for α and passes the burden on to the reader.

Part II
Building the Classical Linear Regression Model

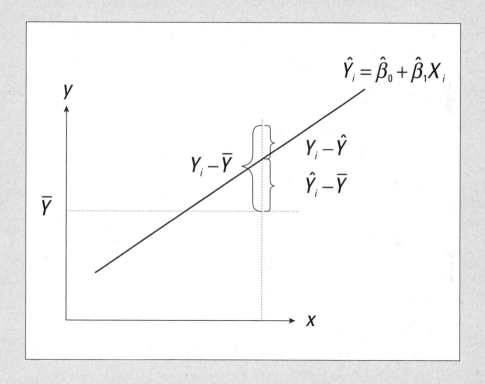

In this part . . .

- ✔ Recognize how econometric techniques help you make estimates about economic relationships by relating economic theory to econometric models.

- ✔ Grasp the fundamental ideas behind the most common technique used to quantify economic relationships: the ordinary least squares (OLS) technique, also known as regression analysis.

- ✔ Estimate simple regression models by hand and on the computer and interpret the results of regression analysis with the help of econometric software.

- ✔ Get acquainted with the assumptions of the classical linear regression model (CLRM) that define a "standard situation" in econometrics and understand their role in proving the Gauss-Markov theorem.

- ✔ Find out precisely how a normal distribution is used in econometrics and the importance of the normality assumption for tests of statistical significance and calculations of forecast error.

Chapter 4

Understanding the Objectives of Regression Analysis

*E*conometric techniques help you make estimates about economic relationships. For example, you can use your knowledge of economic theory to predict that having more disposable income leads to increased consumption for normal goods, but you need econometrics to determine how much consumption rises for a given increase in income. In other words, the wisdom you acquired in your introductory and intermediate economics courses helps you form hypotheses about the direction (positive or negative signs) of various relationships, but econometrics assists you in estimating their magnitude.

The purpose of this chapter is twofold: to provide you with an overview of the most common technique used to quantify economic relationships, called *regression analysis,* and to explain how to organize the data you'll use for your analysis.

In order to apply econometrics effectively, you need some background in both economics and statistics. If you need a refresher of economic theory, check out *Economics For Dummies* by Sean Masaki Flynn (John Wiley & Sons, Inc.). For a review of the relevant statistical concepts, refer to Chapters 2 and 3 of this book.

Making a Case for Causality

Econometrics is typically used for one of the following objectives:

✔ Predicting or forecasting future events

✔ Explaining how one or more factors affect some outcome of interest

Although some econometrics problems have both objectives, in most cases you use econometric tools for one aim or the other.

Regardless of the objective for using econometrics, econometric studies generally have one characteristic in common: the specification of a model. *Model specification* consists of selecting an outcome of interest or dependent variable (typically labeled as *Y*) and one or more independent factors (or explanatory variables, usually labeled with *X*s). In addition, model specification also, refers to choosing an appropriate functional form (a topic that I discuss in Chapter 8).

Independent variables are the factors that cause changes in your dependent variable, not the other way around. Because most situations in economics (and in some business fields like marketing and accounting) involve cause-and-effect scenarios, applied work in econometrics pays careful attention to the variables chosen to be dependent and independent. If the relationship between cause variables and effect variables isn't obvious, you should utilize your common sense and knowledge of economics to justify the causal assumptions of your model.

Justifying your model means that you should be able to explain why it makes sense to think of your dependent variable as being caused by the independent variables you've selected. In some cases, that connection may be obvious, but in other cases you may need to provide a detailed explanation. For example, if you have state data and your dependent variable is the average amount of time unemployed workers are without a job, you'd want to include independent variables that capture the skill traits of workers and other state characteristics that may influence unemployment spell length. Average education and work experience levels are characteristics that, according to human capital theory, should help workers reduce the amount of time they're unemployed. These are justifiable independent variables and won't require much explanation because of their direct connection with the outcome of interest. On the other hand, state policies, such as welfare assistance and unemployment insurance, have a less obvious connection. Nevertheless, they're likely to influence worker decision making and be important causal factors. It's likely, however, that you'll need to invest more time explaining how they're related to the outcome and why their inclusion among the independent variables makes sense.

Keep in mind that regression analysis identifies the direction (sign ±) and strength (magnitude) of the relationship between the variables in your model. But the strength of the statistical relationship does not imply causality. Figure 4-1 shows the scatter plot of monthly ice cream production in the United States and drowning deaths in Florida single residence pools in 2006. You can see that drowning and ice cream production have a strong positive relationship (trend line is upward sloping, so both variables move in the same direction [deaths increase, ice cream increase]), but you don't have a strong case for one *causing* the other simply because they're correlated (ice cream affects drowning?). It's simply an example of *spurious correlation,* which occurs when two variables coincidentally have a statistical relationship (positive or negative) but one doesn't cause the other.

Ice Cream and Drowning Scatter, 2006

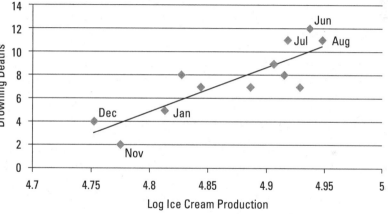

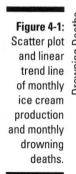

Figure 4-1: Scatter plot and linear trend line of monthly ice cream production and monthly drowning deaths.

Causation cannot be proven by statistical results. Your results can be used to support a hypothesis of causality, but only after you've developed a model that is well grounded in economic theory and/or good common sense.

Getting Acquainted with the Population Regression Function (PRF)

Before you begin with regression analysis, you need to identify the *population regression function* (PRF). The PRF defines reality (or your perception of it) as it relates to your topic of interest. To identify it, you need to determine your dependent and independent variables (and how they'll be measured) as well as the mathematical function describing how the variables are related.

Setting up the PRF model

After you narrow down your topic or question of interest, you're ready to develop your model using the following steps:

1. **Provide the general mathematical specification of your model.**

   The general specification denotes your dependent variable and all the independent (or explanatory) variables that you believe affect the dependent variable in your population of interest.

   Suppose that three variables affect the dependent variable. The general specification will look something like $Y = f(X_1, X_2, X_3)$, where Y is the dependent variable and the Xs represent the independent variables, which you believe directly affect (or cause) fluctuations in the Y variable.

    Unless the reasoning is obvious, provide some justification for the variables chosen as independent variables and for the functional form of the specification (see Step 2). Doing so helps you avoid misspecification, which occurs if you omit important variables or include irrelevant variables (I cover the details of misspecification issues in Chapter 8).

2. **Derive the econometric specification of your model.**

   In this step, you take the variables identified in Step 1 and develop a function that can be used to calculate econometric results. This functional form is known as the *population regression function* (PRF). In this step, you're also acknowledging that the relationship you hypothesized in Step 1 is expected to exist when you look at the average of the data; not for every single observation.

   Assume you have reason to believe that the model is linear. It will look like this: $E(Y|X_1, X_2, X_3) = \beta_0 + \beta_1 X_1 + \beta_2 X_2 + \beta_3 X_3$.

   In this function, the *conditional mean operator* $E(Y|X_1, X_2, X_3)$ indicates that the relationship is expected to hold, on average, for given values of the independent variables. The intercept term β_0, also called the *constant,* is the expected mean value of Y when all Xs are equal to zero. The other βs represent the partial slopes (effects). These partial slopes tell you how much your dependent variable changes when you change the independent variable by one unit but hold the value of the other independent variables constant. (This idea of changing one thing and keeping the rest the same is the *ceteris paribus*, or all else equal, condition that you're familiar with from your introductory economics courses.)

   Depending on the particular phenomenon you're analyzing, a nonlinear relationship using squared terms, logs, or another method instead of the linear function $E(Y|X_1, X_2, X_3) = \beta_0 + \beta_1 X_1 + \beta_2 X_2 + \beta_3 X_3$ may be more appropriate (these alternatives are described in Chapter 8).

The specification you choose is assumed to describe the "true" relationship, so be sure to justify it using sound economic theory and common sense.

3. **Specify the random nature of your model.**

   This step clarifies that the relationship you've assumed in Steps 1 and 2 holds on average but may contain errors when a specific observation is chosen at random from the population. This is known as the *stochastic population regression function* and is written as $Y_i = \beta_0 + \beta_1 X_{1i} + \beta_2 X_{2i} + \beta_3 X_{3i} + \varepsilon_i$, where the i subscripts denote any randomly chosen observation and ε_i represents the stochastic (or random) error term associated with that observation. Note that *stochastic* is simply statistics jargon for *random*.

   Regardless of how you choose to represent the PRF, the random error term represents the difference between the observed value of your dependent variable and the conditional mean of the dependent variable derived from your model. This value is positive if the observed value is above the conditional mean and negative if it is below.

The random error can result from one or more of the following factors:

✔ Insufficient or incorrectly measured data

✔ A lack of theoretical insights to fully account for all the factors that affect the dependent variable

✔ Applying an incorrect functional form; for example, assuming the relationship is linear when it's quadratic

✔ Unobservable characteristics

✔ Unpredictable elements of behavior

If you have several explanatory variables, you can save time by writing the econometric model using some mathematical shorthand. With algebraic notation, it would look like one of the following two functions:

$$Y_i = \beta_0 + \beta_1 X_{i1} + \beta_2 X_{i2} + \dots + \beta_p X_{ip} + \varepsilon_i$$

$$Y_i = \beta_0 + \sum_{k=1}^{p} \beta_k X_{ik} + \varepsilon_i$$

Walking through an example

This section is all about illustrating the steps used to develop the population regression function with an example. Suppose you're interested in explaining the variation in exam scores for an entire group of econometrics students. Economic theory suggests that input will have a positive effect on output. In this case, common sense suggests that study hours are an appropriate input and exam scores be used as an output, so the general model is $S = f(H)$, where S is exam score and H is study hours (number of hours students spent studying).

The art of econometrics is the way you use additional insights to specify the econometric model. Often those theoretical insights are vague or don't exist at all, so some experimentation may be required. For simplicity, assume in this case that the relationship is linear. Then the PRF is $E(S|H) = \beta_0 + \beta_1 H$ and the stochastic PRF is $S_i = \beta_0 + \beta_1 H_1 + \varepsilon_i$.

Table 4-1 contains the population data of exam scores and study hours for my econometrics students.

Table 4-1	Study Hours and Individual Exam Scores for Population of Econometrics Students
Study Hours, H	*Scores, S*
1	25, 30, 35, 40, 45
2	35, 40, 44, 50, 55, 58
3	49, 54, 60, 64, 68
4	50, 63, 65, 73, 78, 83, 85
5	72, 77, 80, 86, 88, 95

Using the data in Table 4-1, you can calculate the conditional means (the average exam score for each level of study hours) and the resulting PRF. The conditional means are as follows:

$$E(S|H=1) = \frac{25+30+35+40+45}{5} = 35$$

$$E(S|H=2) = \frac{35+40+44+50+55+58}{6} = 47$$

$$E(S|H=3) = \frac{49+54+60+64+68}{5} = 59$$

$$E(S|H=4) = \frac{50+63+65+73+78+83+85}{7} = 71$$

$$E(S|H=5) = \frac{72+77+80+86+88+95}{6} = 83$$

The PRF must pass through the conditional means, so those values can be used to calculate the slope.

On average, the students increase their exam scores by 12 points for every additional hour of studying. You can determine the intercept value (value of S when $H = 0$) by extrapolating back to zero study hours, and then you can write the PRF as $E(S|H) = 23 + 12H$.

Figure 4-2 illustrates the data, conditional means, and PRF. You can write the stochastic version of the PRF in Figure 4-2 as $S_i = 23 + 12H_i + \varepsilon_i$. This representation emphasizes that the observed value for your dependent variable from an observation picked at random is likely to be different from the conditional mean for that group. Some students earn scores above the conditional mean (positive random error) and some below (negative random error).

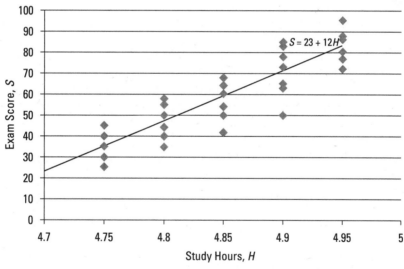

Figure 4-2: Population regression function with scatter plot of individual population observations.

In most applications, you won't have population data. Consequently, you'll need to make some sensible assumptions about the model and work with sample data to *estimate* your PRF. Because sample data may contain only one Y value for a given X value, calculating conditional means makes no sense and you'll need to use a different technique. That's where Chapter 5 comes to the rescue. Head there for details on estimating regression functions using sample data.

Collecting and Organizing Data for Regression Analysis

After you develop the econometric model and population regression function that you'd like to estimate (as I describe in the earlier section "Getting Acquainted with the Population Regression Function (PRF)"), you must compile the data and prepare it for regression analysis. In general, you'll utilize one of four types of data:

- ✔ Cross-sectional
- ✔ Time series
- ✔ Panel (longitudinal)
- ✔ Pooled cross-sectional

I cover each of these types of data in more detail in the following sections.

Although most econometric techniques can be applied to any data structure, some situations require specialized techniques that allow you to deal with special features of the data. Chapter 12 addresses issues that arise mainly when you use time-series data; Chapters 16 and 17 cover methods that can be applied when you use panel (longitudinal) data.

Taking a snapshot: Cross-sectional data

Cross-sectional data contains measurements for individual observations (persons, households, firms, counties, states, countries, or what have you) at a given point in time.

A linear regression function using cross-sectional data is typically written this way: $Y_i = \beta_0 + \beta_1 X_{i1} + \beta_2 X_{i2} + \ldots + \beta_p X_{ip} + \varepsilon_i$.

The i subscripts represent the individual units providing the measurements for each variable.

You can use these types of models for testing microeconomic hypotheses, so they tend to be popular in labor economics, industrial organization, urban economics, and other micro-based fields.

When using cross-sectional data, you assume that the observations represent a *random* draw from your population of interest. Sometimes the data for the individual observations must be collected over a period of days or weeks, but you can usually ignore these timing differences with cross-sectional data.

Table 4-2 shows how you organize cross-sectional data in preparation for estimating your econometric model. *Note:* Econometric software programs typically require that the variables be aligned in columns, with the observations (or measurements) following in rows.

Table 4-2   Cross-Sectional Data for a Random Sample of Movies Released in 2009

i	Title	Box Office Revenue (in $mil)	Viewer Approval Rating	Budget (in $mil)
1	Crazy Heart	39	91	7
2	A Serious Man	9	89	7
3	A Single Man	9	86	7
4	An Education	13	94	7.5
5	Sunshine Cleaning	12	71	8
⋮	⋮	⋮	⋮	⋮
115	Harry Potter and the Half-Blood Prince	302	83	250

Source: www.imdb.com and www.rottentomatoes.com

In order to save space, I skip from the fifth observation in the data to the last observation (a procedure that I replicate in some other tables). All of the other observations have the same structure, so keep in mind that this dataset contains a total of 115 observations.

Cross-sectional data is typically collected through surveys. The most popular cross-sectional datasets include the Current Population Survey (CPS), the American Community Survey (ACS), and extracts from the decennial census. If your research question is highly specialized, you may need to devise your own survey and collect the cross-sectional data needed for your analysis.

Looking at the past to explain the present: Time-series data

Time-series data contains measurements on one or more variables (such as gross domestic product, interest rates, or unemployment rates) over time in a given space (like a specific country or state).

A linear regression function using time series data is generically written as

$$Y_t = \beta_0 + \beta_1 X_{i1} + \beta_2 X_{i2} + \ldots + \beta_p X_{tp} + \varepsilon_t$$

where the *t* subscripts represent the period of time in which the measurement was observed.

You can utilize these models for identifying trends and examining seasonal adjustments, so their use tends to be most popular among macroeconomists (I cover these types of econometric models in Chapter 15).

Patterns in time-series data can convey important information, so make sure your data is organized in chronological order. Also, when ordering the data, pay particular attention to the *frequency* with which it was collected. Typical frequencies are daily, weekly, monthly, quarterly, or yearly. You'll be able to use the ordering of the data to identify trends and the frequency to examine changes that are unique to specific periods (election year, holidays, and so on).

Table 4-3 shows how to organize time-series data concerning labor force statistics in preparation for estimating your econometric model. The variables should be aligned in columns with a measurement for each unit of time. The observations (or measurements) follow chronologically in rows.

Table 4-3		**Monthly Time-Series Data**		
t	*Year*	*Month*	*Unemployment Rate*	*Underemployment Rate*
1	2002	January	5.7	9.5
2	2002	February	5.7	9.5
⋮	⋮	⋮	⋮	⋮
12	2002	December	6.0	9.8
13	2003	January	5.8	10.0
⋮	⋮	⋮	⋮	⋮
120	2011	December	8.5	15.2

Source: www.bls.gov

Time-series data can be compiled by businesses, but the most popular series are typically collected by government agencies. The Federal Reserve, Census Bureau, Department of Commerce, Department of Energy, and Bureau of Labor Statistics are all excellent sources for time-series data.

Combining the dimensions of space and time: Panel or longitudinal data

Panel data (also referred to as *longitudinal data*) contains a time series for each cross-sectional unit in the sample. The data contains measurements for individual observations (persons, households, firms, counties, states, countries, or other) over a period of time (days, months, quarters, or years). Consequently, panel data contains both cross-sectional and time-series characteristics.

A linear regression function using panel data is generically written this way:

$$Y_{it} = \beta_0 + \beta_1 X_{it1} + \beta_2 X_{it2} + \ldots + \beta_p X_{itp} + \varepsilon_{it}$$

The *i* subscripts represent the individual units, and the *t* subscripts represent the period of time in which the measurement was observed.

You can use these models to control for numerous characteristics (both observed and unobserved) of the cross-sectional units as well as lags and trends that may be present over time. Consequently, both microeconomists and macroeconomists use this type of data. (You can learn about specific types of panel econometric models in Chapter 17.)

The collection of panel data begins with a random, cross-sectional draw from your population of interest. Then the same cross-sectional units are followed over a period of time with some predetermined frequency.

Table 4-4 shows how you'd organize panel data (in this case concerning the same 50 Major League Baseball players in 2003 and 2004) in preparation for estimating your econometric model. Your variables should be aligned in columns, with the observations (or measurements) in rows. The observations should be ordered so that data collected over time is adjacent to each of your cross-sectional units.

Table 4-4				Panel Data		
Obs	i	t	Name	Year	Batting Average	Years in MLB
1	1	1	Carlos Baerga	2003	0.343	14
2	1	2	Carlos Baerga	2004	0.235	15
3	2	1	Tony Clark	2003	0.232	9
4	2	2	Tony Clark	2004	0.221	10
⋮	⋮	⋮	⋮		⋮	⋮
99	50	1	Todd Zeile	2003	0.257	15
100	50	2	Todd Zeile	2004	0.233	16

Source: www.seanlahman.com

Panel data is typically collected through surveys. The most popular panel datasets include the National Longitudinal Survey (NLS), the Panel Study of Income Dynamics (PSID), and the Survey of Income and Program Participation (SIPP).

Joining multiple snapshots: Pooled cross-sectional data

If a cross sectional survey collects the same information on multiple occasions from different individual units, you can combine the data to create a *pooled cross section*. A pooled cross section combines independent cross-sectional data that has been collected over time.

The advantage of pooled cross-sectional data is that more observations tend to improve the accuracy of econometric estimates and the added time element allows you to explore both static and dynamic elements (I discuss some applications using pooled cross-sectional data in Chapter 16).

Simply because your dataset contains both a cross-sectional and time-series component doesn't make it a panel dataset. In some cases, you may be able to increase the number of observations for your analysis by combining randomly sampled cross sections of individuals collected in different points in time, but it isn't a panel dataset unless the same individual units are observed in each subsequent time period.

Treat pooled cross-sectional data simply as a larger version of a cross-sectional dataset, because the data lacks the special feature of observing the same cross-sectional unit on multiple occasions. In Table 4-5, you're working with pooled cross section data for a random sample of Major League Baseball players: 50 players from 2005 and 50 players from 2006. The table shows how you would organize a pooled cross section by year in preparation for estimating your econometric model.

Table 4-5			Pooled Cross Section Data			
Obs	**i**	**t**	**Name**	**Year**	**Batting Average**	**Years in MLB**
1	1	1	Moises Alou	2005	0.321	16
2	2	1	Paul Bako	2005	0.250	8
⋮	⋮	⋮	⋮	⋮	⋮	⋮
50	50	1	Eric Young	2005	0.275	14
51	51	2	Sandy Alomar	2006	0.217	19
52	52	2	Geoff Blum	2006	0.254	8
⋮	⋮	⋮	⋮	⋮	⋮	⋮
100	100	2	Preston Wilson	2006	0.269	9

Source: www.seanlahman.com

You'll want to keep track of the time period in which you collected data for each individual unit.

In addition to increasing your observations, a pooled cross section allows you to identify changes over time (on average across all individual units) and observe policy analysis across different time periods. To accomplish this, keep any variables that track the time component.

Chapter 5

Going Beyond Ordinary with the Ordinary Least Squares Technique

. . . .

In This Chapter

▶ Getting acquainted with the least squares principle

▶ Pinpointing the residuals

▶ Estimating regression coefficients

▶ Interpreting the magnitude of regression coefficients

▶ Measuring the overall regression fit

. . . .

*R*egression analysis refers to techniques that allow you to estimate economic relationships using data. The method used most frequently is commonly known as *ordinary least squares* (OLS). In this chapter, you discover how to estimate simple regression models with manual calculations and computer calculations. You also find out how to interpret simple and multiple regression models using output from STATA.

Although the OLS technique is popular and relatively simple (in comparison to other available methods), the application of it through manual calculations can become quite complicated when you start adding more independent (explanatory) variables to your regression model. You can improve your understanding of the OLS technique by working through the algebraic manipulations you see throughout this chapter, but you must also learn how to apply OLS using STATA with realistic models and real-world data. (For more information on this software, see Chapter 1.)

Note: In this chapter I assume that you grasp the fundamental difference between parameters and estimates/statistics (see Chapter 3 for a review of these topics). I also assume that you've thought about your need to perform regression analysis (the goals of which I cover in Chapter 4).

Defining and Justifying the Least Squares Principle

When you need to estimate a sample regression function (SRF), the most common econometric method is the ordinary least squares (OLS) technique, which uses the least squares principle to fit a prespecified regression function through your sample data. The *least squares principle* states that the SRF should be constructed (with the constant and slope values) so that the sum of the squared distance between the observed values of your dependent variable and the values estimated from your SRF is minimized (the smallest possible value).

Although sometimes alternative methods to OLS are necessary, in most situations, OLS remains the most popular technique for estimating regressions for the following three reasons:

- **Using OLS is easier than the alternatives.** Other techniques, including generalized method of moments (GMM) and maximum likelihood (ML) estimation, can be used to estimate regression functions, but they require more mathematical sophistication and more computing power. These days you'll probably always have all the computing power you need, but historically it did limit the popularity of other techniques relative to OLS.

- **OLS is sensible.** By using squared residuals, you can avoid positive and negative residuals canceling each other out and find a regression line that's as close as possible to the observed data points.

- **OLS results have desirable characteristics.** A desirable attribute of any estimator is for it to be a good predictor. When you use OLS, the following helpful numerical properties are associated with the results:

  - The regression line always passes through the sample means of Y and X or $\bar{Y} = \hat{\beta}_0 + \hat{\beta}_1\bar{X}$.

  - The mean of the estimated (predicted) Y value is equal to the mean value of the actual Y or $\bar{\hat{Y}} = \bar{Y}$.

  - The mean of the residuals is zero, or $\bar{\hat{\varepsilon}} = 0$.

  - The residuals are uncorrelated with the predicted Y, or $\sum_{i=1}^{n}\left(Y_i - \bar{Y}\right)\hat{\varepsilon}_i = 0$.

  - The residuals are uncorrelated with observed values of the independent variable, or $\sum_{i=1}^{n}\hat{\varepsilon}_i X_i = 0$.

The OLS properties are used for various proofs in econometrics, but they also illustrate that your predictions will be perfect, on average. This conclusion follows from the regression line passing through the sample means, the mean of your predictions equaling the mean of your data values, and from the fact that your average residual will be zero.

Estimating the Regression Function and the Residuals

The regression function is usually expressed mathematically in one of the following ways:

- **Basic notation:** $Y_i = \beta_0 + \beta_1 X_{i1} + \beta_2 X_{i2} + \ldots + \beta_p X_{ip} + \varepsilon_i$
- **Summation notation:** $Y_i = \beta_0 + \sum_{k=1}^{p} \beta_k X_{ik} + \varepsilon_i$
- **Matrix notation** (which I don't use in this book): $Y = X\beta + \varepsilon$

The Y variable represents the outcome you're interested in, called the dependent variable, and the Xs represent all the independent (or explanatory) variables (turn to Chapters 4 and 8 for information on how you go about determining which variables to include). Your objective now is to estimate the population regression function (PRF) using your sample data.

When working on real-world econometric problems, you usually specify a PRF with a dependent variable and several independent variables. For example, suppose you're interested in the number of hamburgers purchased during the lunch hour at school cafeterias. Microeconomic theory suggests that sales should be influenced by the price of the hamburgers along with other factors, such as the price of other food items, the price of soft drinks, and so on. With that in mind, you may want to specify your PRF using hamburger sales as the dependent variable and all other relevant factors as the independent variables.

To visualize the OLS regression and get a basic understanding of the fundamental concept, assume now that the dependent variable (hamburger sales) is influenced by only one explanatory variable (the price of hamburgers). The sample regression function (SRF) is expressed as $Y_i = \hat{\beta}_0 + \hat{\beta}_1 X_i + \hat{\varepsilon}_i$, where Y is hamburger sales and X is the price. In this case, the SRF is a line, with the value for $\hat{\beta}_0$ estimating the intercept and $\hat{\beta}_1$ estimating the value of the slope.

Notice how the mathematical representation of the SRF uses hats (^) above the coefficients and error term. I use this symbol to denote that these numbers are estimates of their true population values, but keep in mind that some textbooks use English (Latin) letters to represent sample regression coefficients and other estimates.

Obtaining Estimates of the Regression Parameters

Before you start estimating regression coefficients using mathematical tools, you can get a good idea of the relationship between the intercept, slope, and the residuals by examining the components of the sample regression function graphically. Figure 5-1 shows a scatter plot of Y and X values, the sample regression line (SRL) containing the estimated (or *predicted*) Y values, and the estimated errors.

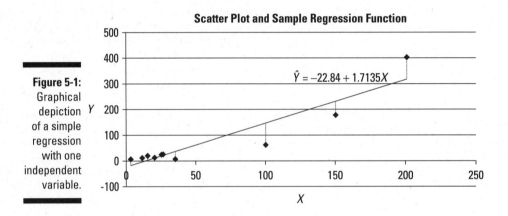

Figure 5-1:
Graphical
depiction
of a simple
regression
with one
independent
variable.

The regression line superimposed on the scatter plot in Figure 5-1 was derived using the ordinary least squares (OLS) technique. You can imagine sketching a random line through the points, calculating the sum of squared *residuals* (distance from the observed values — the diamonds — to the line), and moving the line and repeating this process until you find a line placement that achieves the smallest possible value for that sum. The problem is that you can make infinitely small adjustments to the line placement, which means you'd be sketching lines forever trying to find that magical value. Fortunately, a mathematical solution to this problem exists. Simply determine the formulas necessary to find the coefficient values and then calculate, as explained in the following sections. You get a regression line based on estimates that are great — in fact, they're perfect, on average.

Finding the formulas necessary to produce optimal coefficient values

Changes to a regression line also change the *residuals* (distance from the observed values to the line). The more appropriate the values you choose for the intercept and slope of that line, the smaller the squared residuals. If the value of the regression coefficients is inappropriately large or small, the squared residuals will be too large.

Figure 5-2 illustrates how the sum of squared residuals can respond to changes in coefficient values. The coefficient value is measured along the horizontal axis, and the sum of squared residuals is represented by the vertical axis. If the value of the regression coefficient is too low, the line won't have a good fit and the sum of squared residuals will be high. The same outcome occurs if the value of the regression coefficient is too high. ***Note:*** Your regression may consist of several coefficients (an intercept and slope coefficients), so this graph is a two-dimensional simplification.

Figure 5-2: An optimal set of coefficient values achieves the smallest sum of squared residuals.

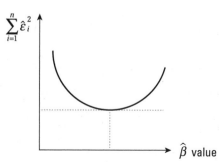

The objective of OLS is to produce those optimal regression coefficients. Because the coefficients have an infinite number of possible values, you can't rely on eyeballing it. Math to the rescue!

You can write the objective of OLS this way:

$$\min \sum_{i=1}^{n} \hat{\varepsilon}_i^2$$

which can be rewritten as

$$\min \sum_{i=1}^{n} \left(Y_i - \hat{Y}_i \right)^2$$

where $\hat{Y}_i$ is the estimated (or predicted) Y value from the regression. The final step in setting up the derivation of the regression coefficients is to substitute the equation of the SRL for the predicted Y values to obtain

$$\min \sum_{i=1}^{n}\left(Y_i - \hat{\beta}_0 - \hat{\beta}_1 X_i\right)^2$$

From here, you can use calculus to differentiate this equation with respect to the first regression coefficient (β_0) and set it equal to zero; then differentiate with respect to the other regression coefficient (β_1) and set it to zero. The result is two equations with two unknowns. Using algebra, you can then solve for the two regression coefficients.

The calculus and somewhat complicated algebraic manipulations result in easy-to-use formulas for calculating the regression coefficients (estimates of the slope and intercept). Calculate the slope first with

$$\hat{\beta}_1 = \frac{\sum_{i=1}^{n}\left(X_i - \bar{X}\right)\left(Y_i - \bar{Y}\right)}{\sum_{i=1}^{n}\left(X_i - \bar{X}\right)^2}$$

Then calculate the intercept with $\hat{\beta}_0 = \bar{Y} - \hat{\beta}_1\bar{X}$.

As you can see from the formulas, you need to first use the sample data to calculate the mean of the dependent variable ($\bar{Y}$) and the mean of the independent variable ($\bar{X}$).

Calculating the estimated regression coefficients

After you have the formulas for the coefficients that achieve the smallest sum of squared residuals, you're ready to start calculating either by hand or by using computer software. I cover both methods in the following sections.

Man and machine can produce the same results, but the machines allow you to produce results much more quickly.

Doing the math by hand

If you're going to be performing OLS estimation calculations by hand, I strongly recommend using a table to keep yourself organized. You're less likely to make mistakes this way.

Table 5-1 contains sample (or raw) data on hamburger sales (Y) and price (X) at five different school cafeterias (i). Each variable is housed in a column, and each observation is located in a row. Columns 1, 2, and 3 contain your sample data, and Columns 4, 5, 6, and 7 contain the intermediate calculations you use to arrive at the OLS regression coefficients.

Table 5-1   Calculation of Estimated Regression Coefficients

(1)	(2)	(3)	(4)	(5)	(6)	(7)
i	Y_i	X_i	$Y_i - \bar{Y}$	$X_i - \bar{X}$	$\left(X_i - \bar{X}\right)^2$	$\left(X_i - \bar{X}\right)\left(Y_i - \bar{Y}\right)$
1	100	1	38.2	−2	4	−76.4
2	80	2	18.2	−1	1	−18.2
3	63	3	1.2	0	0	0
4	45	4	−16.8	1	1	−16.8
5	21	5	−40.8	2	4	−81.6
Sum:	309	15	0	0	10	−193
Mean:	61.8	3				

Using Table 5-1, you can estimate the following regression coefficients:

$$\hat{\beta}_1 = \frac{\sum_{i=1}^{n}\left(X_i - \bar{X}\right)\left(Y_i - \bar{Y}\right)}{\sum_{i=1}^{n}\left(X_i - \bar{X}\right)^2} = \frac{-193}{10} = -19.3$$

$$\hat{\beta}_0 = \bar{Y} - \hat{\beta}_1\bar{X} = 61.8 - (-19.3)(3) = 119.7$$

The resulting SRF or equation of the line is $\hat{Y}_i = 119.7 - 19.3X_i$.

TIP

When you're computing regression coefficients by hand, you can use the properties $\bar{\hat{Y}} = \bar{Y}$ and $\bar{\hat{\varepsilon}} = 0$ to check your calculations. Alternatively, as shown in Figure 5-3, you can use STATA to estimate the regression coefficients and simply check your final answer.

. reg y x

Source	SS	df	MS		Number of obs =	5
					F(1, 3) =	803.94
Model	3724.9	1	3724.9		Prob > F =	0.0001
Residual	13.9	3	4.63333333		R-squared =	0.9963
					Adj R-squared =	0.9950
Total	3738.8	4	934.7		Root MSE =	2.1525

y	Coef.	Std. Err.	t	P>|t|	[95% Conf. Interval]	
x	−19.3	.6806859	−28.35	0.000	−21.46625	−17.13375
_cons	119.7	2.25758	53.02	0.000	112.5154	126.8846

Figure 5-3: STATA results using the OLS regression technique.

As you work through your table, periodically pause to make sure your intermediate calculations are correct. I'm sure you recall from statistics that the sum of deviations from the mean must be equal to zero. Then, you know that a zero must appear at the bottom of Columns 4 and 5. Always make sure you meet this requirement before you continue with your final calculations.

Computing on the computer

When you want to perform a regression with several independent variables, the formulas for calculating the regression coefficients become increasingly complex and typically require matrix algebra. Of course, more observations (sample points) also make manual calculations tedious. You'll want to let computer software do the heavy lifting for you in these cases.

Econometric software is not only useful with a simple regression model but also absolutely essential when you include additional independent variables and/or use data with numerous observations. STATA, one of the most popular econometrics software programs, can immediately produce the regression results you seek.

In order to truly appreciate the capability of the computer and the specialized software to generate regression results, take a look at a *multiple regression* (a regression model that contains more than one explanatory variable).

A movie studio is interested in gaining a better understanding of movie success. The studio execs provide you with a dataset containing 580 observations (movies). For each movie, you're given its box office revenue (in millions of dollars) and a measure of film quality through viewer approval (measured on a scale that can go from 0 to 100 percent viewer approval) and its budget (in millions of dollars). Table 5-2 provides a snapshot of the data for 10 of the 580 movies.

Table 5-2	First Ten Observations in Movie Dataset			
Observation	*Title*	*Box Office Revenue (in mil $)*	*Viewer Approval Rating*	*Budget (in mil $)*
1	Fireproof	33	40	0.5
2	Transamerica	9	76	1
3	The Lives of Others	11	93	2
4	The Visitor	9	90	4
5	The Gospel	16	32	5
6	The Wrestler	26	98	6

Observation	Title	Box Office Revenue (in mil $)	Viewer Approval Rating	Budget (in mil $)
7	Akeelah and the Bee	19	83	6
8	Thank You for Smoking	25	86	6.5
9	Friends with Money	13	71	6.5
10	Crash	55	76	6.5

Source: www.imdb.com *and* www.rottentomatoes.com

You use the complete dataset (containing all 580 observations) to perform an econometric analysis. With your understanding of economic theory, you determine that movie revenue is likely to depend on the quality of the film as perceived by moviegoers along with the studio's efforts to use well-known actors, cutting-edge special effects, exotic locations, and so on. Given the available data, you determine that both viewer ratings and the film's budget are sensible explanatory variables.

You use the OLS technique to produce the results, but because of the number of explanatory variables and observations, you want to rely exclusively on the computer for the calculations.

Using two *X* variables (X1 is viewer approval rating and X2 is budget), you can quickly obtain the multiple regression results in Figure 5-4.

Figure 5-4:
STATA
multiple
regression
output for
the movie
revenue
example.

```
. regress Y X1 X2

      Source |       SS       df       MS              Number of obs =     580      Sample
-------------+------------------------------           F(  2,   577) =  310.05      size
       Model | 1588188.67      2   794094.334           Prob > F      =  0.0000
    Residual | 1477786.25    577   2561.15468           R-squared     =  0.5180      R-sq
-------------+------------------------------           Adj R-squared =  0.5163
       Total | 3065974.92    579   5295.29347           Root MSE      =  50.608      Adj. R-sq

------------------------------------------------------------------------------
           Y |      Coef.   Std. Err.      t    P>|t|     [95% Conf. Interval]
-------------+----------------------------------------------------------------
          X1 |   .4138258   .0784313     5.28   0.000     .2597802    .5678713
          X2 |    1.11124   .0465035    23.90   0.000     1.019903    1.202577
       _cons |  -8.394324   4.668307    -1.80   0.073    -17.56327    .7746213
------------------------------------------------------------------------------
```

$\hat{\beta}s$

With these results, you're now prepared to provide the movie studio with some insights into film success — provided you know how to interpret the output. I explain how to do just that in the next section.

Interpreting Regression Coefficients

In most cases, you estimate a regression with the hope of gaining insight into the behavior of some phenomenon that interests you. The primary strength of regression analysis is being able to identify what factors affect that phenomenon and the magnitude of their effect. This information is powerful. Use it! The following sections explain how.

Seeing what regression coefficients have to say

Slope coefficients tell you the estimated direction of the impacts (positive/increase or negative/decrease) that your independent variables have on your dependent variable. They also tell you by how much your dependent variable changes (value or magnitude) when one of your independent variables increases or decreases.

The slope coefficient measures the change in your dependent variable for a 1-unit change in your explanatory variable. Suppose you calculate the following regression results using data on hamburger sales and prices from school cafeterias.

$$\hat{Y}_i = 119.7 - 19.3X_i$$

The slope coefficient is –19.3, which implies that a 1-unit increase in X is associated with a 19.3-unit decrease in Y. More specifically, the slope in this example implies that a \$1 increase in the price of hamburgers results in about 19 fewer hamburgers being sold. The literal interpretation of the intercept coefficient is the value of the dependent variable when the explanatory variables are all equal to zero. In the hamburger sales example, you would estimate hamburger consumption to be about 120 (119.7 ≈ 120) units if the school cafeterias were serving them for free or price was zero dollars.

Ignoring the intercept term in real-world scenarios

Problems in econometrics textbooks may ask you about the intercept term, but it's usually ignored in applied work, because situations where all of the explanatory variables equal zero are unlikely to occur. In applied situations, you're estimating regressions with two or more explanatory variables. If you want to obtain an accurate estimate of a variable's marginal effect on your dependent variable, then you need to make sure you adequately control for other factors that may simultaneously affect your variable of interest. Ignoring other variables can result in biased regression results (a topic I cover later in Chapter 8).

When you estimate a regression model with two or more independent (explanatory) variables, you have a *multiple regression* and the coefficients are called *partial slope coefficients.* Partial slope coefficients provide an estimate of the change in the dependent variable for a 1-unit change in the explanatory variable, assuming the value of all other variables in the regression model hold constant. The goal here is to disentangle the effects that numerous variables may have on the outcome of interest and isolate their impact.

If you refer to the preceding section's example of estimating movie revenue, you can see an interpretation of coefficients in the multiple regression. The STATA results ($\hat{Y}_i = -8.39 + 0.41X_{i1} + 1.11X_{i2}$) shown in Figure 5-4 suggest that a percentage-point increase in the viewer rating increases movie revenue by \$0.41 million ($\hat{\beta}_1 = 0.41$) (or \$410,000), holding movie budget constant. Also, a \$1 million increase in the movie budget increases film revenue by \$1.11 million ($\hat{\beta}_2 = 1.11$) (or \$1,110,000), holding viewer rating constant.

When interpreting the results of multiple regressions, make sure you're using the units in which the variables are measured. For example, if X_1 represents viewer ratings and viewer ratings are measured as a percentage, you need to remember that a percentage point is 1 unit. People looking at your work may not know (or may not remember) how the variables are measured, so without the appropriate units, any value is difficult (if not impossible) to interpret accurately. ***Note:*** Because the variables used in your regression analysis aren't likely to all be measured in the same units, try to avoid comparing coefficient values for different variables.

Standardizing regression coefficients

Comparing coefficient values is not as straightforward as you may first think. Here are a few reasons why:

- ✔ In standard OLS regression, the coefficient with the largest magnitude is not necessarily associated with "the most important" variable.

- ✔ Coefficient magnitudes can be affected by changing the units of measurement; in other words, scale matters.

- ✔ Even variables measured on similar scales can have different amounts of variability.

For some variables, a unit change may represent a large amount, whereas it may be of marginal importance for other variables. Suppose you're examining the success of college students through their grade point averages. You may hypothesize that high school grade point average (GPA) and SAT score helps you predict college success. If you estimate a multiple regression, the coefficient for SAT score is much smaller than the coefficient for GPA. The reason is not because SAT has a smaller impact (even though it may) but because a 1-unit change in SAT score is insignificant in comparison to a 1-unit change in GPA.

If you want to compare coefficient magnitudes in a multiple regression, you need to calculate the *standardized regression coefficients*. You can do so in two ways:

- ✔ Calculating a *Z*-score for every variable of every observation and then performing OLS with the *Z* values rather than the raw data

- ✔ Obtaining the OLS regression coefficients using the raw data and then multiplying each coefficient by $\left(\dfrac{\hat{\sigma}_{X_k}}{\hat{\sigma}_Y} \right)$

Start by modifying the original SRF: $Y_i = \hat{\beta}_0 + \hat{\beta}_1 X_{i1} + \hat{\beta}_2 X_{i2} + \ldots + \hat{\beta}_p X_{ip} + \hat{\varepsilon}_i$.

Then subtract the average value of each variable from every observation to get this equation:

$$Y_i - \bar{Y} = \hat{\beta}_1 \left(X_{i1} - \bar{X}_1 \right) + \hat{\beta}_2 \left(X_{i2} - \bar{X}_2 \right) + \ldots + \hat{\beta}_p \left(X_{ip} - \bar{X}_p \right) + \left(\hat{\varepsilon}_i - \bar{\hat{\varepsilon}} \right)$$

Notice that the constant drops out from the right-hand side of the equation because you're basically subtracting 1 from 1. Next, divide both sides by the estimated standard deviation of the dependent variable:

$$\frac{Y_i - \bar{Y}}{\hat{\sigma}_Y} = \hat{\beta}_1 \left(\frac{X_{i1} - \bar{X}_1}{\hat{\sigma}_{X_1}} \right) \left(\frac{\hat{\sigma}_{X_1}}{\hat{\sigma}_Y} \right) + \hat{\beta}_2 \left(\frac{X_{i2} - \bar{X}_2}{\hat{\sigma}_{X_2}} \right) \left(\frac{\hat{\sigma}_{X_2}}{\hat{\sigma}_Y} \right) + \ldots + \hat{\beta}_p \left(\frac{X_{ip} - \bar{X}_p}{\hat{\sigma}_{X_p}} \right) \left(\frac{\hat{\sigma}_{X_p}}{\hat{\sigma}_Y} \right) + \frac{\hat{\varepsilon}_i}{\hat{\sigma}_Y}$$

The preceding equation takes advantage of one of the desirable OLS properties, namely that the average residual is zero (for the rest of the desirable OLS properties, see the earlier section "Defining and Justifying the Least Squares Principle"). A little mathematical manipulation ensures that you're still performing the same operation to both sides of the equation, which allows you to arrive at the final step $Z_Y = \hat{b}_1 Z_{X_1} + \hat{b}_2 Z_{X_2} + \ldots + \hat{b}_p Z_{X_p} + \hat{u}_i$, where you've defined the standardized regression coefficients as $\hat{b}_k = \hat{\beta}_k \left(\frac{\hat{\sigma}_{X_k}}{\hat{\sigma}_Y} \right)$.

Standardized regression coefficients are also known as *beta coefficients*. This convention can be confusing, because the Greek letter beta is also used for the regular OLS coefficients. Unfortunately, this terminology has been commonly adopted by econometricians and most textbooks.

In practice, you rely on the econometrics software to calculate the standardized regression coefficients. For instance, in the movie revenue example, you select **Statistics ➪ Linear models and related ➪ Linear regression** from the menu bar or type "regress Y X1 X2, beta" on the STATA command line to produce the results shown in Figure 5-5.

Figure 5-5:
STATA output with standardized (or beta) coefficients and regular OLS coefficients.

```
. regress Y X1 X2, beta
```

Source	SS	df	MS
Model	1588188.67	2	794094.334
Residual	1477786.25	577	2561.15468
Total	3065974.92	579	5295.29347

Number of obs =	580
F(2, 577) =	310.05
Prob > F =	0.0000
R-squared =	0.5180
Adj R-squared =	0.5163
Root MSE =	50.608

Y	Coef.	Std. Err.	t	P>|t|	Beta
X1	.4138258	.0784313	5.28	0.000	.1528903
X2	1.11124	.0465035	23.90	0.000	.6924274
_cons	-8.394324	4.668307	-1.80	0.073	.

Regular OLS coefficients and standardized regression coefficients do not have the same meaning. The standardized regression coefficient estimates the standard deviation change in your dependent variable for a 1-standard-deviation change in the independent variable, holding other variables constant.

Using the results from Figure 5-5 (column labeled *beta*), you can say that a 1-standard-deviation increase in viewer ratings increases revenue by 0.15 standard deviations if you hold the film budget constant. A 1-standard-deviation increase in film budget increases movie revenue by 0.69 standard deviations, holding viewer ratings constant. Because you're now using a standard deviation change for all the explanatory variables, you can compare the beta coefficients. Consequently, you can also say that the impact of movie budget on revenue is about five times larger than that of viewer ratings.

Measuring Goodness of Fit

After you've estimated a regression, you need to be able to gauge how well that regression fits the data. In most settings, a measure of fit compares the predicted values of the dependent variable, which you get by using the estimated regression function, to the actual values of the dependent variable in the data.

To properly measure goodness of fit, you first need to break down, or *decompose,* the variation in the dependent variable into explained and unexplained (or residual) parts. Then (in most cases) you can go about using the coefficient of determination, also known as *R-squared,* to determine fit. However, R-squared doesn't always indicate the quality of what the regression is telling you. In this section I walk you through each step of measurement.

Decomposing variance

If the value of the dependent variable were similar for every observation (regardless of the values of other variables), then a prediction equal to the average value would be sensible and you'd have no reason to complicate your life with regression analysis. But the very reason you perform regression analysis is because quite a bit of variation can exist between one observed value and another. Using economic theory and common sense, you develop a regression model that (hopefully) helps you explain why some of that variation exists.

The variation in your dependent variable can be *decomposed,* or separated, into different pieces. In econometrics, decomposing variance means that you take all the variation in your dependent variable and separate it into a part that's explained by your regression and a part that remains unexplained.

Figure 5-6 illustrates some sample data points: the mean value of the dependent variable (at the dashed horizontal line), an observed *Y* value (at the dot), and the estimated regression line. You can see how variation in the dependent variable (the difference between the observed Y value and the mean value) can be decomposed into two parts; One is the contribution of your regression analysis in explaining this variation (the difference between the regression line and the mean value) and the other part is unexplained or residual variation (the difference between the observed Y value and the regression line).

Figure 5-6:
The variation in the dependent variable can be decomposed into explained and unexplained (or residual) parts.

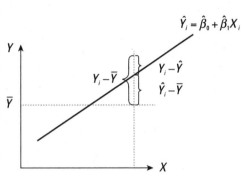

Consider one randomly chosen observation so you can examine the variation of the observed value from its mean. The distance of an observation from its mean can be characterized by $Y_i - \bar{Y} = \left(\hat{Y}_i - \bar{Y}\right) + \left(Y_i - \hat{Y}_i\right)$.

The left-hand-side is the total difference, but some of that difference is explained by the regression (or independent variable). The independent variable's influence on variation is the first component on the right-hand-side of the equation. The second component is what remains unexplained. It's what you already know as the residual, which means you can rewrite the equation as $Y_i - \bar{Y} = \left(\hat{Y}_i - \bar{Y}\right) + \hat{\varepsilon}_i$.

The decomposition of variation into explained and residual components for one observation must be extended to the entire sample in order to provide a measure of overall fit.

Measuring proportion of variance with R^2

The measure of fit most commonly used with OLS regression is the *coefficient of determination,* which is more commonly known as *R-squared.* R-squared measures the proportion of variation in the dependent variable that's explained by variation in the independent variables. Because it's a ratio, its value must be between 0 and 1.

You calculate R-squared by generalizing the decomposition in $Y_i - \bar{Y} = \left(\hat{Y}_i - \bar{Y}\right) + \hat{\varepsilon}_i$ so that it includes all the observations in the data. In order to avoid positive and negative residuals from canceling each other out, you must square both sides of the equation and then apply summation to include all the observations.

This manipulation of summing and squaring plus a few algebraic steps ultimately provide a measure for each component of variance, as seen in the following equation:

$$\sum_{i=1}^{n}\left(Y_i - \bar{Y}\right)^2 = \sum_{i=1}^{n}\left(\hat{Y}_i - \bar{Y}\right)^2 + \sum_{i=1}^{n}\hat{\varepsilon}_i^2$$

The left-hand-side is called the *total sum of squares* (TSS), and the right-hand side is the sum of the *explained sum of squares* (ESS) and *residual sum of squares* (RSS). If you write this equation out and perform one additional algebraic manipulation, you end up with the formula for the R-squared value.

$$TSS = ESS + RSS$$

$$\frac{ESS}{TSS} = 1 - \frac{RSS}{TSS}$$

TIP

The ratio on the left-hand side measures the explained variation as a fraction of the total and is, therefore, the R-squared value.

$$R^2 = \frac{ESS}{TSS} = 1 - \frac{RSS}{TSS}$$

Because the OLS technique seeks to minimize the RSS, it's essentially fitting the line (or function) that maximizes the R-squared value.

Returning to the movie revenue example and the regression results in Figure 5-4, you see that the R-squared value is included in any standard regression output. With the reported value of 0.5180, you can say that 51.8 percent of the variation in movie revenue is explained by viewer ratings and film budget.

Adjusting the goodness of fit in multiple regression

A surefire way to increase R-squared (or regression fit) is to add more explanatory variables to the model. If you examine the following formula for the R-squared value, you can see why this is the case.

$$R^2 = \frac{ESS}{TSS} = 1 - \frac{RSS}{TSS}$$

Suppose you begin with a model that has one explanatory variable. The regression produces certain values for the residuals (*RSS*) and, consequently, some R-squared value. Now, imagine that you add another explanatory variable to the model. This new explanatory variable can help you explain more of the variation in the dependent variable (*RSS* decreases) or be of no use at all (*RSS* remains the same). It can't, however, take away any ability that the first explanatory variable has in explaining variation in the dependent variable.

If you increase the number of explanatory variables in a regression model, your R-squared value increases or remains the same (if the additional variable has no impact on the dependent variable), but it can never cause your R-squared value to decrease.

You may be tempted to continue adding more variables and, as a result, increase the R-squared value. However, doing so has a cost. When you add more variables, you lose *degrees of freedom* (the number of observations above and beyond the number of estimated coefficients). Fewer degrees of freedom make your estimates less reliable (for more on this topic, turn to Chapter 6). This issue is addressed with *adjusted R-squared,* which is defined as

$$\bar{R}^2 = 1 - \frac{\dfrac{RSS}{n-p-1}}{\dfrac{TSS}{n-1}} = 1 - \left(1 - R^2\right)\left(\frac{n-1}{n-p-1}\right)$$

where *RSS* is the residual sum of squares, *TSS* is the total sum of squares, *n* is the number of observations, and *p* is the number of independent variables in the model.

When additional variables are added to the regression, adjusted R-squared can increase, remain the same, and even decrease depending on whether the increase in R-squared is large enough to outweigh the loss in degrees of freedom (increase in *p*). If it is, the adjusted R-squared value increases. If not, adjusted R-squared remains the same or decreases.

Because the adjusted R-squared equation includes the degrees of freedom "penalty" for additional explanatory variables, sometimes researchers compare the fit of various models with the adjusted R-squared rather than the unadjusted R-squared.

In order to compare two models on the basis of R-squared (adjusted or not), the dependent variable and sample size must be the same.

Evaluating fit versus quality

Although regression fit is important and R-squared is a commonly reported result, it is only one measure of regression quality.

Here are a few reasons why you shouldn't use R-squared (adjusted or not) as the only measure of your regression's quality:

- A regression may have a high R-squared but have no meaningful interpretation because the model equation isn't supported by economic theory or common sense.
- Using a small dataset or one that includes inaccuracies can lead to a high R-squared value but deceptive results.
- Obsessing over R-squared may cause you to overlook important econometric problems.

In economic settings, a high R-squared (close to 1) is more likely to indicate that something is wrong with the regression instead of showing that it's of high quality.

High R-squared values may be associated with regressions that violate assumptions (which I cover in Chapter 6) and/or have nonsensical results (coefficients with the wrong sign, unbelievable magnitudes, and so on.). When evaluating regression quality, give these outcomes more weight than the R-squared.

Chapter 6

Assumptions of OLS Estimation and the Gauss-Markov Theorem

· ·

In This Chapter

▶ Defining the assumptions of ordinary least squares (OLS) regression

▶ Illustrating the difference between good and bad statistical estimates

▶ Understanding the role of each OLS assumption in proving the Gauss-Markov theorem

· ·

*E*conometricians seek to find the best way to estimate economic relationships. That best method depends on what they think the relationship is between the variables and on what type of data is being utilized for the analysis. In this chapter, I discuss the assumptions of the most basic technique used in applied econometrics, the ordinary least squares (OLS) technique, and explain how the assumptions are important in producing reliable results.

OLS is the most popular method of performing regression analysis because in standard situations, its results are optimal. In this chapter, you discover exactly which assumptions define a *standard situation* in econometrics and which characteristics classify an estimation technique as *optimal.* You also find out the role of technical assumptions in showing that OLS achieves those criteria. (***Note:*** I'm assuming you already have a basic understanding of regression mechanics and are familiar with how to interpret OLS results, but if you need to review these concepts, you can turn to Chapter 5.)

Characterizing the OLS Assumptions

When deciding whether OLS is the *best* technique for your estimation problem, some requirements must be met. They're called the *OLS assumptions* or the *classical linear regression model* (CLRM). Here's the complete set:

✔ The model is linear in parameters and has an additive error term.

✔ The values for the independent variables are derived from a random sample of the population and contain variability.

✔ No independent variable is a perfect linear function of any other independent variable(s) (no perfect collinearity).

✔ The model is correctly specified and the error term has a zero conditional mean.

✔ The error term has a constant variance (no heteroskedasticity).

✔ The values of the error term aren't correlated with each other (no autocorrelation or no serial correlation).

If you encounter a situation where one (or more) of the CLRM assumptions fails, then OLS may not be the best estimation technique. When that occurs, econometricians typically propose some precise modification to the OLS technique or offer a completely different alternative.

In applied situations, some assumptions are violated more frequently than others. I devote entire chapters to a discussion of the methods used to detect when those specific assumptions fail and how to proceed if they do. Specifically, I tackle collinearity in Chapter 10, heteroskedasticity in Chapter 11, and autocorrelation in Chapter 12. In the following sections, however, I explain the facets of the CLRM so you know exactly what you're assuming about your model and/or dataset when you use OLS estimation.

Linearity in parameters and additive error

When a model is linear in parameters and has an additive error term, it typically means that you can write the population regression function (PRF) as $Y_i = \beta_0 + \beta_1 X_{i1} + \beta_2 X_{i2} + \ldots + \beta_p X_{ip} + \varepsilon_i$, where Y is your dependent variable, the Xs are your independent variables, the βs are your partial slope coefficients (parameters of interest), and ε is your random error term.

A model doesn't have to be a linear function in order to satisfy the *linear in parameters* assumption. A couple examples of nonlinear functions that are linear in parameters include

✔ $Y_i = \beta_0 + \beta_1 X_i + \beta_2 X_i^2 + \varepsilon_i$

✔ $Y_i = \beta_0 + \beta_1 \left(\dfrac{1}{X_i} \right) + \varepsilon_i$

You can estimate these types of models using the OLS technique.

However, you can't use OLS to estimate a model that isn't linear in parameters, like the function $Y_i = \beta_0 + X_i^{\beta_1} + \varepsilon_i$.

When the parameters (βs) you're trying estimate are in the exponents of the function, OLS can't be used. In some cases, you can perform a log transformation to linearize the function and then use OLS (I discuss this topic in Chapter 8). However, in many scenarios, the log transformation may not work or won't be feasible.

Other techniques, such as *maximum likelihood* (ML) estimation, can be used when the function you need to estimate is not linear in parameters. Specific examples of models that are nonlinear in parameters and the use of ML estimation are discussed at length in Chapters 13 and 14.

Random sampling and variability

Strictly speaking, the CLRM assumes that the values of the independent variables are fixed in repeated random samples. In other words, every sample from a given population is assumed to contain the same values for the independent variables even though the values of the dependent variable change from sample to sample. This assumption can be, and is often, weakened. The more common version of the assumption is that the values of the independent variable are random from sample to sample but independent of the error term. The weaker version is equivalent asymptotically (with large samples) because the likelihood that you're missing relevant values for the independent variables decreases as the sample size increases.

You need variation in the independent variable to estimate its regression coefficient. If it has no variation, the coefficient for that variable is undefined.

This assumption isn't likely to hold when you use lagged values of your dependent variable as an independent variable (*autoregression;* see Chapter 15 for details on this topic) or when the value of your dependent variable simultaneously affects the value of one (or more) of your independent variables (*simultaneous equations*). Therefore, OLS is inappropriate in these situations. You must modify it or use something else anytime one or more assumptions don't hold.

Imperfect linear relationships among the independent variables

In econometrics, you want to avoid using data in situations where two (or more) of your independent variables have exact relative movements. When changes in the value of one independent variable are matched by a relative movement (positive or negative) in one or more of your other independent variables, you have a *multicollinearity* (or *perfect collinearity*) problem and you can't estimate the model with those variables included in the regression.

For example, suppose I have a dataset with five observations and two variables (X_1 and X_2). The values for X_1 are 2, 5, 6, 10, and 12, and the values for X_2 are 7, 13, 15, 23, and 27. These two variables exhibit perfect collinearity because $X_2 = 2X_1 + 3$. This is one type of linear function, but there are many possibilities.

You can have a multicollinearity problem even if the units of measurement for the variables are quite different. The *relative* relationship is what causes multicollinearity, not the *absolute* relationship.

A perfect collinear relationship between two independent variables, X_1 and X_2, could be expressed as $X_2 = \alpha_0 + \alpha_1 X_1$, where α_1 captures the relative co-movement of the two variables.

Usually, multicollinearity with more than two variables occurs because you create new variables and fail to account for their relationship when including them in your regression model. Be careful not to create variables that are perfect linear functions of other variables.

Suppose I want to explain earnings differentials among workers in a population where individuals attend school or work (they're never unemployed or without work). I want to use workers' wages as my dependent variable with age (X_1), years of education (X_2), and years of work experience (X_3) as the independent variables. Because individuals work immediately when they finish school in the population, I create a work experience variable by subtracting 6 (the assumed age when they started school) and their years of education from their age. So their work experience is $X_3 = X_1 - X_2 - 6$.

This equation expresses a perfect collinear relationship, because when age increases, so does experience (holding other variables constant). Similarly, if years of education increase, then experience decreases (holding other variables constant). Avoid creating these types of variables unless you plan on using the newly created variable in place of one of the others. For example, you may want to use the experience variable instead of age in the regression.

If you have perfect collinearity, the software program you use to calculate regression results can't estimate the regression coefficients. The reason for this is that perfect collinearity causes you to lose linear independence and the computer can't identify the unique effect of each variable because they move in unison with one another.

If you don't have perfect collinearity, you're not out of the woods just yet. *High collinearity,* which occurs when there's a *strong relationship* (as opposed to a *perfect relationship*) between two or more independent variables, can also be problematic. In applied cases, *high collinearity* is much more common than perfect collinearity. I discuss this issue in Chapter 10.

Error term has a zero conditional mean; correct specification

Your error term has a zero conditional mean when, for any given value for independent variable(s), the average value of the error is zero. (Reminder: The error term is the difference between the actual value of the dependent variable and the value from the population regression function.)You can write this mathematically as $E(\varepsilon|X_i) = 0$.

If the conditional mean of the error is zero, that implies that no relationship (or correlation) can exist between the error term and the X values. The assumption that $E(\varepsilon|X_i) = 0$ is one of the CLRM assumptions that may fail if you have

- **Misspecification:** This occurs when you fail to include a relevant independent variable or you use an incorrect functional form. Specification issues are addressed in detail in Chapter 8.

- **A restricted dependent variable:** In other words, you're using a qualitative or limited dependent variable. For example, you may be interested in modeling the outcome of a *yes/no* response from a survey (qualitative data measured with a 1 or 0 value), or you may want to explain injury rates on professional football teams (limited data measured on a percent scale from 0 to 100). Qualitative dependent variables are discussed in Chapter 13, and limited dependent variables are examined in Chapter14.

Figure 6-1 provides a comparison of a situation when the $E(\varepsilon|X_i) = 0$ assumption holds and when it fails. The graph on the left side of Figure 6-1 illustrates a situation where the mean of the error is zero at any X value. However, the graph on the right side of Figure 6-1 displays a scenario in which the mean of the error is not zero at all X values.

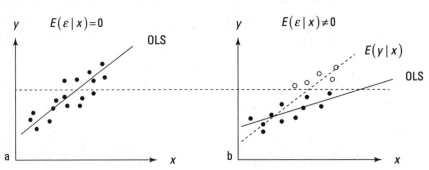

Figure 6-1: Regression function with a zero conditional mean error term (a) and with a nonzero conditional mean (b).

Sometimes the assumption $E(\varepsilon|X_i) = 0$ is confused with the notion that the average residual (estimated error) is zero $\left(E(\hat{\varepsilon}) = 0\right)$. Even if the overall mean of the residual is zero $\left(E(\hat{\varepsilon}) = 0\right)$, the conditional mean of the error $E(\varepsilon|X_i)$ may not be zero.

Error term has a constant variance

The CLRM also relies on the variance of the error term being constant. *Homoskedasticity* refers to a situation in which the error has the same variance regardless of the value(s) taken by the independent variable(s). Econometricians usually express homoskedasticity as $Var(\varepsilon|X_i) = \sigma_\varepsilon^2 \forall i$. In Figure 6-2, I show the regression of a model satisfying the CLRM assumptions and a graphical depiction of homoskedasticity. Notice when the error term is homoskedastic, the dispersion of the error remains the same over the range of observations.

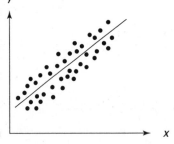 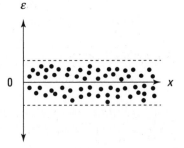

Figure 6-2: A model with a constant (homoskedastic) error variance.

If the error term is *heteroskedastic,* the dispersion changes over the range of observations. *Heteroskedasticity* occurs when the variance of the error term changes in response to a change in the value(s) of the independent variable(s). Econometricians typically express heteroskedasticity as $Var(\varepsilon|X_i) = \sigma_{\varepsilon i}^2$.

In Figure 6-3, I graph a situation where heteroskedasticity is present. The pattern depicted in Figure 6-3 is only one among many possible patterns. Any error variance that doesn't resemble that shown in Figure 6-2 is likely to be heteroskedastic.

Figure 6-3:
A model
with a
changing
(hetero-
skedastic)
error
variance.

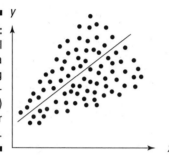
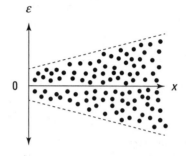

WARNING! Heteroskedasticity is a common problem for OLS regression estimation, especially with cross-sectional and panel data. You usually have no way of knowing in advance if it's going to be present, but there are several tests to check for it and several ways to correct if you find evidence of it in your regression. Turn to Chapter 11 for the full scoop on these heteroskedasticity topics.

Correlation of error observations is zero

REMEMBER The observations are assumed to be randomly drawn, so the error values should be independent and not related to one another. If the errors have a relationship, then you have *autocorrelation* (or *serial correlation*) and have violated a CLRM assumption. Here's what it looks like when the assumption holds:

$$Cov(\varepsilon_t, \varepsilon_s) = 0 \forall t \neq s$$

and when it fails:

$$Cov(\varepsilon_t, \varepsilon_s) \neq 0 \forall t \neq s$$

where ε represents the error term, while the t and s subscripts identify the time period in which the error is observed.

In Figure 6-4, I use time-series data to show a scatter plot of the possible error values in t and $t - 1$. In this figure, the assumption of no autocorrelation holds ($Cov(\varepsilon_t, \varepsilon_s) = 0$). How can you tell? Well, when no autocorrelation exists, you can't see a clear relationship between the error values.

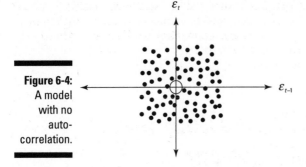

Figure 6-4:
A model
with no
auto-
correlation.

If autocorrelation does exist, you may find that it's positive $(Cov(\varepsilon_t, \varepsilon_s) > 0)$, as in the example in Figure 6-5. When you have positive autocorrelation, positive error values tend to be followed by other positive errors, and vice versa.

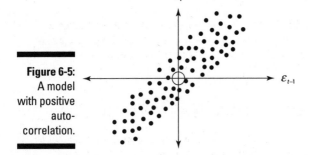

Figure 6-5:
A model
with positive
auto-
correlation.

Another possibility is negative autocorrelation $(Cov(\varepsilon_t, \varepsilon_s) < 0)$, like the case in Figure 6-6. When you have negative autocorrelation, a positive error value tends to followed by negative errors, and vice versa.

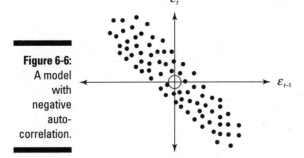

Figure 6-6:
A model
with
negative
auto-
correlation.

Autocorrelation can be quite common when you're estimating models with time-series data, because when observations are collected over time, they're unlikely to be independent from one another. In other words, if something occurs today, its influence isn't likely to be completely absorbed today. (For more details on autocorrelation, see Chapter 12.)

Relying on the CLRM Assumptions: The Gauss-Markov Theorem

Most theorems in statistics and mathematics rely on a set of assumptions, and the Gauss-Markov theorem is no different. It relies on the CLRM assumptions I walk you through earlier in this chapter.

The Gauss-Markov theorem states that the ordinary least squares (OLS) estimators are the best linear unbiased estimators (BLUE) given the assumptions of the classical linear regression model (CLRM).

The following material shows how each component of the Gauss-Markov theorem is derived. I devote one section to each of the first three letters in BLUE (best, linear, and unbiased), although not in that order.

Proving the Gauss-Markov theorem

To understand why OLS is best in some situations, you may find it useful to see how each component of the Gauss-Markov theorem is derived. The following sections illustrate each part of the theorem's proof using a simple regression model (with one independent variable). In each part of the proof, I draw your attention to the importance of at least one of the CLRM assumptions.

In graduate econometrics courses, the proof of the Gauss-Markov theorem is often extended to the multivariate case. You need to be comfortable with matrix algebra before you go there.

Linearity of OLS

In the sample regression function (SRF) $\hat{Y}_i = \hat{\beta}_0 + \hat{\beta}_1 X_i$, the estimators are calculated with the following formulas

$$\hat{\beta}_1 = \frac{\sum_{i=1}^{n}(X_i - \bar{X})(Y_i - \bar{Y})}{\sum_{i=1}^{n}(X_i - \bar{X})^2}$$

$$\hat{\beta}_0 = \bar{Y} - \hat{\beta}_1 \bar{X}$$

If you don't recall how these formulas are derived, you can refresh your memory in Chapter 5.

The proof of the linearity property can be simplified by defining

$$c_i = \frac{\left(X_i - \bar{X}\right)}{\sum\limits_{i=1}^{n}\left(X_i - \bar{X}\right)^2}$$

I begin by working with $\hat{\beta}_1$ and substituting with c_i to get

$$\hat{\beta}_1 = \sum_{i=1}^{n} c_i \left(Y_i - \bar{Y}\right) = c_1\left(Y_1 - \bar{Y}\right) + c_2\left(Y_2 - \bar{Y}\right) + \ldots + c_n\left(Y_n - \bar{Y}\right)$$

The c_i can be treated as constants because, according to one of the CLRM assumptions, the X values in repeated random sampling are the same. Consequently, $\hat{\beta}_1$ is a linear combination of the observed Y values.

I proceed in a similar fashion with $\hat{\beta}_0$ and substitute for $\hat{\beta}_1$ to get

$$\hat{\beta}_0 = \bar{Y} - \left(\frac{\sum\limits_{i=1}^{n}\left(X_i - \bar{X}\right)\left(Y_i - \bar{Y}\right)}{\sum\limits_{i=1}^{n}\left(X_i - \bar{X}\right)^2}\right)\bar{X}$$

Using c_i, I simplify this to

$$\hat{\beta}_0 = \bar{Y} - \left(\sum_{i=1}^{n} c_i \left(Y_i - \bar{Y}\right)\right)\bar{X}$$

and with one more algebraic step, I arrive at

$$\hat{\beta}_0 = \bar{Y} - \bar{X}\left(c_1\left(Y_1 - \bar{Y}\right) + c_2\left(Y_2 - \bar{Y}\right) + \ldots + c_n\left(Y_n - \bar{Y}\right)\right)$$

which shows that $\hat{\beta}_0$ is also a linear function of the Y values.

In the sample regression function $\hat{Y}_i = \hat{\beta}_0 + \hat{\beta}_1 X_i$, the $\hat{\beta}$ terms are linear estimators because they are linear combinations of the observed values for the dependent variable (Y_i).

Expected value of OLS coefficients

In the sample regression function (SRF) $\hat{Y}_i = \hat{\beta}_0 + \hat{\beta}_1 X_i$, the estimators are calculated with the following formulas:

$$\hat{\beta}_1 = \frac{\sum_{i=1}^{n}(X_i - \bar{X})(Y_i - \bar{Y})}{\sum_{i=1}^{n}(X_i - \bar{X})^2}$$

$$\hat{\beta}_0 = \bar{Y} - \hat{\beta}_1 \bar{X}$$

If you take $\hat{\beta}_1$ and substitute the population regression function (PRF) for Y_i, you get

$$\hat{\beta}_1 = \frac{\sum_{i=1}^{n}(X_i - \bar{X})(\beta_0 + \beta_1 X_i + \varepsilon_i - \bar{Y})}{\sum_{i=1}^{n}(X_i - \bar{X})^2}$$

After several algebraic manipulations, you can arrive at

$$\hat{\beta}_1 = \beta_1 + \frac{\sum_{i=1}^{n}\varepsilon_i(X_i - \bar{X})}{\sum_{i=1}^{n}(X_i - \bar{X})^2}$$

Then apply the expectations operator to both sides:

$$E(\hat{\beta}_1) = E\left(\beta_1 + \frac{\sum_{i=1}^{n}\varepsilon_i(X_i - \bar{X})}{\sum_{i=1}^{n}(X_i - \bar{X})^2}\right)$$

and using expected value properties (see Chapter 2), work through the following steps:

$$E(\hat{\beta}_1) = E(\beta_1) + E\left(\frac{\sum_{i=1}^{n}\varepsilon_i(X_i - \bar{X})}{\sum_{i=1}^{n}(X_i - \bar{X})^2}\right)$$

$$E(\hat{\beta}_1) = \beta_1 + \frac{Cov(\varepsilon, X)}{Var(X)}$$

The CLRM assumption that the conditional mean of the error is zero implies that no relationship exists between the error term and the X values, so $Cov(\varepsilon, X) = 0$. Therefore, the slope coefficient $\hat{\beta}_1$ is unbiased because $E(\hat{\beta}_1) = \beta_1$.

Now you can work with the intercept term and begin with this formula:

$$\hat{\beta}_0 = \bar{Y} - \hat{\beta}_1 \bar{X}$$

Using the property that the regression line must pass through the means of X and Y, substitute for $\bar{Y}$ and get

$$\hat{\beta}_0 = \beta_0 + \beta_1 \bar{X} - \hat{\beta}_1 \bar{X}$$

$$\hat{\beta}_0 = \beta_0 + \bar{X}\left(\beta_1 - \hat{\beta}_1\right)$$

Then you can apply the expectations operator to both sides:

$$E\left(\hat{\beta}_0\right) = E\left(\beta_0 + \bar{X}\left(\beta_1 - \hat{\beta}_1\right)\right)$$

and after a few algebraic manipulations, you get

$$E\left(\hat{\beta}_0\right) = \beta_0 + E\left(\bar{X}\right)\left(E(\beta_1) - E\left(\hat{\beta}_1\right)\right)$$

You simplify this expression by using the fact that $E\left(\bar{X}\right) = \mu_X$ and $E\left(\hat{\beta}_1\right) = \beta_1$ to complete the proof:

$$E\left(\hat{\beta}_0\right) = \beta_0 + \mu_X(\beta_1 - \beta_1)$$

$$E\left(\hat{\beta}_0\right) = \beta_0$$

In the sample regression function $\hat{Y}_i = \hat{\beta}_0 + \hat{\beta}_1 X_i$, the $\hat{\beta}$ terms are unbiased because on average they equal their true parameter values; $E\left(\hat{\beta}_1\right) = \beta_1$ and $E\left(\hat{\beta}_0\right) = \beta_0$.

In Figure 6-7, you can see the difference between a biased and an unbiased estimator of regression coefficients.

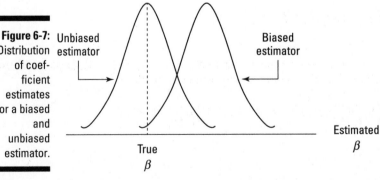

Figure 6-7: Distribution of coefficient estimates for a biased and unbiased estimator.

Unbiased estimator

Biased estimator

Estimated β

True β

If an estimator is unbiased, it doesn't mean $\hat{\beta} = \beta$. Instead, it means that $E\left(\hat{\beta}\right) = \beta$. You can see in Figure 6-7 that the estimated coefficients from some random sample are not likely to equal their true value. However, on average, the estimates equal the true value.

Variance of OLS coefficients

In the sample regression function (SRF) $\hat{Y}_i = \hat{\beta}_0 + \hat{\beta}_1 X_i$, the estimators are calculated with the following formulas:

$$\hat{\beta}_1 = \frac{\sum_{i=1}^{n}\left(X_i - \bar{X}\right)\left(Y_i - \bar{Y}\right)}{\sum_{i=1}^{n}\left(X_i - \bar{X}\right)^2}$$

$$\hat{\beta}_0 = \bar{Y} - \hat{\beta}_1 \bar{X}$$

The OLS estimators are linear functions of the observed values, so you can write their formulas this way:

$$\hat{\beta}_k = \sum_{i=1}^{n} c_i\left(Y_i - \bar{Y}\right)$$

where

$$c_i = \frac{\left(X_i - \bar{X}\right)}{\sum_{i=1}^{n}\left(X_i - \bar{X}\right)^2}$$

for $\hat{\beta}_c = \hat{\beta}_1$. I focus on the slope term $\hat{\beta}_1$ and define an alternative estimator:

$$\tilde{\beta}_1 = \sum_{i=1}^{n} w_i\left(Y_i - \bar{Y}\right)$$

where w_i doesn't necessarily equal c_i. I substitute the SRF into this equation and apply the variance operator to both sides and get

$$Var\left(\tilde{\beta}_1\right) = Var\left(\sum_{i=1}^{n} w_i\left(Y_i - \bar{Y}\right)\right)$$

Here, utilize the CLRM assumption that X is fixed in repeated samples and the property that X is not correlated with the error term to get

$$Var\left(\tilde{\beta}_1\right) = \sum_{i=1}^{n} w_i^2 Var\left(\beta_0 + \beta_1 X_i + \varepsilon_i - \bar{Y}\right) = \sum_{i=1}^{n} w_i^2 Var\left(\varepsilon_i\right)$$

Using the CLRM assumptions of homoskedasticity (constant variance) and no autocorrelation (no correlation among the error values), you can write the variance of $\tilde{\beta}_1$ as

$$Var\left(\tilde{\beta}_1\right) = \sigma_\varepsilon^2 \sum_{i=1}^{n} w_i^2$$

After several algebraic steps, you can rewrite the variance of $\tilde{\beta}_1$ as

$$Var\left(\tilde{\beta}_1\right) = \sigma_\varepsilon^2 \sum_{i=1}^{n} \left(w_i - \frac{\left(X_i - \bar{X}\right)}{\sum_{i=1}^{n}\left(X_i - \bar{X}\right)^2} \right)^2 + \sigma_\varepsilon^2 \left(\frac{1}{\sum_{i=1}^{n}\left(X_i - \bar{X}\right)^2} \right)$$

If you let

$$w_i = \frac{\left(X_i - \bar{X}\right)}{\sum_{i=1}^{n}\left(X_i - \bar{X}\right)^2} = c_i$$

then

$$Var\left(\tilde{\beta}_1\right) = \frac{\sigma_\varepsilon^2}{\sum_{i=1}^{n}\left(X_i - \bar{X}\right)^2} = Var\left(\hat{\beta}_1\right)$$

If you allow $w_i \neq c_i$ so that the estimator is something other than OLS, then $Var\left(\tilde{\beta}_1\right) > Var\left(\hat{\beta}_1\right)$.

In the sample regression function $\hat{Y}_i = \hat{\beta}_0 + \hat{\beta}_1 X_i$, the $\hat{\beta}$ terms are efficient (in other words, *best*) because their variance is the smallest among all such estimators.

In Figure 6-8, I illustrate the difference between a more efficient and less efficient estimator.

The variance of your OLS estimators is influenced by a three factors:

- ✔ **The variance of the error term, σ_ε^2:** The larger the variance of the error, the larger the variance of the OLS estimates and vice versa (holding everything else constant).
- ✔ **The variance of X, $\sum_{i=1}^{n}\left(X_i - \bar{X}\right)^2$:** The larger the sample variance of X, the smaller the variance of the OLS estimates and vice versa (holding everything else constant).

✔ **Multicollinearity:** As the correlation between two or more independent variables approaches 1, the variance of the OLS estimates becomes increasingly large and approaches infinity.

Figure 6-8:
Distribution of coefficient estimates for two unbiased estimators with different variance.

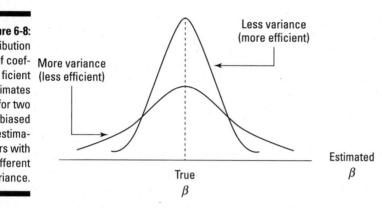

More variance (less efficient)

Less variance (more efficient)

True β

Estimated β

The efficiency characteristic of an estimator is not only relevant with unbiased estimators. Even if an estimator is biased, more efficiency (less variance) can be valuable if the bias is small.

In Figure 6-9, I illustrate an unbiased estimator that isn't very efficient and a biased estimator that is much more efficient.

Figure 6-9:
Distribution of coefficients for an unbiased estimator with a large variance and a biased estimator with a small variance.

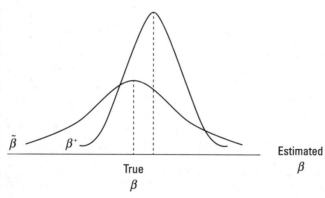

$\tilde{\beta}$ β^+

True β

Estimated β

Even though the estimator β^+ in Figure 6-9 is biased, you'd have a better chance of producing an estimate that is close to the true value with β^+ than you'd have with $\tilde{\beta}$. In some cases, econometricians have to weigh the cost of using a biased estimator against the benefits of using a more efficient estimator.

In practice, you're probably going to get only one sample to estimate your regression coefficients. In that case, you want to maximize your chances of producing an estimate that's close to the true parameter value. A more efficient estimator increases the probability that an estimate from a single sample is close to the true value.

OLS coefficients: Best when BLUE

Given the assumptions of the CLRM, the OLS estimators (or coefficients) are best linear unbiased estimators (BLUE).

- ✔ *Best* means achieving the smallest possible variance among all similar estimators.
- ✔ *Linear* indicates that the estimates are derived using linear combinations of the data values.
- ✔ *Unbiased* means the estimators (coefficients) on average equal their true parameter values.

When you put all these pieces together, you have the Gauss-Markov theorem.

When judging how good or bad an estimator is, econometricians usually evaluate the amount of bias and variance of that estimator. The BLUE property of OLS estimators is viewed as the gold standard. When a CLRM assumption fails (which happens regularly in applied situations), you either have to adjust OLS for that failure or use an entirely different estimation technique.

Econometricians have devised methods to deal with failures of the CLRM assumptions, but they aren't always successful in proving that the alternative method produces a BLUE. In those cases, they usually settle for an *asymptotic* property known as *consistency*. Estimators are consistent if, as the sample size approaches infinity, the variance of the estimator gets smaller and the value of the estimator approaches the true population parameter value.

Summarizing the Gauss-Markov theorem

Each part of the Gauss-Markov theorem relies on at least one CLRM assumption. In Table 6-1, I list the CLRM assumptions required to show that OLS estimators are BLUE. I also indicate their use in proving each part of the theorem, typical violations, and in which chapter I cover specific violations of CLRM assumptions.

Table 6-1	Summary of Gauss-Markov Assumptions			
Assumption	**Expression**	**Used to Prove OLS Estimators Are**	**Common Violations**	**Chapter Covering Assumption Violation**
Linearity in model parameters	$Y_i = \beta_0 + \beta_1 X_{i1} + \beta_2 X_{i2} + \ldots \beta_p X_{ip} + \varepsilon_i$	Linear Unbiased	Misspecification	8
Observations of independent variable(s) are fixed in repeated samples	N/A	Linear Unbiased Best	Autoregression	15
No perfect collinearity	$\sum_{i=1}^{n} \left(X_i - \bar{X} \right)^2 \neq 0$	Best	High collinearity	10
Conditional mean of the error is zero	$E\left(\varepsilon \mid X_i \right) = 0$	Unbiased	Misspecification	10
Error has a constant variance (homoskedasticity)	$Var\left(\varepsilon \mid X_i \right) = \sigma_\varepsilon^2 \; \forall i$	Best	Cross-sectional data	11
Error observations are not correlated (no autocorrelation)	$Cov(\varepsilon_t, \varepsilon_s) = 0, t \neq s$	Best	Time-series data	12

Chapter 7

The Normality Assumption and Inference with OLS

• •

In This Chapter

▶ Understanding what the normal distribution implies

▶ Deriving hypothesis testing procedures for regression coefficients

▶ Determining whether regression results are statistically significant

▶ Using the normal distribution to determine forecast/prediction error

• •

*W*hen you use ordinary least squares (OLS) regression for hypothesis testing and/or prediction and forecasting, you always assume that the distribution of the unobserved error is normal. However, the idea of assuming a normal distribution is often misunderstood. That's what this chapter clears up. It helps you understand precisely how a normal distribution is used in econometrics and the importance of the normality assumption for tests of statistical significance and calculations of forecast error. You also get to check out some example scenarios in which the assumption is likely to be reasonable and others for which it's likely to fail.

Note: In this chapter, I assume that you already have a basic understanding of regression mechanics and are familiar with interpretation of OLS results. If you need to review these concepts, please refer to Chapter 5.

Describing the Role of the Normality Assumption

The normality assumption in econometrics (and in the context of OLS specifically) doesn't imply that all variables used in the analysis are expected to be normally distributed. Instead, the assumption focuses on the distribution of the error term, ε. (That little error term is of critical importance in econometrics. As Chapter 6 explains, you need several assumptions about it to prove that the OLS estimators are unbiased and efficient, per the Gauss-Markov theorem.)

The normality assumption in econometrics states that, for any given X value, the error term follows a normal distribution with a zero mean and constant variance. This assumption is written in mathematical notation as

$$\varepsilon \mid X \sim N\left(0, \sigma_\varepsilon^2\right)$$

Two of the classical linear regression model (CLRM) assumptions (covered in Chapter 6) are that the conditional mean of the error is zero and that the error term has a constant variance (homoskedasticity). Those assumptions are also included in the normality assumption.

Another important characteristic of the normality assumption is that it isn't required for performing OLS estimation. It's necessary only when you want to produce confidence intervals and/or perform hypothesis tests with your OLS estimates.

In Figure 7-1, you can see a graphical depiction of the normality assumption.

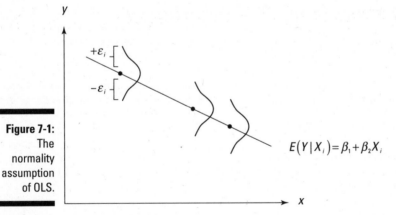

Figure 7-1:
The normality assumption of OLS.

The error term contains the influence of many different forces (random variables) that affect your dependent variable (Y) and aren't captured by your independent variables (Xs). The central limit theorem indicates that the sum or mean of random variables is normally distributed as long as many random variables are present and the influence of any one random variable is small (check out Chapter 3 if you need to review the central limit theorem and its implications).

In some applications, the assumption of a normal distribution for the error term may be difficult to justify. These situations typically involve a dependent variable (Y) that has limited or highly skewed values. A *limited* dependent variable is one whose potential values are restricted, which can result from natural limits or artificial constraints on the variable. For example, the number of times an individual votes in a six-year period takes on a limited number of integer values and is zero for a large fraction of individuals. Variables like wages and prices tend to be highly skewed or may also have limited values with minimum wages, floors, ceilings, and so on. In some cases, you can use log values to obtain a distribution that's approximately normal. Econometricians have also shown that with *large* sample sizes, normality is not a major issue because the OLS estimators are approximately normal even if the errors are not normal.

In the following sections, you find out how the normality of the error term is passed on to the OLS estimators. Additionally, I show you how the assumption of a normal distribution for the error term subsequently allows you to produce statistics that use other popular probability distributions.

The error term and the sampling distribution of OLS coefficients

In a simple regression model (with one independent or X variable), you calculate the OLS coefficients using these formulas:

$$\hat{\beta}_1 = \frac{\sum_{i=1}^{n}\left(X_i - \bar{X}\right)\left(Y_i - \bar{Y}\right)}{\sum_{i=1}^{n}\left(X_i - \bar{X}\right)^2}$$

and

$$\hat{\beta}_0 = \bar{Y} - \hat{\beta}_1 \bar{X}$$

In Chapter 6, I illustrate the following derivation:

$$\hat{\beta}_1 = \frac{\sum_{i=1}^{n}\left(X_i - \bar{X}\right)\left(Y_i - \bar{Y}\right)}{\sum_{i=1}^{n}\left(X_i - \bar{X}\right)^2} = \frac{\sum_{i=1}^{n}\left(X_i - \bar{X}\right)\left(\beta_0 + \beta_1 X_i + \varepsilon_i - \bar{Y}\right)}{\sum_{i=1}^{n}\left(X_i - \bar{X}\right)^2} = \beta_1 + \frac{\sum_{i=1}^{n}\varepsilon_i\left(X_i - \bar{X}\right)}{\sum_{i=1}^{n}\left(X_i - \bar{X}\right)^2}$$

which shows that the estimated slope term is a linear function of the error term (ε). Because the intercept term is a linear function of the slope term, it also follows that the intercept term is a linear function of the error term. Therefore, all OLS coefficients are a linear function of the error term. The error term is assumed to be normally distributed, which implies that the estimates of your $\hat{\beta}$ terms also follow a normal distribution. This last point is derived from a property of normally distributed random variables that you may have discussed in your statistics class; that is, a linear combination of a normally distributed random variable results in another normally distributed random variable.

A linear function of a normally distributed random variable is itself normally distributed. If you assume that the error term is normally distributed ($\varepsilon \sim N(0,\sigma_\varepsilon^2)$), then that implies that the OLS estimators are normally distributed ($\hat{\beta}_k \sim N(\beta_k,\sigma_{\hat{\beta}_k}^2)$).

In Figure 7-2, I illustrate a normally distributed OLS estimator.

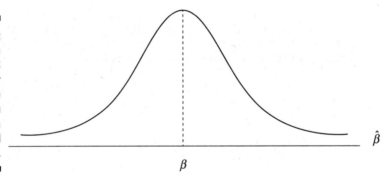

Figure 7-2:
Distribution of OLS estimator when the error term follows a normal distribution.

Every sample that's randomly drawn from some population is likely to yield different values for your OLS coefficients ($\hat{\beta}$ terms). If you assume that the error term has a normal distribution, you're also assuming that the sampling distribution of the coefficients looks like Figure 7-2.

I use a model with one independent variable (univariate) to keep the algebra manageable, but with matrix algebra I can extend the model in Figure 7-2 to show many independent variables (multivariate).

Revisiting the standard normal distribution

Any normally distributed random variable can be converted to a standard normal. When you convert a normal random variable with mean (μ) and variance (σ^2) to a standard normal, those parameters are shifted so that the mean is 0 and the variance is 1.

The generic formula to convert a normally distributed random variable (RV) to a standard normal (Z) is

$$Z = \frac{RV - E(RV)}{SD(RV)}$$

where RV is any normally distributed random variable, $E(RV)$ is the expected value or mean of the random variable, and $SD(RV)$ is the standard deviation of the random variable.

The distribution of your OLS coefficients ($\hat{\beta}$s) is normal; in mathematical notation $\hat{\beta}_k \sim N\left(\beta_k, \sigma^2_{\hat{\beta}_k}\right)$. Consequently, the standard normal distribution for OLS estimators can be defined as

$$Z_k = \frac{\hat{\beta}_k - \beta_k}{\sigma_{\hat{\beta}_k}}$$

where the standard deviation of the estimator ($\sigma_{\hat{\beta}_k}$) is a function of the variation in the X values and the variance of the error term (σ^2_ε). I provide more details about the variance of the error in Chapter 6.

In order to apply the standard normal distribution to OLS estimators, you need to know the true value of the error term's variance. In an econometrics class, this value may be provided. In practice, the true variance of the error isn't known, which means you need to estimate it. I explain the procedure for performing this calculation in the next section.

Deriving a chi-squared distribution from the random error

The OLS coefficients (the $\hat{\beta}$ terms) have a sampling distribution because randomly drawn samples from a population of interest yield different values for the dependent variable (Y). These different values change your estimated intercept and slope coefficients from sample to sample.

The assumption that the error term is normally distributed also implies that the sampling distributions of your $\hat{\beta}$s are also normally distributed. However, in order to work with any normally distributed random variable, you must know its mean and variance. For the OLS coefficients, this information is usually written as $\hat{\beta}_k \sim N\left(\beta_k, \sigma^2_{\hat{\beta}_k}\right)$.

The variance of an estimator provides a measure of how much the estimator is likely to change from one sample to another. For the OLS estimators in a model with one independent variable, the variances are

$$\sigma_{\hat{\beta}_1}^2 = \frac{\sigma_\varepsilon^2}{\sum_{i=1}^{n}\left(X_i - \bar{X}\right)^2}$$

$$\sigma_{\hat{\beta}_0}^2 = \left(\frac{\sum_{i=1}^{n} X_i^2}{n\sum_{i=1}^{n}\left(X_i - \bar{X}\right)^2}\right)\sigma_\varepsilon^2$$

In practice, the true variance of the error (σ_ε^2) isn't known, but you can estimate it by calculating the *variance of the regression* or *mean square error* (MSE). Here's the formula:

$$\hat{\sigma}_\varepsilon^2 = \frac{\sum_{i=1}^{n}\hat{\varepsilon}_i^2}{n-p-1}$$

The number of independent variables are represented by p, and $n-p-1$ is known as the residual degrees of freedom.

The square root of this value is known as the *standard error of the regression,* or *root mean square error* (RMSE):

$$\hat{\sigma}_\varepsilon = \sqrt{\hat{\sigma}_\varepsilon^2} = \sqrt{\frac{\sum_{i=1}^{n}\hat{\varepsilon}_i^2}{n-p-1}}$$

As you would when calculating the sample variance of any random variable, you must divide by the degrees of freedom. The degrees of freedom represent the number of independent values used when producing the variance estimate; in other words, it's the number of observations minus the number of estimates that must be produced before the sample variance is calculated. In the case of a residual variance, you first need to estimate the regression function before you can calculate each residual. That means you lose degrees of freedom p plus the intercept (or constant).

REMEMBER

If you replace the known error variance (σ_ε^2) in the calculation of $\sigma_{\hat{\beta}_1}^2$ and $\sigma_{\hat{\beta}_0}^2$ with the estimated (or residual) variance ($\hat{\sigma}_\varepsilon^2$), you get the estimated variances of the OLS coefficients

$$\hat{\sigma}_{\hat{\beta}_1}^2 = \frac{\hat{\sigma}_\varepsilon^2}{\sum_{i=1}^{n}\left(X_i - \bar{X}\right)^2}$$

and

$$\hat{\sigma}_{\hat{\beta}_0}^2 = \left(\frac{\sum_{i=1}^{n}X_i^2}{n\sum_{i=1}^{n}\left(X_i - \bar{X}\right)^2}\right)\hat{\sigma}_\varepsilon^2$$

The square root of these estimated variances ($\hat{\sigma}_{\hat{\beta}_k} = \sqrt{\hat{\sigma}_{\hat{\beta}_k}^2}$) provides the *standard errors of the coefficients*.

In Table 7-1, data for the dependent variable (Y) and the independent variable (X) are in the first two columns. With these values and the OLS technique, you can obtain the sample regression function $\hat{Y}_i = 119.7 - 19.3X_i$. (If you need to review these calculations, I calculate the OLS coefficients using the same data in Chapter 5.)

Table 7-1			Calculation of Coefficient Standard Errors				
(1)	*(2)*	*(3)*	*(4)*	*(5)*	*(6)*	*(7)*	*(8)*
i	Y_i	X_i	X_i^2	$\left(X_i - \bar{X}\right)^2$	$\hat{Y}_i$	$\hat{\varepsilon}_i$	$\hat{\varepsilon}_i^2$
1	100	1	1	4	100.4	−0.4	0.16
2	80	2	4	1	81.1	−1.1	1.21
3	63	3	9	0	61.8	1.2	1.44
4	45	4	16	1	42.5	2.5	6.25
5	21	5	25	4	23.2	−2.2	4.84
Sum:	309	15	55	10	309	0	13.9
Mean:	61.8	3					

Beginning with Column 4 of Table 7-1, proceed with the intermediate steps to calculate the standard errors of the coefficients. Using the work in the table, you can obtain the MSE:

$$\hat{\sigma}_{\varepsilon}^2 = \frac{\sum_{i=1}^{n}\hat{\varepsilon}_i^2}{n-p-1} = \frac{13.9}{3} = 4.6333\overline{3}$$

The numerator is derived using the values in Table 7-1, and the denominator is calculated by using the number of observations (5) for n and the number of X variables (1) for p. After you have the MSE, you can obtain the estimated variances of the coefficients:

$$\hat{\sigma}_{\hat{\beta}_1}^2 = \frac{\hat{\sigma}_{\varepsilon}^2}{\sum_{i=1}^{n}\left(X_i - \bar{X}\right)^2} = \frac{4.6333}{10} = 0.4633$$

$$\sigma_{\hat{\beta}_0}^2 = \left(\frac{\sum_{i=1}^{n}X_i^2}{n\sum_{i=1}^{n}\left(X_i - \bar{X}\right)^2}\right)\hat{\sigma}_{\varepsilon}^2 = \left(\frac{55}{(5)(10)}\right)(4.6333) = 5.0966$$

Then you find the standard errors of the coefficients:

$$\hat{\sigma}_{\hat{\beta}_1} = \sqrt{0.4633} = 0.6807$$

$$\hat{\sigma}_{\hat{\beta}_0} = \sqrt{5.0966} = 2.2576$$

Using the "regress" command in STATA, I can quickly produce the OLS results, which you see in Figure 7-3. STATA (and most econometrics software packages) includes the coefficients, MSE, RMSE, and standard errors of the coefficients.

. regress y x

Source	SS	df	MS	Number of obs	=	5
				F (1,3)	=	803.94
Model	3724.9	1	3724.9	Prob > F	=	0.0001
Residual	13.9	3	4.63333333	R-squared	=	0.9963
				Adj R-squared	=	0.9950
Total	3738.8	4	934.7	Root MSE	=	2.1525

y	Coef.	Std. Err.	t	P>|t|	[95% Conf. Interval]
x	-19.3	.6806859	-28.35	0.000	-21.46625 -17.13375
_cons	119.7	2.25758	53.02	0.000	112.5154 126.8846

Figure 7-3: STATA OLS output includes the MSE, RMSE, and coefficient standard errors.

MSE

RMSE

$\sigma_{\hat{\beta}_k}$

The variance of the error (σ_ε^2) is a parameter. In other words, there's some true, but unknown, value for this in the population as a whole. The MSE, however, is an estimate of the error variance. Like all estimators, you never know exactly what value will be derived, because it varies from sample to sample. The assumption that the error is normally distributed implies that the MSE and the estimated variances of the coefficients are the square of a normal, so they have a chi-squared (χ^2) distribution with $n - p - 1$ degrees of freedom.

OLS standard errors and the t-distribution

When you assume that the error term is normally distributed, that translates into a normal distribution of your OLS estimators. You could express this as

$$\hat{\beta}_k \sim N\left(\beta_k, \sigma_{\hat{\beta}_k}^2\right)$$

Consequently, each of your OLS estimators can be transformed to a standard normal. In other words,

$$\frac{\hat{\beta}_k - \beta_k}{\sigma_{\hat{\beta}_k}} \sim N(0,1)$$

In practice, the standard deviation of the estimator isn't known, so you use its estimate (the standard error). When you replace the standard deviation of the estimator ($\sigma_{\hat{\beta}_k}$) with the standard error ($\hat{\sigma}_{\hat{\beta}_k}$), the appropriate probability distribution becomes t instead of standard normal. This can be written as

$$\frac{\hat{\beta}_k - \beta_k}{\hat{\sigma}_{\hat{\beta}_k}} \sim t_{n-p-1}$$

The reason $\frac{\hat{\beta}_k - \beta_k}{\hat{\sigma}_{\hat{\beta}_k}}$ has a t-distribution is because the numerator is a normal distribution while the parameter $\sigma_{\hat{\beta}_k}$ in the denominator is replaced by the estimator $\hat{\sigma}_{\hat{\beta}_k}$. This estimator is derived from $\hat{\sigma}_{\hat{\beta}_k}^2$, so it has a square root of a chi-squared distribution. The degrees of freedom $(n - p - 1)$ for this t-distribution come from the standard error estimate in the denominator.

Testing the Significance of Individual Regression Coefficients

After you estimate a regression and have your OLS estimates, you want to know what conclusions can be drawn from your results. At the very start of the process, you selected the variables in your model based on your knowledge of economic theory along with a healthy dose of common sense, and now that you've obtained results, what do they suggest about your hypothesized relationships? What is the probability that results like the ones you produced were the result of chance? In order to address these questions, you need to test the individual significance of your regression coefficients.

A regression coefficient is *statistically significant* (meaning the results didn't happen just by chance) if you can provide solid evidence that the true parameter value isn't zero. In order to provide strong evidence that the true parameter value isn't zero, you need to show that it's highly unlikely that the X variable associated with that coefficient has no effect on your dependent (Y) variable.

The most common test of statistical significance for the OLS coefficients is the following two-sided test: H_0: $\beta_k = 0$ and H_1: $\beta_k \neq 0$ where H_0 represents the null hypothesis that the true parameter value is zero and H_1 is the alternative hypothesis. Although this two-sided test (using zero as the hypothesized value) is the most common hypothesis test for regression coefficients, any value can be used (if you're having trouble recalling these concepts from your statistics class, you can go to Chapter 3 for an overview).

Sometimes you may be interested in performing a one-sided test, such as

$$H_0: \beta_k \leq 0 \; H_1: \beta_k > 0$$

or

$$H_0: \beta_k \geq 0 \; H_1: \beta_k < 0$$

In economics, theory may rule out some numerical possibilities and imply that the relationship (slope coefficient) has a particular sign (positive or negative). For example, income should always have some positive effect on consumption. If you're only interested in rejecting a null hypothesis if the evidence goes in a particular direction, then a one-sided test is appropriate.

You can't determine the *importance* of a variable or the *magnitude* of its effect by the statistical significance of the coefficient. Some coefficients that are highly statistically significant may be of little importance, so keep in mind that statistical significance provides only evidence of a positive or negative effect. For magnitude and importance, you want to focus on the value of the coefficient and perhaps calculate the standardized regression coefficient (see Chapter 5 for a discussion of this).

Interpreting the meaning of your coefficient estimates helps you determine economic significance. Do the coefficients represent unit changes? Percent changes? Are some of the variables measures in hundreds or thousands? Keep these things in mind, provide a verbal description of your results, and make the connection to the economic theory that motivated your estimation in order to drive home economic significance.

In the following sections, I guide you through two approaches that can be chosen for hypothesis testing and show you how statistical significance is determined from your results.

Picking an approach

You can report the statistical significance of your coefficients (the result of your hypothesis test) with either the confidence interval approach or the test of significance approach. The former provides you with a range of possible values for your estimator in repeated sampling, and the latter gives you a test statistic that's used to determine the likelihood of your hypothesis.

Confidence interval approach

A confidence interval provides a range (lower and upper limit) of values that would contain the true value (parameter) a certain percentage of time. If you need to review the concept of a confidence interval, I discuss the details in Chapter 3.

The confidence interval for a regression coefficient is given by

$$f\left(\hat{\beta}_k - \left(t_{\alpha/2,n-p-1}\right)\left(\hat{\sigma}_{\hat{\beta}_k}\right) \le \beta_k \le \hat{\beta}_k + \left(t_{\alpha/2,n-p-1}\right)\left(\hat{\sigma}_{\hat{\beta}_k}\right)\right) = 1-\alpha$$

where $1 - \alpha$ is the level of confidence, $\hat{\beta}_k$ is the estimated coefficient, $\hat{\sigma}_{\hat{\beta}_k}$ is the standard error of the coefficient, and $t_{\alpha/2,n-p-1}$ is the appropriate t value. You can find the t value by using the t-distribution table in the Appendix and choosing $n - p - 1$ as your degrees of freedom (if your recollection of the t-distribution is foggy, you can visit Chapter 3).

Suppose your estimated slope coefficient is –19.3, its standard error is 0.6807, and the degrees of freedom are 3. With this information you can calculate a 95 percent confidence interval as follows:

$$f(-19.3 - (3.182)(0.6807) \le \beta_1 \le -19.3 + (3.182)(0.6807)) = 1 - 0.05$$

where the value 3.182 is pulled from the t table in the Appendix by going to the row with 3 degrees of freedom ($n - p - 1 = 5 - 1 - 1 = 3$) and 0.025 tail density ($\alpha/2 = 0.05/2 = 0.025$).

$$f(-21.47 \le \beta_1 \le -17.13) = 0.95$$

Therefore, you can be confident that, in repeated samples, your estimated coefficient will fall between –21.47 and –17.13 95 percent of the time. The calculation of a 95 percent confidence interval is a conventional norm (and STATA chooses it as the default), but other common confidence intervals are 90 and 99 percent.

Similarly, a confidence interval can be calculated for the intercept (β_0) or any other coefficient (β_k) using the same formula. In your STATA output, as shown in Figure 7-3, you'll find the confidence intervals to the right of the estimated coefficients, standard errors, and *t*-statistics.

If the hypothesized value is not contained in your calculated confidence interval, then your coefficient is statistically significant (meaning you can reject the null hypothesis).

Test of significance approach

The test of significance is the most common approach econometricians use to test hypotheses about coefficients. For individual coefficients, a *t*-test is typically performed.

You can conduct a *t*-test for any of your coefficients with the following steps:

1. **Estimate the coefficient ($\hat{\beta}_k$) and standard error ($\hat{\sigma}_{\hat{\beta}_k}$).**

2. **Calculate the *t-statistic* with the formula** $t = \dfrac{\hat{\beta}_k - \beta_k}{\hat{\sigma}_{\hat{\beta}_k}}$**, where β_k is the hypothesized value of the coefficient (usually zero).**

3. **Determine the level of significance (α) at which you want to perform the test and obtain the *critical t* value from the *t*-distribution table.**

   Recall that a critical *t*-value is the reference value chosen from the *t*-distribution (table) at the appropriate level of significance and degrees of freedom (you can find the *t* table in the Appendix).

4. **Compare your *t-statistic* to your *critical t* and reject the null hypothesis (or consider your coefficient *statistically significant*) if you're in the critical region.**

   See Chapter 3 if you need to review the concept of a critical region.

As in the preceding section, suppose your estimated slope coefficient is –19.3, its standard error is 0.6807, and the degrees of freedom are 3. In order to perform a two-tailed test of significance (which assumes that the true value of the coefficient is zero) at the 5 percent level (meaning a 95 percent confidence level), you must calculate the *t*-statistic as follows:

$$t = \frac{-19.3}{0.6807} = -28.35$$

Next, you want to compare the calculated *t* (–28.35) to the critical *t* from the table (3.182). For a two-sided test, the critical value is on both the left and right side of the distribution, so the critical region is defined by values less than –3.182 and greater than +3.182. Your *t*-statistic is in the critical region, so the variable associated with that coefficient is *statistically significant* at the 5 percent level.

One quick way of examining *t*-statistics in regression output, such as that in Figure 7-3, is to see if their absolute value is greater than 2. As a rule of thumb, *t*-statistics with an absolute value greater than 2 indicate that the variable is statistically significant.

Choosing the level of significance and p-values

The 10, 5, and 1 percent levels of significance are the most common for testing the statistical significance of individual regression coefficients. However, any level of significance chosen for a confidence interval or test of significance exposes you to type I and type II errors.

A *type I error* is rejecting a hypothesis that's true, and a *type II error* is failing to reject a hypothesis that's false. If you choose a higher level of significance, you increase the chances of committing a type I error. And if you choose a lower level of significance, you increase the chances of committing a type II error.

Researchers may pass on the burden of committing type I or type II errors to readers by doing one of two things:

✔ **Present regression results in a table with asterisks next to the coefficients of each variable.** Usually, one asterisk (*) indicates that the coefficient is significant at the 10 percent level, two asterisks (**) indicate significance at the 5 percent level, and three asterisks (***) are used if it's significant at the 1 percent level.

✔ **Report the *p*-value associated with the calculated *t*-statistic.** The *p*-value is the lowest level of significance at which the null hypothesis could be rejected and is probably the most useful way of summarizing the strength (or weakness) of a statistical significance test. Econometrics software programs routinely report *p*-values for each estimated coefficient.

Analyzing Variance to Determine Overall or Joint Significance

Because so many independent variables (*X*s) can simultaneously affect your dependent variable (*Y*), fully observing and accounting for all of them in a regression model is impossible. Some cases may have many unobservable characteristics, which leads to a relatively low R-squared value. However, that doesn't mean that what you've explained is inconsequential or unimportant. You can use tests of *overall* (or *joint*) *significance* to determine if the variation in your *Y* variable explained by all (or some subset) of your variables is nontrivial. The following sections illustrate how you use variance calculations to produce *F*-statistics that allow you to perform hypothesis tests of overall and joint significance.

Normality, variance, and the F distribution

One reason why you perform regression analysis is to help you explain variation in some outcome of interest, and that outcome is your dependent (*Y*) variable.

After you introduce some independent variables and estimate a regression, you can identify other components of variance; namely, those parts of the total variance in *Y* that can be explained by variation in the *X*s you added to the regression model or that remain unexplained (this concept is discussed in more detail in Chapter 5). The normality assumption also ensures that these variances have a chi-squared distribution. In other words, the explained and unexplained variations from a regression model have a chi-squared distribution under the assumption that the conditional distribution of *Y* is normal $(Y \mid X \sim N(\beta_0 + \beta_1 X_{i1} + \beta_2 X_{i2} + \ldots, \sigma_Y^2))$, which is equivalent to assuming that the error term is normally distributed $(\varepsilon \mid X \sim N(0, \sigma_\varepsilon^2))$.

In order to see how changes to your model affect explained variation, you want to compare the different components of variance. You can do so by calculating the ratio of the variances and, as a result, generating an *F*-distribution that allows you to draw some conclusions about the likelihood that your model has a significant impact on the components of variance.

The reported F-statistic from OLS

The R-squared value is a measure of overall fit for a regression model, but it doesn't tell you whether the amount of explained variation is statistically significant (in Chapter 5, I discuss how you calculate and interpret the R-squared). This situation is similar to individual regression coefficients, because you don't know by simply looking at the value of a regression coefficient whether it's statistically significant.

Despite a low R-squared value, your model may explain a significant amount of variation in your dependent variable. The opposite may also be true; a high R-squared value may not be statistically significantly different from zero.

The null and alternative hypotheses to test for a regression model's overall significance are

$$H_0: \beta_1 = \beta_2 = \ldots = \beta_p = 0$$

$H_1: H_0$ is not true

Overall significance only examines the impact of the slope coefficients (not the intercept term) and is tested using the following F-statistic:

$$F = \frac{\dfrac{ESS}{p}}{\dfrac{RSS}{n-p-1}}$$

In this equation, the explained sum of squares is $ESS = \sum_{i=1}^{n}\left(\hat{Y}_i - \bar{Y}\right)^2$, and the residual sum of squares is $RSS = \sum_{i=1}^{n}\hat{\varepsilon}_i^2$.

The number of sample observations is n, and p is the number of independent variables in the regression model. The degrees of freedom are p in the numerator and $n - p - 1$ in the denominator.

With some algebraic manipulation, the F-statistic of overall significance can also be written using the R-squared values as follows:

$$F = \frac{\dfrac{R^2}{p}}{\dfrac{\left(1-R^2\right)}{\left(n-p-1\right)}}$$

I have a small dataset on demand (or sales) for a good (*qtydemX*), the price of that good (*priceX*), and the price of a related good (*priceY*). In Figure 7-4, I use the "list" command in STATA to show you the values for the individual observations. In addition, Figure 7-4 displays STATA's regression output which, by default, includes the F-test for overall significance. In this example, the *F*-statistic is 5.03 and the *p*-value is 0.055, so I can reject the hypothesis that the independent variables have no collective influence on the dependent variable at the 5.5 percent level of significance (or with 94.5 percent confidence). *Note:* All econometrics software packages, as part of the standard regression output, display the sum of squares (explained, residual, and total), the *F*-statistic, and the *p*-value associated with the test of overall significance.

```
. list qtydemX priceX
```

	qtydemX	priceX
1.	6216	3.59
2.	8253	3.23
3.	8038	2.6
4.	7476	2.89
5.	5911	3.77
6.	7950	3.64
7.	6134	2.82
8.	5868	2.96
9.	3160	4.24
10.	5872	3.69

Figure 7-4:
The analysis of variance (ANOVA) section of STATA's regression output contains the measures needed for the *F*-statistic.

ANOVA

```
. regress qtydemX priceX
```

Source	SS	df	MS	Number of obs	=	10
				F (1,8)	=	5.03
Model	8109106.14	1	8109106.14	Prob > F	=	0.0552
Residual	12893875.5	8	1611734.43	R-squared	=	0.3861
				Adj R-squared	=	0.3094
Total	21002981.6	9	2333664.62	Root MSE	=	1269.5

qtydemX	Coef.	Std. Err.	t	P>|t|	[95% Conf. Interval]	
priceX	-1820.482	811.6086	-2.24	0.055	-3692.055	51.09078
_cons	12573.67	2742.748	4.58	0.002	6248.882	18898.46

In models with numerous independent variables, many of the variables can be individually statistically insignificant. Remember that individual significance doesn't rule out the possibility that they're collectively significant. Some variables, in combination with others, can have a strong collective influence even though their individual impact is small.

Slope coefficients and the relationship between t and F

If the degrees of freedom in the numerator of an F-value equal 1, then the square of a t-distribution approximately equals an F-distribution. In the context of regression analysis, this implies $\left(t_{n-p-1}\right)^2 = F_{1,n-p-1}$ if $p = 1$.

In a simple regression model (with one independent variable), the t-test of significance for the slope coefficient is the same as the F-test for overall significance.

If you have one independent variable, the null hypothesis for the test of individual significance (t-test) is $H_0: \beta_1 = 0$. But this is also the test of overall significance (F-test) because the entire model's influence on your dependent variable rests on the influence of one variable.

Figure 7-5 shows STATA output for a simple regression model where the demand (or sales) for a good is the dependent variable (*qtydemX*) and the price of that good is the independent variable (*priceX*).

. regress qtydemX priceX

Figure 7-5: In a simple regression model, the *p*-value for overall significance is identical to the *p*-value for the slope coefficient.

Source	SS	df	MS	Number of obs	=	10
				F (1,3)	=	5.03
Model	8109106.14	1	8109106.14	Prob > F	=	0.0552
Residual	12893875.5	8	1611734.43	R-squared	=	0.3861
				Adj R-squared	=	0.3094
Total	21002981.6	9	2333664.62	Root MSE	=	1269.5

qtydemX	Coef.	Std. Err.	t	P>|t|	[95% Conf. Interval]	
priceX	-1820.482	811.6086	-2.24	0.055	-3692.055	51.09078
_cons	12573.67	2742.748	4.58	0.002	6248.882	18898.46

The t-test for the slope coefficient and the F-test shown in Figure 7-5 produce the same result. Both have a *p*-value of 0.055. In models with only one independent variable, the t-test and F-test always produce the same *p*-value.

Joint significance for subsets of variables

In addition to testing for overall significance, the F-test can be useful in other situations. The most common is to examine the joint significance of a subset of variables in a regression model that includes several independent variables.

Testing the joint significance of a subset of variables in a regression model is accomplished by generalizing the F-test of overall significance to

$$F = \frac{\dfrac{RSS_r - RSS_{ur}}{q}}{\dfrac{RSS_{ur}}{n-p-1}}$$

where RSS_r is the RSS for the *restricted* model (the model with fewer independent variables), RSS_{ur} is the RSS for the *unrestricted* model (the model with more independent variables), n is the number of sample measurements, p is the number of independent variables in the unrestricted model, and q is the number of independent variables contained in your unrestricted model that are not contained in your restricted model.

The F-test of overall significance is a special case of the more general test. In that case, $q = p$ because the restricted model contains no independent variables in a test of overall significance.

Suppose you're interested in explaining variation in movie box office revenue. You develop a model using the movie's budget, critic reviews, and MPAA rating as independent variables. You use the MPAA ratings to generate three dummy variables indicating whether the movie received a PG, PG-13, or R rating (see Chapter 9 for an in-depth discussion of dummy variables). The model can be estimated without the ratings dummies (restricted) and with the ratings variables (unrestricted). Figure 7-6 shows the results produced from estimating both the restricted and unrestricted models using STATA.

You can use the results in Figure 7-6 to test the statistical significance of MPAA ratings in affecting movie revenue. The t-statistics suggest that none of the ratings have an *individually* significant impact on revenue. But do they have an impact *collectively*? To answer this question, calculate the following F-statistic:

$$F = \frac{\dfrac{1,477,786.25 - 1,460,517.34}{3}}{\dfrac{1,460,517.34}{580-5-1}} = 2.26$$

The critical value on the F-distribution is $F_{.05,3,574} = 2.62$, so you don't have enough evidence to claim that MPAA ratings are collectively significant at the 5 percent level.

Restricted model:

`. regress grossbox_mil budget_mil crit`

Source	SS	df	MS		Number of obs	=	580
					F (2,577)	=	310.05
Model	1588188.67	2	794094.334		Prob > F	=	0.0000
Residual	1477786.25	577	2561.15468		R-squared	=	0.5180
					Adj R-squared	=	0.5163
Total	3065974.92	579	5295.29347		Root MSE	=	50.608

grossbox_mil	Coef.	Std. Err.	t	P>|t|	[95% Conf. Interval]	
budget_mil	1.11124	.0465035	23.90	0.000	1.019903	1.202577
crit	.4138258	.0784313	5.28	0.000	.2597802	.5678713
_cons	-8.394324	4.668307	-1.80	0.073	-17.56327	.7746213

Unrestricted model:

`. regress grossbox_mil budget_mil crit PG13 r`

Source	SS	df	MS		Number of obs	=	580
					F (2,577)	=	310.05
Model	1605457.58	5	321091.516		Prob > F	=	0.0000
Residual	1460517.34	574	2544.45529		R-squared	=	0.5180
					Adj R-squared	=	0.5163
Total	3065974.92	579	5295.29347		Root MSE	=	50.608

grossbox_mil	Coef.	Std. Err.	t	P>|t|	[95% Conf. Interval]	
budget_mil	1.07877	.0485923	22.20	0.000	.9833294	1.17421
crit	.459252	.0806962	5.69	0.000	.3007561	.6177479
pg	-30.55521	36.27839	-0.84	0.400	-101.8098	40.69938
PG13	-24.55272	35.83444	-0.69	0.494	-94.93534	45.8229
r	-36.22161	35.81987	-1.01	0.312	-106.5756	34.1324
_cons	20.81916	35.93415	0.58	0.563	-49.75931	91.39762

Figure 7-6: STATA estimates of a restricted and unrestricted model of movie revenue.

In STATA, you can test the significance of subsets of your independent variables in fewer steps. Specifically, you can estimate your unrestricted model and then use the "test *var1 var2*..." command to perform the *F*-test. Doing so with my sample of movies has the results in Figure 7-7.

The benefits of using STATA for this calculation are enhanced accuracy, faster calculations, and a reported *p*-value for the test. The result in Figure 7-7 suggests that you can reject the hypothesis that MPAA ratings have no collective impact on movie revenue at the 8 percent (0.0802) level of significance.

```
. regress grossbox_mil budget_mil crit pg PG13 r
```

Source	SS	df	MS
Model	1605457.58	5	321091.516
Residual	1460517.34	574	2544.45529
Total	3065974.92	579	5295.29347

```
                              Number of obs =     580
                              F (5,574)     =  126.19
                              Prob > F      =  0.0000
                              R-squared     =  0.5236
                              Adj R-squared =  0.5195
                              Root MSE      =  50.443
```

grossbox_mil	Coef.	Std. Err.	t	P>|t|	[95% Conf. Interval]	
budget_mil	1.07877	.0485923	22.20	0.000	.9833294	1.17421
crit	.459252	.0806962	5.69	0.000	.3007561	.6177479
pg	-30.55521	36.27839	-0.84	0.400	-101.8098	40.69938
PG13	-24.55272	35.83444	-0.69	0.494	-94.93534	45.8299
r	-36.22161	35.81987	-1.01	0.312	-106.5756	34.1324
_cons	20.81916	35.93415	0.58	0.563	-49.75931	91.39762

Figure 7-7: STATA regression output followed by a joint test of statistical significance for a subset of the independent variables.

```
. test pg PG13 r

 ( 1) pg = 0
 ( 2) PG13 = 0
 ( 3) r = 0

      F(3, 574) = 2.26
      Prob > F = 0.0802
```

Applying Forecast Error to OLS Predictions

After you apply the OLS technique to estimate your regression function, the results can be used to make predictions about the dependent variable. Your predictions won't be perfect, so when you're using regression for forecasting, you need to provide some measure of accuracy. In the subsequent sections, you apply regression results to make predictions, figure out how much variability your predictions will have, and use estimated prediction error to produce forecast confidence intervals.

Mean prediction and forecast error

The population regression function (PRF) passes through the conditional means of the dependent variable (Y). For a simple regression model, the conditional mean for a specific value of the independent variable (X_0) is

$$E(Y|X_0) = \beta_0 + \beta_1 X_0$$

In practice, you estimate the conditional mean for a specific X value using your sample regression function (SRF) $\hat{Y}_0 = \hat{\beta}_0 + \hat{\beta}_1 X_0$ by plugging in any potential value of your independent variable for X_0. The resulting $\hat{Y}_0$ is known as the *mean prediction*.

If you apply the expected value operator to both sides of the SRF, you get

$$E\left(\hat{Y}_0\right) = E\left(\hat{\beta}_0\right) + E\left(\hat{\beta}_1\right) X_0$$

With the classical linear regression model (CLRM) assumptions, the estimated regression coefficients are unbiased (see Chapter 6 for a description and proof of this result). If the coefficients are unbiased, then $E\left(\hat{Y}_0\right) = \beta_0 + \beta_1 X_0$ and $E\left(Y \mid X_0\right) = E\left(\hat{Y}_0\right)$.

The predicted value of the dependent variable from your SRF ($\hat{Y}$) is an unbiased estimator of the true conditional mean ($E(Y \mid X)$), but this estimation only proves that the two are equal on average. Any particular prediction you produce from a SRF is likely to contain *forecast error* (the difference between the true conditional mean and the predicted value) even though, on average, the forecast error is zero.

Variance of mean prediction

The variance of an estimate (or prediction) provides a numerical value that describes how much a prediction changes from one sample to another.

Given that your *mean prediction* from a SRF contains forecast error, you want to know how much variability your prediction contains. The less variability, the more reliable your forecast.

In applied situations, you're likely to get only one sample (or opportunity) to make a prediction. A smaller variance for your prediction increases the chances that your forecast is close to the true value and decreases the chances of having a large forecast error.

In order to derive the variance of the mean prediction, begin with the SRF at a specific X value and apply the variance operator to get

$$Var\left(\hat{Y}_0\right) = Var\left(\hat{\beta}_0 + \hat{\beta}_1 X_0\right)$$

Using the variance properties, you can rewrite the variance of the mean prediction as

$$\sigma_{\hat{Y}_0}^2 = Var\left(\hat{\beta}_0\right) + X_0^2 Var\left(\hat{\beta}_1\right) + 2X_0 Cov\left(\hat{\beta}_0, \hat{\beta}_1\right)$$

The covariance of the estimated regression coefficients is

$$Cov\left(\hat{\beta}_0, \hat{\beta}_1\right) = -\bar{X}\left(\frac{\sigma_\varepsilon^2}{\sum_{i=1}^n \left(X_i - \bar{X}\right)^2}\right)$$

If you substitute this and the components of $Var\left(\hat{\beta}_0\right)$ and $Var\left(\hat{\beta}_1\right)$ into the variance equation, you have

$$\sigma_{\hat{Y}_0}^2 = \left(\frac{\sum_{i=1}^n X_i^2}{n\sum_{i=1}^n \left(X_i - \bar{X}\right)^2}\right)\sigma_\varepsilon^2 + X_0^2 \left(\frac{\sigma_\varepsilon^2}{\sum_{i=1}^n \left(X_i - \bar{X}\right)^2}\right) + 2X_0 \left(\frac{-\bar{X}\sigma_\varepsilon^2}{\sum_{i=1}^n \left(X_i - \bar{X}\right)^2}\right)$$

Note: See the earlier section "Deriving a chi-squared distribution from the random error" if you don't know how to calculate the variance of the coefficients.

After several algebraic steps, you can reduce this equation to

$$\sigma_{\hat{Y}_0}^2 = \sigma_\varepsilon^2 \left(\frac{1}{n} + \frac{\left(X_0 - \bar{X}\right)^2}{\sum_{i=1}^n \left(X_i - \bar{X}\right)^2}\right)$$

where σ_ε^2 represents the variance of the error term.

In practice, you don't know the true variance of the error, so you can calculate the estimated variance of the mean prediction using

$$\hat{\sigma}_{\hat{Y}_0}^2 = \hat{\sigma}_\varepsilon^2 \left(\frac{1}{n} + \frac{\left(X_0 - \bar{X}\right)^2}{\sum_{i=1}^n \left(X_i - \bar{X}\right)^2}\right)$$

where $\hat{\sigma}_\varepsilon^2$ is the variance of the residuals or estimated variance of the error (see the earlier section "Deriving a chi-squared distribution from the random error" if you need help calculating the variance of the residuals).

The variance of your prediction is smallest near the mean value of your independent variable(s). If you make predictions using values for your independent variable(s) that deviate from their mean, the variance of your prediction increases exponentially.

All predictions are not the same: The prediction confidence interval

If you're able to calculate the variance of a parameter prediction and you know the distribution of the parameter, then you can construct a confidence interval.

For the mean prediction of a dependent variable in a regression model, the confidence interval is defined as $\hat{Y}_0 \pm \left(t_{\alpha/2,n-p-1}\right)\left(\hat{\sigma}_{\hat{Y}_0}\right)$, where $\hat{\sigma}_{\hat{Y}_0}$ is the standard error of the mean prediction.

A unique characteristic of this confidence interval is the changing standard error of the prediction; smallest at the mean value of X and increasing exponentially as X deviates from the mean.

The assumption that the error term follows a normal distribution ensures that the OLS estimators ($\hat{\beta}$ terms) are also normally distributed (see the earlier section "Describing the Role of the Normality Assumption" if you can't recall how this works). The mean prediction ($\hat{Y}$) is a linear function of the estimators, so it also has a normal distribution. The *t*-distribution is used to construct the confidence interval because you rely on the estimated variance of the error to calculate the variance of the prediction rather than the true variance of the error.

The nature of the confidence interval for the OLS mean prediction is best illustrated with econometrics software. In STATA, I use the pull-down menu in Graphics and then click on Twoway graph. A small window opens in which I choose Create followed by Linear prediction w/CI. Figure 7-8 shows the resulting graph. It contains all the mean predictions (the regression line) and the confidence interval (the shaded area).

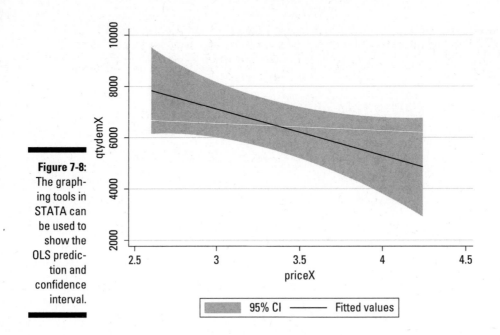

Figure 7-8:
The graph-
ing tools in
STATA can
be used to
show the
OLS predic-
tion and
confidence
interval.

Notice that the area of the confidence interval for your prediction is smallest at the average X value and increases exponentially as you move away from the mean in either direction.

Part III

Working with the Classical Regression Model

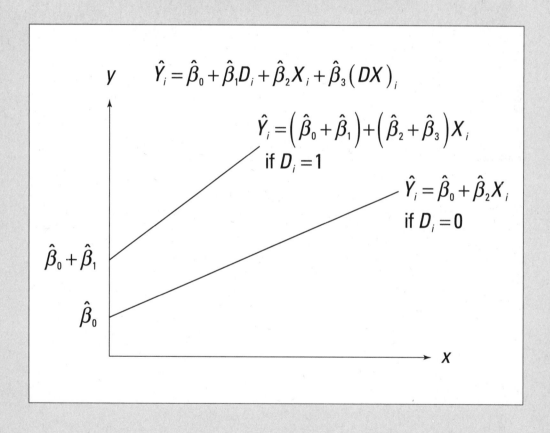

$$\hat{Y}_i = \hat{\beta}_0 + \hat{\beta}_1 D_i + \hat{\beta}_2 X_i + \hat{\beta}_3 (DX)_i$$

$$\hat{Y}_i = \left(\hat{\beta}_0 + \hat{\beta}_1 \right) + \left(\hat{\beta}_2 + \hat{\beta}_3 \right) X_i$$
if $D_i = 1$

$$\hat{Y}_i = \hat{\beta}_0 + \hat{\beta}_2 X_i$$
if $D_i = 0$

$\hat{\beta}_0 + \hat{\beta}_1$

$\hat{\beta}_0$

In this part . . .

- ✔ Model nonlinear relationships and estimate functions with traditional techniques.

- ✔ Examine specification issues, determine the best approach for dealing with them when they occur, and strengthen faith in your results.

- ✔ Discover how to turn qualitative data into quantitative data that you can use as independent (or explanatory) variables.

- ✔ Estimate the impact of qualitative characteristics on quantitative outcomes.

Chapter 8

Functional Form, Specification, and Structural Stability

. . . .

In This Chapter

▶ Understanding how to use and interpret nonlinear regression functions

▶ Transforming common nonlinear functions in economics into linear functions

▶ Testing for specification issues and checking the reliability of your results

. . . .

*Y*ou typically choose the dependent variable in a particular analysis based on the economic question or puzzle that you're interested in exploring and your prior knowledge of economic theory. However, you have to think about several additional questions to determine whether you have a good econometric model. In particular, you need to ask:

▸ What independent variables or factors are likely to affect my outcome or variable of interest (dependent variable)?

▸ Do I expect the variables to have a linear (that is, constant or straight-line) impact on the dependent variable, or are some of them likely to have a nonlinear effect?

Your answers to these questions address what econometricians call *specification issues.* The best ways to deal with specification issues for an individual problem can be controversial and far from obvious, but you aren't without help. In this chapter, I show you some strategies that help you address these questions carefully and, consequently, make your results more convincing. I also expose you to various paths and criteria that can be considered in approaching these questions systematically and formulating your econometric model.

Employing Alternative Functions

Because economic relationships are rarely linear, you may want to allow your econometric model to have some flexibility. Linear functions are the easiest to interpret, but they also impose restrictions on the nature of the relationship between your dependent (Y) and independent (X) variables insofar as they force the effect of the X variable(s) on the Y variable to be constant over all values of X. One way you can allow for more flexibility in the effect of the independent variable(s) is by specifying your econometric model using polynomials; that is, as a nonlinear function. In this section, I show you different ways that you can use polynomials.

Quadratic function: Best for finding minimums and maximums

With a quadratic function, you allow the effect of the independent variable (X) on the dependent variable to change. As the value of X increases, the impact of the dependent variable increases or decreases.

The mathematical representation of an econometric model with a quadratic function is $Y_i = \beta_0 + \beta_1 X_i + \beta_2 X_i^2 + \varepsilon_i$.

If you estimate this type of regression, several outcomes are possible for your coefficients. However, the two most common results are as follows:

- $\hat{\beta}_1 > 0$ and $\hat{\beta}_2 > 0$
- $\hat{\beta}_1 > 0$ and $\hat{\beta}_2 < 0$

If $\hat{\beta}_1$ and $\hat{\beta}_2$ in the estimated regression $\hat{Y}_i = \hat{\beta}_0 + \hat{\beta}_1 X_i + \hat{\beta}_2 X_i^2$ are both positive, then your estimated regression line looks like the one shown in Figure 8-1a. If $\hat{\beta}_1$ is positive and $\hat{\beta}_2$ is negative in the estimated regression $\hat{Y}_i = \hat{\beta}_0 + \hat{\beta}_1 X_i + \hat{\beta}_2 X_i^2$, then Figure 8-1b is an approximate depiction of the regression curve.

A total variable cost (TVC) or total cost (TC) curve may display the shape shown in Figure 8-1a, whereas a short-run total product (TP) curve is likely to display the sort of behavior shown in Figure 8-1b if marginal product is diminishing at any level of input. (These concepts were covered in your microeconomics course. Check out *Economics For Dummies,* by Sean Masaki Flynn [Wiley], if you need a refresher.)

Figure 8-1:
A quadratic
function
with an
increasing
slope (a)
and with a
decreasing
slope (b).

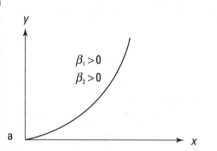

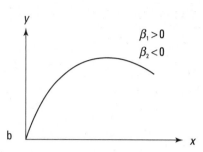

Cubic functions: Good for inflexion

Like when using a quadratic function, with a cubic function, you allow the effect of the independent variable (X) on the dependent variable (Y) to change. As the value of X increases (or decreases), the impact of the dependent variable may increase or decrease. However, unlike a quadratic function, this relationship changes at some unique value of X. In other words, at some specific point, a decreasing effect becomes increasing or an increasing effect becomes decreasing. The point at which this occurs is called the *inflexion point.*

The mathematical representation of an econometric model with a cubic function is $Y_i = \beta_1 X_i + \beta_2 X_i^2 + \beta_3 X_i^3 + \varepsilon_i$. If you estimate this type of regression, numerous outcomes are possible for your coefficients. However, the two most common results lead to either of the following curves:

✔ A decreasing slope followed by an increasing slope, as shown in Figure 8-2a

✔ An increasing slope followed by a decreasing slope, as shown in Figure 8-2b

Figure 8-2:
A cubic
function with
a decreas-
ing and then
increasing
slope (a)
and with an
increasing
and then
decreasing
slope (b).

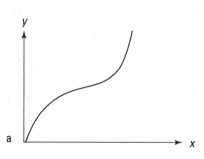

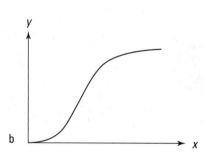

Among many other possibilities, Figure 8-2a depicts the potential shape of a total variable cost (TVC) or total cost (TC) curve. Figure 8-2b approximates a short-run total product (TP) curve if initially marginal productivity is increasing and then it diminishes.

Inverse function: Limiting the value of the dependent variable

If you believe that the outcome (dependent variable) you're modeling is likely to approach some value asymptotically (as X approaches zero or infinity), then an inverse function may be the way to go. Inverse functions can be useful if you're trying to estimate a Phillips curve (the inverse relationship between inflation and unemployment rates) or a demand function (the inverse relationship between price and quantity demanded), among other economic phenomena where the variables are related inversely.

Here is the mathematical representation of an inverse function econometric model: $Y_i = \beta_0 + \beta_1 \frac{1}{X_i} + \varepsilon_i$

If you estimate this type of regression, you're likely to see one of the following three outcomes (which I also show you in Figure 8-3):

- $\hat{\beta}_0 > 0$ and $\hat{\beta}_1 > 0$. The graph in Figure 8-3a shows an inverse function with Y approaching positive infinity as X approaches zero and Y approaching $\hat{\beta}_0$ as X approaches infinity.

- $\hat{\beta}_0 < 0$ and $\hat{\beta}_1 > 0$. The graph in Figure 8-3b depicts an inverse function with Y approaching positive infinity as X approaches zero and Y approaching some negative value $\left(\hat{\beta}_0\right)$ as X approaches infinity.

- $\hat{\beta}_0 > 0$ and $\hat{\beta}_1 < 0$. The graph in Figure 8-3c shows an inverse function with Y approaching some positive value $\left(\hat{\beta}_0\right)$ as X approaches positive infinity and Y approaching negative infinity as X approaches zero.

Figure 8-3: Three graphical representations of inverse functions.

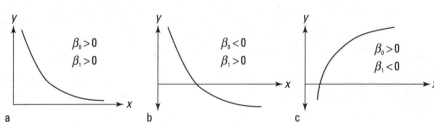

Giving Linearity to Nonlinear Models

In some cases, the models you're working with aren't linear in parameters. Examples include Cobb-Douglas production functions and constant-elasticity demand curves that you worked with in your microeconomics class. In other cases, you may be working with models in which the variables used in the analysis cause the normality assumption of OLS to fail (I cover this assumption in Chapter 7). This failure typically occurs when the variables are measured in dollars or some other large scale (like population figures). For both of these cases, log transformations may come to the rescue. I break down the different options available in the following sections.

Working both sides to keep elasticity constant: The log-log model

Using natural logs for variables on both sides of your econometric specification is called a *log-log model*. This model is handy when the relationship is nonlinear in parameters, because the log transformation generates the desired linearity in parameters (you may recall that linearity in parameters is one of the OLS assumptions; if not, flip to Chapter 6).

In principle, any log transformation (natural or not) can be used to transform a model that's nonlinear in parameters into a linear one. All log transformations generate similar results, but the convention in applied econometric work is to use the natural log. The practical advantage of the natural log is that the interpretation of the regression coefficients is straightforward (a topic that I discuss later in this section).

Consider the demand function $Q = \alpha P^{\beta}$ where Q is the quantity demanded, α is a shifting parameter, P is the price of the good, and the parameter β is less than zero for a downward-sloping demand curve. If $\beta = -1$, you can recognize the function as a specific type of demand curve with elasticity equal to -1 at all points; that is, you have a unitary elastic demand curve.

A demand curve of the form $Q = \alpha P^{\beta}$ has a constant elasticity (equal to $-\beta$), but the value of that elasticity may not be known. Using data, you can estimate the parameters (α and β), but you must transform the function in order to make estimates using the OLS technique.

If your model is not linear in parameters, sometimes a log transformation achieves linearity.

A generic form of a constant elasticity model can be represented by

$$Y_i = \alpha X_i^\beta$$

If you take the natural log of both sides, you end up with

$$\ln Y_i = \ln(\alpha) + \beta \ln X_i$$

You treat $\ln(\alpha)$ as the intercept. You end up with the following model:

$$\ln Y_i = \beta_0 + \beta_1 \ln X_i$$

You can estimate this model with OLS by simply using natural log values for the variables instead of their original scale.

After estimating a log-log model, such as the one in this example, the coefficients can be used to determine the impact of your independent variables (X) on your dependent variable (Y). The coefficients in a log-log model represent the *elasticity* of your Y variable with respect to your X variable. In other words, the coefficient is the estimated *percent change* in your dependent variable for a *percent change* in your independent variable.

Using calculus with a simple log-log model, you can show how the coefficients should be interpreted. Begin with the model $\ln Y = \beta_0 + \beta_1 \ln X$ and differentiate it to obtain $\frac{\delta Y}{Y} = \beta_1 \frac{\delta X}{X}$. The term on the right-hand side ($\frac{\delta X}{X}$) is the percent change in X, and the term on the left-hand side ($\frac{\delta Y}{Y}$) is the percent change in Y, so β_1 measures the elasticity.

Suppose you obtain the estimates $\ln \hat{Y}_i = 4.81 - 0.85 \ln X_i$, where Y is sales and X is price. The elasticity is –0.85, so a 1 percent increase in the price is associated with a 0.85 percent decrease in quantity demanded (sales), on average.

If you estimate a log-log regression, a few outcomes for the coefficient on X (β_1) produce the most likely relationships:

- $\hat{\beta}_1 > 1$: Figure 8-4a shows this log-log function in which the impact of the independent variable is positive and becomes larger as its value increases.

- $0 < \hat{\beta}_1 < 1$: Figure 8-4b shows a log-log function in which the impact of the independent variable is positive but becomes smaller as its value increases.

- $\hat{\beta}_1 < 0$: Figure 8-4c shows a log-log function where the impact of the dependent variable is negative.

Figure 8-4:
Three
depictions
of a log-log
function.

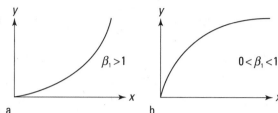
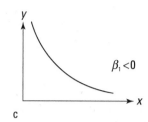

$\beta_1 > 1$ $0 < \beta_1 < 1$ $\beta_1 < 0$

a   b   c

Although regression coefficients are sometimes referred to as *partial-slope coefficients,* in a log-log model the coefficients don't represent the slope (or unit change in your Y variable for a unit change in your X variable).

Making investments and calculating rates of return: The log-linear model

If you use natural log values for your dependent variable (Y) and keep your independent variables (X) in their original scale, the econometric specification is called a *log-linear model.* These models are typically used when you think the variables may have an exponential growth relationship, For example, if I put some cash in a saving account, I expect to see the effect of compounding interest with an exponential growth of my money! The original model in these types of scenarios isn't linear in parameters, but a log transformation generates the desired linearity (see Chapter 6 for more on this standard OLS assumption).

Consider the following model of value in a savings fund that depends on your initial investment, your return, and the length of time in which the funds are invested: $Y_t = Y_0(1 + r)^t$, where Y_t represents the value of the fund at time t, Y_0 is the initial investment in the savings fund, and r is the growth rate.

Labor economists are also interested in similar functions because individuals usually have some initial earning power that can be supplemented with investments in skill acquisition. These *human capital functions* deal with the amount of money an individual can expect to earn depending on his or her initial abilities and investments in education, training, experience, and so on.

A generic exponential growth function can be written as $Y = Y_0(1 + r)^X$, where the value of Y for a given X can be derived only if the growth rate (r) is known. The growth rate can be estimated, but a log transformation must be used to estimate using OLS.

If you begin with an exponential growth model and take the log of both sides, you end up with $ln\ Y = ln\ Y_0 + Xln\ (1 + r)$, where $ln\ Y_0$ is the unknown constant and $ln\ (1 + r)$ is the unknown growth rate plus 1 (in natural log form). You end up with the following model:

$$ln\ Y = \beta_0 + \beta_1 X$$

You can estimate this model with OLS by simply using natural log values for the dependent variable (Y) and the original scale for the independent variables (X). It's known as a *log-linear model*.

After estimating a log-linear model, the coefficients can be used to determine the impact of your independent variables (X) on your dependent variable (Y). The coefficients in a log-linear model represent the estimated *percent change* in your dependent variable for a *unit change* in your independent variable. The coefficient β_1 provides the *instantaneous rate of growth*.

Using calculus with a simple log-linear model, you can show how the coefficients should be interpreted. Begin with the model $ln\ Y = \beta_0 + \beta_1 X$ and differentiate it to obtain $\frac{\delta Y}{Y} = \beta_1 \delta X$. The term on the right-hand-side (δX) is the unit-change in X, and the term on the left-hand-side ($\frac{\delta Y}{Y}$) is the percent change in Y, so β_1 provides the *instantaneous rate of growth* for Y associated with a unit change in X.

The *compounded growth rate* is considered to be a more accurate estimate of the impact of X. After estimating a log-linear model, you can calculate the compounded growth rate (r) as $r = e^{\beta_1} - 1$.

Suppose you obtain the estimated regression $ln\ \hat{Y}_i = 1.79 + 0.08X_i$, where Y is an individual's wage and X is her years of education. The 0.08 value for β_1 indicates that the instantaneous return for an additional year of education is 8 percent and the compounded return is 8.3 percent ($e^{0.08} - 1 = 0.083$).

If you estimate a log-linear regression, a couple outcomes for the coefficient on X (β_1) produce the most likely relationships:

- ✔ $\beta_1 > 0$: This log-linear function illustrates a positive impact from the independent variable, as shown in Figure 8-5a.

- ✔ $\beta_1 < 0$: This log-linear function depicts a negative impact from the independent variable, as shown in Figure 8-5b.

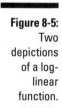

Figure 8-5:
Two
depictions
of a log-
linear
function.

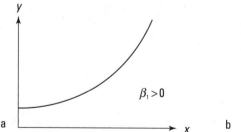

$\beta_1 > 0$

$\beta_1 < 0$

a

b

Regression coefficients in a log-linear model don't represent the slope.

Decreasing the change of the dependent variable: The linear-log model

If you use natural log values for your independent variables (X) and keep your dependent variable (Y) in its original scale, the econometric specification is called a *linear-log model* (basically the mirror image of the log-linear model discussed earlier in this chapter). These models are typically used when the impact of your independent variable on your dependent variable decreases as the value of your independent variable increases. The behavior of the function is similar to a quadratic, but it's different in that it never reaches a maximum or minimum Y value.

The original model is not linear in parameters, but a log transformation generates the desired linearity. (Recall that linearity in parameters is one of the OLS assumptions, which I discuss in Chapter 6.)

Consider the following model of consumption spending, which depends on some autonomous consumption and income:

$$Y = \beta_0 + \beta_1 \ln X$$

where Y represents consumption spending, β_0 is autonomous consumption (consumption that doesn't depend on income), X is income, and β_1 is the estimated effect of income on consumption.

I suspect that you're familiar with the relationship between income and consumption. In your principles of economics courses, you probably referred to it as an *Engel curve*. You may not have seen the mathematical function behind it, but you've seen the graphical depiction.

The estimation of consumption functions isn't the only use of linear-log functions. Economists tend to use these functions anytime that the unit changes in the dependent variable are likely to be less than the unit changes in the independent variables.

If you begin with a function of the form $e^Y = e^{\beta_0} X^{\beta_1}$, where the value of Y for a given X can be derived only if the impact (β_1) is known, then you can estimate the impact using OLS only if you use a log transformation. If you take the natural log of both sides, you end up with $Y = \beta_0 + \beta_1 \ln X$ where β_0 is the unknown constant and β_1 is the unknown impact of X. You can estimate this with OLS by simply using natural log values for the independent variable (X) and the original scale for the dependent variable (Y).

After estimating a linear-log model, the coefficients can be used to determine the impact of your independent variables (X) on your dependent variable (Y). The coefficients in a linear-log model represent the estimated *unit change* in your dependent variable for a *percentage change* in your independent variable.

Using calculus with a simple linear-log model, you can see how the coefficients should be interpreted. Begin with the model $Y = \beta_0 + \beta_1 \ln X$ and differentiate it to obtain $\delta Y = \beta_1 \frac{\delta X}{X}$. The term on the right-hand-side ($\frac{\delta X}{X}$) is the percent change in X, and the term on the left-hand-side (δY) is the unit change in Y.

In economics, many situations are characterized by diminishing marginal returns. The linear-log model usually works well in situations where the effect of X on Y always retains the same sign (positive or negative) but its impact decreases.

Suppose, using a random sample of schools districts, you obtain the following regression estimates:

$$\hat{Y}_i = 450.2 + 65.32 \ln X_i$$

where Y is the average math SAT score and X is the expenditure per student. The estimated coefficient $\hat{\beta}_1 = 65.32$ implies that a 1 percent increase in expenditure per student increases the average math SAT score by 0.65 points.

If you estimate a linear-log regression, a couple outcomes for the coefficient on X (β_1) produce the most likely relationships:

- $\beta_1 > 0$: Figure 8-6a shows a linear-log function where the impact of the independent variable is positive.

- $\beta_1 < 0$: Figure 8-6b shows a linear-log function where the impact of the independent variable is negative.

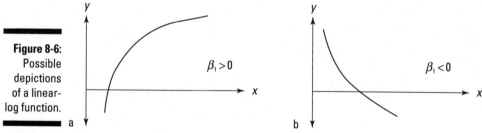

$\beta_1 > 0$

$\beta_1 < 0$

a

b

As with log-log and log-linear models, the regression coefficients in linear-log models don't represent slope.

Checking for Misspecification

The art of econometrics lies in finding the appropriate specification or functional form to model your particular outcome of interest. The choices made regarding functional form and the selection of independent variables should be based on economic theory and common sense. However, in many cases, the theory can be vague about the specific elements of a model's specification.

Given the uncertainty that you face when settling on the model and determining the results you'll present in applied econometrics, you have to consider the impact of excluding variables, using inappropriate variables, or choosing the wrong functional form.

Too many or too few: Selecting independent variables

One of the most important decisions you make when specifying your econometric model is which variables to include as independent variables. In the following sections, you find out what problems can occur if you include too few or too many independent variables in your model, and you see how this misspecification affects your results.

Omitting relevant variables

If a variable that belongs in the model is excluded from the estimated regression function, the model is misspecified and may cause bias in the estimated coefficients.

Part III: Working with the Classical Regression Model

REMEMBER

You have an omitted variable bias if an excluded variable has some effect (positive or negative) on your dependent variable and it's correlated with at least one of your independent variables.

The mathematical nature of specification bias can be expressed using a simple model. Suppose the true population model is given by

$$Y_i = \beta_0 + \beta_1 X_{i1} + \beta_2 X_{i2} + \varepsilon_i$$

where X_1 and X_2 are the two variables that affect Y. But due to ignorance or lack of data, instead you estimate this regression:

$$Y_i = \alpha_0 + \alpha_1 X_{i1} + u_i$$

which omits X_2 from the independent variables. The expected value of $\hat{\alpha}_1$ in this situation is

$$E(\hat{\alpha}_1) = \beta_1 + \beta_2 \delta_1$$

But this equation violates the Gauss-Markov theorem because $E(\hat{\alpha}_1) \neq \beta_1$ (I discuss the components of the Gauss-Markov theorem in Chapter 6). The magnitude of the bias can be expressed as

$$Bias(\hat{\alpha}_1) = \beta_2 \delta_1$$

where β_2 if the effect of X_2 on Y and δ_1 is the slope from this regression:

$$X_{i2} = \delta_0 + \delta_1 X_{i1} + v_i$$

which captures the correlation (positive or negative) between the included and excluded variable(s).

I summarize the direction of omitted variable bias in Table 8-1.

Table 8-1	Summary of Omitted Variable Bias	
Impact of Omitted Variable on Dependent Variable	**Correlation between Included and Omitted Variable:**	
	Positive	*Negative*
Positive	Positive bias	Negative bias
Negative	Negative bias	Positive bias

In practice, you're likely to have some omitted variable bias because it's impossible to control for everything that affects your dependent variable. However, you can increase your chances of minimizing omitted variable bias by avoiding simple regression models (with one independent variable) and including the variables that are likely to be the most important theoretically (and possibly, but not necessarily statistically) in explaining the dependent variable.

Including irrelevant variables

If a variable doesn't belong in the model and is included in the estimated regression function, the model is overspecified. If you overspecify the regression model by including an irrelevant variable, the estimated coefficients remain unbiased. However, it has an undesirable effect of increasing the standard errors of your coefficients.

In a simple regression model (with one independent variable), the estimated standard error of the regression coefficient for X is

$$\hat{\sigma}_{\hat{\beta}_1} = \sqrt{\frac{\hat{\sigma}_\varepsilon^2}{\sum_{i=1}^{n}(X_i - \bar{X})^2}}$$

where $\hat{\sigma}_\varepsilon^2$ is the estimated variance of the error and $\sum_{i=1}^{n}(X_i - \bar{X})^2$ is the total variation in X.

If you include additional independent variables in the model, the estimated standard error for any given regression coefficient is given by

$$\hat{\sigma}_{\hat{\beta}_k} = \sqrt{\frac{\hat{\sigma}_\varepsilon^2}{\sum_{i=1}^{n}(X_i - \bar{X})^2(1 - R_k^2)}}$$

where R_k^2 is the R-squared from the regression of X_k on the other independent variables or Xs. Because $0 \leq R_k^2 \leq 1$, the numerator decreases. An irrelevant variable doesn't help explain any of the variation in Y, so without an offsetting decrease in $\hat{\sigma}_\varepsilon^2$, the standard error increases.

Just because your estimated coefficient isn't statistically significant doesn't make it irrelevant. A well-specified model usually includes some variables that are statistically significant and some that aren't. Additionally, variables that aren't statistically significant can contribute enough explained variation to have no detrimental impact on the standard errors.

Sensitivity isn't a virtue: Examining misspecification with results stability

There's no substitute for sound economic theory and good common sense in specifying an econometric model. However, the existence of contesting theories in economics often means you can estimate a relationship in more than one way. The following sections show you how to utilize some conventional tests in econometrics to help you refine your model's specification.

Performing a RESET to test the severity of specification issues

Although your econometric model isn't likely to be perfectly specified, that doesn't imply that specification is a serious issue with your model. A statistical test can be used to examine the severity of certain specification issues.

Ramsey's *regression specification error test* (RESET) can be used to detect specification issues related to omitted variables and certain functional forms. The test is conducted by adding a quartic function of the fitted values of your dependent variable ($\hat{Y}_i^2$, $\hat{Y}_i^3$, and $\hat{Y}_i^4$) to your original regression and then testing the joint significance of the coefficients for the added variables.

The logic of using a quartic of your fitted values is that they serve as proxies for variables that may have been omitted. Because the proxies are essentially nonlinear functions of your *X*s, RESET is also testing misspecification from functional form. The function of your fitted values doesn't have to be limited to a quartic, but this structure has proven useful and is the most common in practice.

You can perform a RESET in three steps:

1. **Estimate the model you want to test for specification error.**

   For example, you may decide to use $Y_i = \beta_0 + \beta_1 X_{i1} + \ldots + \varepsilon_i$.

2. **Obtain the fitted values after estimating your model and estimate.**

   $Y_i = \beta_0 + \beta_1 X_{i1} + \ldots + \alpha \hat{Y}_i^2 + \gamma \hat{Y}_i^3 + \delta \hat{Y}_i^4 + \varepsilon_i$

3. **Test the joint significance of the coefficients on the fitted values of Y_i terms, α, γ, and δ using an *F*-statistic.**

   See Chapter 7 for details on testing joint significance for a subset of variables in a regression model.

Most econometrics software packages have commands that conduct a RESET and save you time. For example, in STATA, after estimating your original model, you can type "estat ovtest" to perform the test.

A RESET allows you to identify whether misspecification is a serious problem with your model, but it doesn't allow you to determine the source. If your RESET result doesn't reject your specification, you can use it to support your claim that specification isn't a major problem with your model. However, a RESET result that rejects the specification of your model can't be used to address any particular specification problem.

Using the Chow test to determine structural stability

Sometimes specification issues arise because the parameters of the model either aren't stable or they change. For example, the marginal propensity to save may change in response to a new capital gains tax, or the returns to education could vary by race and/or gender.

You can use a Chow test to check the structural stability of your model. Here's how to conduct a Chow test for structural stability between any two groups (A and B) in just three steps:

1. **Estimate your model combining all data and obtain the residual sum of squares (RSS_r) with degrees of freedom $n - p - 1$.**

   This is considered the restricted RSS because the model restricts the parameters to be the same for the two groups.

2. **Estimate your model separately for each group and obtain the residual sum of squares for group A, $RSS_{ur,A}$, with degrees of freedom $n_A - p - 1$ and the residual sum of squares for group B, $RSS_{ur,B}$, with degrees of freedom $n_B - p - 1$.**

   These are considered the unrestricted RSS because the model doesn't restrict the parameters to be the same for the two groups.

3. **Compute the F-statistic by using this formula:**

$$F = \frac{\dfrac{RSS_r - \left(RSS_{ur,A} + RSS_{ur,B} \right)}{p+1}}{\dfrac{RSS_{ur,A} + RSS_{ur,B}}{n - 2p - 2}}$$

The null hypothesis for the Chow test is structural stability. The larger the F-statistic, the more evidence you have against structural stability and the more likely the coefficients are to vary from group to group.

The result of the F-statistic for the Chow test assumes homoskedasticity (see Chapter 6 for a discussion of homoskedasticity). Assuming homoskedasticity holds, a large F-statistic only informs you that the parameters vary between the groups, but it doesn't tell you which specific parameter(s) is (are) the source(s) of the structural break.

If structural stability is rejected in your Chow test, then you must obtain coefficient estimates for different time periods or different groups of cross-sectional units. If structural stability isn't rejected, one regression is appropriate in estimating the relationship.

Conducting robustness/sensitivity analysis

One of the most common practices in applied econometrics is the use of robustness analysis to check for specification issues. *Robustness* refers to the sensitivity of the estimated coefficients when you make changes to your model's specification.

Performing robustness/sensitivity analysis requires that you determine which independent variables are of primary interest (also known as *core variables*) for your empirical investigation. Then you estimate numerous regressions with your core variables, but experiment with various combinations of other control variables. If the coefficients of your core variables aren't sensitive (maintain the same sign with similar magnitudes and levels of significance), then the coefficients are considered *robust*. **Note:** Misspecification is considered to be less problematic when your results are robust.

Some econometrics software programs have specific commands that allow you to perform robustness analysis more quickly. For example, in STATA, you can download the "rcheck" and/or "checkrob" programs to automatically perform regressions with various combinations of your independent variables. **Note:** Don't confuse these robustness checks with the ", robust" regression option in STATA. The ", robust" option is useful, but it's not designed to address specification issues; instead, it helps you deal with heteroskedasticity (something I discuss at length in Chapter 11).

Robustness analysis requires that you be cautious about which non-core independent variables are considered for exclusion/inclusion in the various regressions that will examine sensitivity. Some variables, despite not being of primary interest (that is, despite not being core), are likely to be essential control variables that would be included in any analysis of your outcome of interest (you should rely on economic theory and your common sense here). Removing those variables can result in more serious misspecification and cause your core coefficients to appear sensitive.

Chapter 9

Regression with Dummy Explanatory Variables

. . . .

In This Chapter

▶ Converting qualitative information into quantitative data

▶ Estimating differences in means between two groups with regression analysis

▶ Performing regression analysis using qualitative and quantitative data simultaneously

▶ Testing for joint significance

. . . .

*Q*uantitative variables such as years of experience, costs, and prices aren't the only variables that can have a major influence on the dependent variable in a regression model. Qualitative variables — think gender, race, season of the year, and geographical location — can too. In this chapter, I explain how qualitative variables can be used as independent (or explanatory) variables just as readily as quantitative variables in traditional ordinary least squares (OLS) regression. I also show you all the common ways in which qualitative variables are used in econometric analysis and help you figure out how to interpret the coefficient estimates.

Numbers Please! Quantifying Qualitative Information

Estimating an econometric model requires that all the information be quantified. In other words, numbers must be used to characterize both your quantitative and qualitative variables. Quantitative variables are typically coded with numeric values in the raw data, but qualitative variables are likely to require you to perform some quantification manipulation. In this section you find out how to quantify variables when working with two groups or with multiple groups.

Defining a dummy variable when you have only two possible characteristics

In many cases, the qualitative characteristics you want to include in your econometric analysis have two groups (or categories). In general, you have two groups when sample observations have a "this" or "that" option. For example, in most surveys, gender is classified as either male or female.

If a qualitative characteristic has two groups, you need to create one *dummy variable* in order to quantitatively capture that attribute. The dummy variable takes the value of 1 if one of the two characteristics is present and 0 if the other characteristic is observed. The group that's identified (or assigned) 0 values for the created dummy variable is called your *reference* or *base group*.

Table 9-1 illustrates how you can create a dummy variable from your original data. Column 1 contains the movie title, and Column 2 contains the lead actor's name. Column 3 isn't part of the original data, but I create the variable *Female* using the information in Column 2. The variable *Female* is a dummy variable equal to 1 if the lead actor is female and equal to 0 if the lead actor is male. Notice that only one dummy variable is needed to capture two possibilities (in this case, male and female).

Table 9-1	Representing Actor Gender with a Dummy Variable	
1	*2*	*3*
Title	*Lead*	*Female*
Fireproof	Kirk Cameron	0
Transamerica	Felicity Huffman	1
The Wrestler	Mickey Rourke	0
Akeelah and the Bee	Keke Palmer	1
The Last King of Scotland	James McAvoy	0

Source: www.imdb.com

Your econometric results aren't affected by which group you decide to assign a 1 and which group you assign a 0 in your dummy variable.

Juggling multiple characteristics with dummy variables

In some cases, the qualitative characteristics you want to include in your econometric analysis have more than two groups (or categories). In general, you work with several groups when sample observations are classified into one of many possibilities. For example, a firm may be located in the West, Midwest, South, or Northeast region of the country.

In order to quantitatively capture a qualitative attribute with numerous groups (or possibilities), you need to create dummy variables for each group minus 1. The dummy variable takes the value of 1 if a particular characteristic is present and 0 otherwise. In other words, if you have J groups, you need $J - 1$ dummy variables with 1s and 0s to capture all the qualitative information. The group that does not have a dummy variable is identified when all the other dummy values are 0, and it's called your reference or base group.

To see what I mean, check out Table 9-2. With this data, you can create the dummy variables you need from a qualitative variable with several groups. Column 1 contains the movie title, and Column 2 contains the MPAA rating (G, PG, PG13, or R). Columns 3, 4, and 5 aren't part of the original data, but I create them using the information of MPAA rating in Column 2. Notice that the number of dummy variables I need is one less (three) than the number of possible outcomes for the qualitative characteristic (in this case, four: G, PG, PG13, and R).

Table 9-2	Representing MPAA Ratings with Dummy Variables			
1	*2*	*3*	*4*	*5*
Title	*MPAA Rating*	*PG*	*PG13*	*R*
Fireproof	PG	1	0	0
Transamerica	R	0	0	1
The Visitor	PG13	0	1	0
Crash	R	0	0	1
Herbie: Fully Loaded	G	0	0	0

Source: www.imdb.com

The group you choose to assign a 0 all the way across doesn't affect your econometric results. Those observations (in this example, G-rated movies like *Herbie: Fully Loaded*) are important to include and do affect the overall results, because they are all part of the reference group. It doesn't matter, however, which type of movie is chosen to be the reference group.

Finding Average Differences by Using a Dummy Variable

You should recall from your statistics course how to conduct the *t*-test to examine the differences in means between two groups. (If not, I provide a refresher on this technique in Chapter 3.) But what you may not know is that you can use dummy variables and regression analysis to obtain the same results as the *t*-test. The following sections clarify how.

Specification

Even though your econometric model is likely to include both quantitative and qualitative characteristics, I begin with a model that only uses a dummy variable to capture qualitative characteristics and ignores other potential independent variables. This process amounts to identifying differences in means for groups identified by the dummy variable(s), but it's a useful building block to understanding more realistic models that combine qualitative characteristics with quantitative variables.

If the qualitative characteristic that you'd like to use as an independent variable contains only two groups (as discussed in the earlier section "Defining a dummy variable when you have only two possible characteristics"), then an econometric model with a single dummy variable as the only explanatory variable can be expressed as

$$Y_i = \beta_0 + \beta_1 D_i + \varepsilon_i$$

where Y is the dependent variable, β_0 is the intercept (or constant) term, and β_1 is the impact of the characteristic represented by the dummy variable (D). $D_i = 1$ if the specific qualitative characteristic is present and $D_i = 0$ if not.

If the qualitative characteristic you'd like to use as an independent variable has more than two groups (as in the earlier section "Juggling multiple characteristics with dummy variables"), then the econometric model must include $J - 1$ variables to fully capture the possibilities. Suppose you'd like to use a variable with a qualitative characteristic containing four possible outcomes {A, B, C, and D}. The basic econometric model to capture a qualitative characteristic is expressed as

$$Y_i = \beta_0 + \beta_1 D_{iB} + \beta_2 D_{iC} + \beta_3 D_{iD} + \varepsilon_i$$

where $D_{iB} = 1$ if the observation belongs to group B, $D_{iC} = 1$ if the observation belongs to group C, $D_{iD} = 1$ if the observation belongs to group D, and $D_{iB} = D_{iC} = D_{iD} = 0$ if the observation is in group A. By using this equation, you implicitly assign group A as the reference or base group in any two-group comparison.

Interpretation

One useful way of seeing the role of a dummy variable in an econometric model is to interpret the results of a regression using a dummy variable as the only independent variable.

An estimated regression with a dummy variable is generally written as $\hat{Y}_i = \hat{\beta}_0 + \hat{\beta}_1 D_i$, where the $\hat{\beta}$ terms represent the estimated parameters. Because D can only be 0 or 1 for any given observation, $\hat{Y}_i = \hat{\beta}_0$ if $D_i = 0$, and $\hat{Y}_i = \hat{\beta}_0 + \hat{\beta}_1$ if $D_i = 1$.

The predicted Y value $(\hat{Y}_i)$ from a regression represents the estimate of the conditional mean $(E(Y \mid D_i))$. A dummy variable only has two values, so you get two predicted Y values. Therefore, the predicted Y values are equal to the sample means for each group.

To help illustrate the point, I've estimated a model with a dummy variable by using STATA and data collected from hundreds of movies. I used information on lead characters to create a dummy variable *Female* that is equal to 1 if the lead actor is a female and 0 otherwise. Figure 9-1 contains the STATA output from my regression using gross box office revenue (measured in millions of dollars) as my dependent variable and *Female* as my independent variable. The results in Figure 9-1 imply that, on average, revenue for a movie with a female lead is about $16 million less than a movie with a male lead.

If I simply calculate the average revenue for movies with a male lead and movies with a female lead, the difference is perfectly consistent, as you can see in Figure 9-2. In this figure, you can see that the average revenue is about $63 million overall (group "combined"). However, the average revenue is $67.9 million for movies with male leads (group 0) (the value of the intercept in Figure 9-1), whereas the average revenue is $51.5 million for movies with female leads (group 1). The difference in revenue between the two groups is precisely the value of the coefficient for the dummy variable in Figure 9-1. In addition, the reported *t*-statistic (with a value of 2.44) is identical in Figures 9-1 and 9-2.

```
. regress grossbox_mil Female
```

Source	SS	df	MS
Model	31352.5081	1	31352.5081
Residual	3034622.41	578	5250.21178
Total	3065974.92	579	5295.29347

Number of obs	= 580
F (1,578)	= 5.97
Prob > F	= 0.0148
R-squared	= 0.0102
Adj R-squared	= 0.0085
Root MSE	= 72.458

grossbox_mil	Coef.	Std. Err.	t	P>|t|	[95% Conf. Interval]
Female	-16.38719	6.705895	-2.44	0.015	-29.55808 -3.216298
_cons	67.95166	3.544054	19.17	0.000	60.99086 74.91245

Figure 9-1: STATA regression output with a dummy variable as the only independent variable.

```
. ttest grossbox_mil, by(Female)
Two-sample t test with equal variances
```

Group	Obs	Mean	Std. Err.	Std. Dev.	[95% Conf. Interval]
0	418	67.95166	3.88192	79.36603	60.32109 75.58223
1	162	51.56447	3.954892	50.33756	43.75431 59.37462
combined	580	63.37455	3.021559	72.76877	57.43999 69.3091
diff		16.38719	6.705895		3.216298 29.55808

```
diff = mean(0) - mean(1)                              t =    2.4437
Ho: diff = 0                          degrees of freedom =       578

  Ha: diff < 0              Ha: diff != 0                 Ha: diff > 0
Pr(T < t) = 0.9926    Pr(|T| > |t|) = 0.0148       Pr(T > t) = 0.0074
```

Figure 9-2: STATA output containing means for two groups and t-test for differences in means.

You can also estimate a model with dummy variables when the qualitative characteristic has more than two groups. Consider the example shown in Figure 9-3, which uses information on MPAA ratings (G, PG, PG13, and R) to create dummy variables for three of the four groups. Figure 9-3 contains the STATA output from my regression using gross box-office revenue (measured in millions of dollars) as my dependent variable and the dummy variables as my independent variables. Figure 9-3 illustrates that, on average, movies with PG, PG13, and R ratings earn less revenue than G-rated movies. None of the coefficients, however, are statistically significant (I cover statistical significance in Chapter 7). This implies that it's possible for the revenue of movies in the various rating categories to be identical to the revenue of movies in the reference group (G-rated movies).

```
. regress grossbox_mil PG PG13 R
```

Figure 9-3:
STATA
regression
output using
a qualitative
independent
variable
with more
than two
groups.

Source	SS	df	MS		
Model	149803.934	3	49934.6446		
Residual	2916170.99	576	5062.79685		
Total	3065974.92	579	5295.29347		

	Number of obs	=	580
	F (3,576)	=	9.86
	Prob > F	=	0.0000
	R-squared	=	0.0489
	Adj R-squared	=	0.0439
	Root MSE	=	71.153

grossbox_mil	Coef.	Std. Err.	t	P>|t|	[95% Conf. Interval]	
PG	-5.688056	51.11806	-0.11	0.911	-106.0886	94.71247
PG13	-.8399898	50.49174	-0.02	0.987	-100.0104	98.33038
R	-34.31151	50.52665	-0.68	0.497	-133.5504	64.92743
_cons	78.29162	50.313	1.56	0.120	-20.5277	177.1109

Combining Quantitative and Qualitative Data in the Regression Model

Regression analysis allows you to simultaneously utilize qualitative and quantitative information. You can use dummy variables alone to estimate differences in means between groups. But because many characteristics may vary between groups, it's usually important to use the power of regression analysis so you can concurrently consider the impact of quantitative characteristics. In the following sections, I explain how to use both dummy variables (as qualitative variables) and quantitative variables together in a single regression model.

Specification

A useful way to utilize qualitative characteristics in econometrics is to combine them with quantitative variables in a regression. If the qualitative characteristic that you'd like to use as an independent variable contains only two groups, then one dummy variable is used in the econometric model along with any quantitative variables that should be included in the model.

An econometric model with one dummy variable and one quantitative variable can be expressed as

$$Y_i = \beta_0 + \beta_1 D_i + \beta_2 X_i + \varepsilon_i$$

where $D_i = 1$ if the specific qualitative characteristic is present and $D_i = 0$ otherwise, and X is the usual quantitative variable used in Chapters 5 and 8.

If the qualitative characteristic you'd like to use as an independent variable has more than two groups (say J groups), then the econometric model must include $J - 1$ variables to fully capture the possibilities for the qualitative characteristic plus the quantitative variables you're including as independent variables. An econometric model with a qualitative characteristic containing four possible outcomes (such as the four MPAA ratings used previously) and a quantitative variable is expressed as

$$Y_i = \beta_0 + \beta_1 D_{iB} + \beta_2 D_{iC} + \beta_3 D_{iD} + \beta_4 X_i + \varepsilon_i$$

where $D_{iB} = 1$ if the observation belongs to group B, $D_{iC} = 1$ if the observation belongs to group C, $D_{iD} = 1$ if the observation belongs to group D, and $D_{iB} = D_{iC} = D_{iD} = 0$ if the observation is in group A. (X is the quantitative variable.) Tada! You've just implicitly assigned group A as the reference or base group in any two-group comparison.

Interpretation

An estimated regression with one quantitative and one dummy variable is generally written as $\hat{Y}_i = \hat{\beta}_0 + \hat{\beta}_1 D_i + \hat{\beta}_2 X_i$, where the $\hat{\beta}$s represent the estimated parameters, D can be 0 or 1 for any given observation, and X is any numeric value. The predicted Y value is $\hat{Y}_i = \hat{\beta}_0 + \hat{\beta}_2 X_i$ if $D_i = 0$, and $\hat{Y}_i = \left(\hat{\beta}_0 + \hat{\beta}_1 \right) + \hat{\beta}_2 X_i$ if $D_i = 1$.

The coefficient for your dummy variable(s) in a regression containing a quantitative variable shifts the regression function up (if the coefficient is positive) or down (if the coefficient is negative). The same holds true when there's more than one dummy variable.

Figure 9-4 shows a graphical depiction of the resulting regression when the model contains one dummy variable to capture a qualitative characteristic and one quantitative variable.

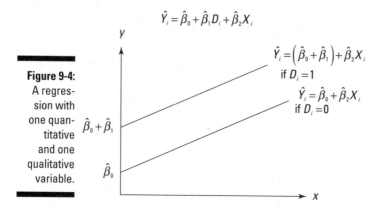

Figure 9-4:
A regression with one quantitative and one qualitative variable.

You can use STATA to estimate a model with a quantitative and dummy variable. Figure 9-5 contains the STATA output from a regression using gross box-office revenue (measured in millions of dollars) as the dependent variable. The dummy variable *Female* (which equals 1 if the lead actor is a female and 0 otherwise) and the quantitative variable movie budget are the independent variables. The results in Figure 9-5 suggest that, holding gender of lead actor constant, every additional dollar in the movie's budget is associated with an additional $1.13 in revenue. Also, holding movie budget constant, a female lead actor has no statistically significant effect on movie revenue because the *t*-statistic for the *Female* coefficient doesn't meet conventionally accepted standards of statistical significance with a *p*-value of 0.545.

. regress grossbox_mil Female budget_mil

Source	SS	df	MS		
Model	1517871.89	2	758935.943		
Residual	1548103.03	577	2683.02086		
Total	3065974.92	579	5295.29347		

	Number of obs	=	580
	F (2,577)	=	282.87
	Prob > F	=	0.0000
	R-squared	=	0.4951
	Adj R-squared	=	0.4933
	Root MSE	=	51.798

grossbox_mil	Coef.	Std. Err.	t	P>|t|	[95% Conf. Interval]	
Female	2.94497	4.863653	0.61	0.545	-6.607652	12.49759
budget_mil	1.133749	.0481663	23.54	0.000	1.039146	1.228351
_cons	9.304207	3.553408	2.62	0.009	2.325016	16.2834

Figure 9-5:
STATA regression output using one quantitative and one dummy variable.

Interacting Quantitative and Qualitative Variables

Interacting qualitative or dummy variables with quantitative variables provides enough flexibility to detect differences between groups overall and differences that may vary depending on the value of the quantitative variable(s). The next sections show you what an interacted econometric model looks like and demonstrate how to apply the model.

Specification

You can use dummy variables as standalone independent variables, but you can also interact them with your quantitative variables to allow for more flexibility in your estimated regression function.

The product of two independent variables is known as an *interaction term*. If the qualitative characteristic that you'd like to use as an independent variable contains only two groups, then independent variables in your interacted model can include one dummy variable, any quantitative variables that should be included in the model, and the product of your dummy variable with at least one quantitative variable.

An interacted econometric model can be expressed as

$$Y_i = \beta_0 + \beta_1 D_i + \beta_2 X_i + \beta_3 (DX)_i + \varepsilon_i$$

where $D_i = 1$ if the specific qualitative characteristic is present and $D_i = 0$ otherwise, X is the quantitative variable, and DX is the interaction term (product of the dummy and quantitative variable for any given observation).

Interpretation

An estimated regression with independent variables that include one dummy, one quantitative, and one interaction variable is generally written as

$$\hat{Y}_i = \hat{\beta}_0 + \hat{\beta}_1 D_i + \hat{\beta}_2 X_i + \hat{\beta}_3 (DX)_i$$

where the $\hat{\beta}$s represent the estimated parameters, D can be 0 or 1 for any given observation, X can be any numeric value, and DX is the product of D and X. The predicted Y value is $\hat{Y}_i = \hat{\beta}_0 + \hat{\beta}_2 X_i$ if $D_i = 0$, and $\hat{Y}_i = \left(\hat{\beta}_0 + \hat{\beta}_1\right) + \left(\hat{\beta}_2 + \hat{\beta}_3\right) X_i$ if $D_i = 1$.

The inclusion of an interaction term in your econometric model allows the regression function to have a different intercept and slope for each group identified by your dummy variables. The coefficient for your dummy variable(s) in a regression shifts the intercept, and the coefficient for your interaction term changes the slope (which is the impact of your quantitative variable).

When you estimate a model with a dummy variable, a quantitative variable, and an interaction term with the dummy and quantitative variables, you end up with one of four possible outcomes:

- ✔ **One regression line:** The dummy and interaction coefficients are zero (meaning they're not statistically significant).

- ✔ **Two regression lines with different intercepts but the same slope:** The coefficient for the dummy variable is significant, but the interaction coefficient is zero (or not statistically significant).

- ✔ **Two regression lines with the same intercept but different slopes:** The dummy coefficient is zero (or not statistically significant), but the interaction coefficient is significant.

- ✔ **Two regression lines with different intercepts and slopes:** The dummy coefficient and the interaction coefficient are both significant.

Figure 9-6 shows a graphical depiction of the resulting regression with an insignificant dummy coefficient but a significant interaction coefficient. *Note:* The dummy coefficient isn't significantly different from zero.

Figure 9-6:
A regression with an interacted quantitative and dummy variable.

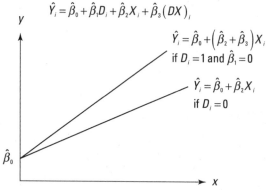

$$\hat{Y}_i = \hat{\beta}_0 + \hat{\beta}_1 D_i + \hat{\beta}_2 X_i + \hat{\beta}_3 (DX)_i$$

$$\hat{Y}_i = \hat{\beta}_0 + \left(\hat{\beta}_2 + \hat{\beta}_3 \right) X_i$$
if $D_i = 1$ and $\hat{\beta}_1 = 0$

$$\hat{Y}_i = \hat{\beta}_0 + \hat{\beta}_2 X_i$$
if $D_i = 0$

Figure 9-7 shows a graphical depiction of the resulting regression with significant dummy and interaction coefficients. In this graph, all coefficients differ significantly from zero.

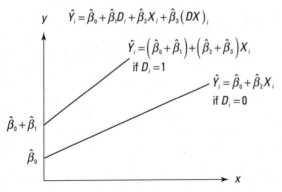

$$\hat{Y}_i = \hat{\beta}_0 + \hat{\beta}_1 D_i + \hat{\beta}_2 X_i + \hat{\beta}_3 (DX)_i$$

$$\hat{Y}_i = \left(\hat{\beta}_0 + \hat{\beta}_1\right) + \left(\hat{\beta}_2 + \hat{\beta}_3\right) X_i$$
if $D_i = 1$

$$\hat{Y}_i = \hat{\beta}_0 + \hat{\beta}_2 X_i$$
if $D_i = 0$

$\hat{\beta}_0 + \hat{\beta}_1$

$\hat{\beta}_0$

Figure 9-7:
A regression with an interacted quantitative and dummy variable.

If you want to estimate a model with a dummy variable, a quantitative variable, and an interacted variable, try using STATA. Figure 9-8 contains the STATA output from my regression using gross box office revenue (measured in millions of dollars) as my dependent variable. One independent variable is the dummy variable labeled *Female* (which equals 1 if the lead actor is a female and 0 otherwise). The other independent variable is the quantitative measurement of the movie budget (labeled *budget_mil*). I create a third variable that is the interaction of my dummy and quantitative variables labeled *budgetXFemale*. The results in Figure 9-8 suggest that every additional dollar in the movie's budget is associated with an additional $1.17 in revenue if the lead actor is male and $0.84 (1.17 – 0.33 = 0.84) if the lead actor is female. Also, when movie budget is zero (or very low), a female lead actor is associated with revenue that is $15.45 million higher, on average.

However, the interaction term estimates that as the movie budget increases, the difference in revenue between movies with female leads and those with male leads declines. If a movie's budget is more than $52 million ($\frac{15.5}{0.3} = 52$), then the revenue will be greater, on average, with a male lead. The average budget for movies in the sample is $47 million. Therefore, low-budget movies tend to earn more revenue with a female lead, and high-budget movies generally earn more revenue with a male lead.

Figure 9-8:
STATA output showing creation of interaction term from original data and regression results using a quantitative variable interacted with a dummy variable.

```
. gen budgetXFemale = budget_mil*Female

. regress grossbox_mil Female budget_mil budgetXFemale
```

Source	SS	df	MS			
				Number of obs	=	580
				F (3,576)	=	192.00
Model	1533007.27	3	511002.422	Prob > F	=	0.0000
Residual	1532967.65	576	2661.40218	R-squared	=	0.5000
				Adj R-squared	=	0.4974
Total	3065974.92	579	5295.29347	Root MSE	=	51.589

grossbox_mil	Coef.	Std. Err.	t	P>|t|	[95% Conf. Interval]	
Female	15.45014	7.138782	2.16	0.031	1.428921	29.47135
budget_mil	1.178223	.0514694	22.89	0.000	1.077132	1.279313
budgetXFemale	-.3387471	.1420477	-2.38	0.017	-.6177416	-.0597525
_cons	7.003623	3.668192	1.91	0.057	-.2010404	14.20829

Interacting Two (or More) Qualitative Characteristics

Interacting two qualitative or dummy variables with each other allows you to detect differences between various combinations of groups. With dummy variables in an econometric model, you can estimate the impact of qualitative characteristics independently, but interacting them provides an opportunity to identify how the presence of multiple characteristics simultaneously affects your dependent variable. In the following sections, I show you how it's done.

Specification

You can interact dummy variables with each other if you have reason to believe that the simultaneous presence of two (or more) characteristics has an additional influence on your dependent variable.

If the qualitative characteristics that you want to use as independent variables require two (or more) sets of dummy variables, then independent variables in your interacted model can include dummy variables, any quantitative variables that should be included in the model, and the product of two (or more) dummy variables.

An econometric model with interacted qualitative characteristics can be expressed as

$$Y_i = \beta_0 + \beta_1 X_i + \beta_2 D_{iA} + \beta_3 D_{iB} + \beta_4 (D_A D_B)_i + \varepsilon_i$$

where X is the quantitative variable, D_A and D_B represent the specific qualitative characteristics, and $D_A D_B$ is the interaction term (product of the two dummy variables for any given observation).

As an example of a situation where the inclusion of an interaction term would be valuable, suppose you're interested in modeling hourly wages to examine discrimination in the labor market. For a sound theoretical model, you include controls for gender and race. Both of these qualitative characteristics would be included in my model as separate dummy variables. However, gender and race could have a combined effect (for example, being both female and non-white) that either magnifies or dampens their individual impact, so you need an interaction term.

Interpretation

An estimated regression with independent variables that include a quantitative variable, at least two dummy variables, and an interaction of dummy variables is generally written as

$$\hat{Y}_i = \hat{\beta}_0 + \hat{\beta}_1 X_i + \hat{\beta}_2 D_{iA} + \hat{\beta}_3 D_{iB} + \hat{\beta}_4 (D_A D_B)_i$$

where the $\hat{\beta}$ terms represent the estimated parameters, X can be any numeric value, D_{iA} and D_{iB} can be 0 or 1 for any given observation, and $(D_A D_B)_i$ is the product of D_{iA} and D_{iB}.

The predicted Y value depends on X and four possible combinations of the dummy variables:

- ✔ $\hat{Y}_i = \hat{\beta}_0 + \hat{\beta}_1 X_i$ if $D_{iA} = 0$ and $D_{iB} = 0$

- ✔ $\hat{Y}_i = \left(\hat{\beta}_0 + \hat{\beta}_2\right) + \hat{\beta}_1 X_i$ if $D_{iA} = 1$ and $D_{iB} = 0$

- ✔ $\hat{Y}_i = \left(\hat{\beta}_0 + \hat{\beta}_3\right) + \hat{\beta}_1 X_i$ if $D_{iA} = 0$ and $D_{iB} = 1$

- ✔ $\hat{Y}_i = \left(\hat{\beta}_0 + \hat{\beta}_2 + \hat{\beta}_3 + \hat{\beta}_4\right) + \hat{\beta}_1 X_i$ if $D_{iA} = 1$ and $D_{iB} = 1$.

The inclusion of interacted dummy variables in your econometric model allows the regression function to have different intercepts for each combination of qualitative attributes. The coefficients for your dummy variables and their interaction shift the intercept by the estimated magnitude.

If you estimate a model with two dummy variables and an interaction between the two characteristics, you end up with one of four possible outcomes:

- ✔ **One regression line:** The dummy and dummy interaction coefficients are zero (or not statistically significant).

- ✔ **Two regression lines:** The coefficient for one dummy variable is significant, but the other dummy coefficient and the interaction coefficient are zero (or not statistically significant).

- ✔ **Three regression lines:** The dummy coefficients are both significant, but the interaction coefficient is zero (not statistically significant).

- ✔ **Four regression lines:** The dummy coefficients and the interaction coefficients are all significant.

Figure 9-9 shows a graphical depiction of the resulting regression of an econometric model with a quantitative variable (X), two significant dummy coefficients, and a significant interacted dummy coefficient.

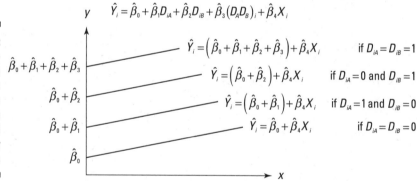

$$y \qquad \hat{Y}_i = \hat{\beta}_0 + \hat{\beta}_1 D_{iA} + \hat{\beta}_2 D_{iB} + \hat{\beta}_3 (D_A D_B)_i + \hat{\beta}_4 X_i$$

$$\hat{Y}_i = \left(\hat{\beta}_0 + \hat{\beta}_1 + \hat{\beta}_2 + \hat{\beta}_3 \right) + \hat{\beta}_4 X_i \qquad \text{if } D_{iA} = D_{iB} = 1$$

$$\hat{Y}_i = \left(\hat{\beta}_0 + \hat{\beta}_2 \right) + \hat{\beta}_4 X_i \qquad \text{if } D_{iA} = 0 \text{ and } D_{iB} = 1$$

$$\hat{Y}_i = \left(\hat{\beta}_0 + \hat{\beta}_1 \right) + \hat{\beta}_4 X_i \qquad \text{if } D_{iA} = 1 \text{ and } D_{iB} = 0$$

$$\hat{Y}_i = \hat{\beta}_0 + \hat{\beta}_4 X_i \qquad \text{if } D_{iA} = D_{iB} = 0$$

Figure 9-9: A regression with a quantitative variable and two interacted dummy variables

$\hat{\beta}_0 + \hat{\beta}_1 + \hat{\beta}_2 + \hat{\beta}_3$

$\hat{\beta}_0 + \hat{\beta}_2$

$\hat{\beta}_0 + \hat{\beta}_1$

$\hat{\beta}_0$

x

Using data collected from movies, I used STATA to estimate a model with a quantitative variable, two dummy variables, and a variable interacting my two dummy variables. Figure 9-10 contains the STATA output from my regression using gross box-office revenue (measured in millions of dollars) as my dependent variable. The movie budget is my quantitative independent variable. As independent variables, I also include the dummy variables *Female* (which equals 1 if the lead actor is a female and 0 otherwise) and *Over40* (which equals 1 if the lead actor's age is over 40 years and 0 otherwise) along with the interaction of those variables, *FemXOver40*.

The results in Figure 9-10 suggest that every additional dollar in the movie's budget is associated with an additional $1.14 in revenue if the lead actor is male and no more than 40 years of age. The actor's gender doesn't appear to have a statistically significant effect (p-value is 0.774), but age is significant at the 9.4 percent level of significance (the p-value is 0.094). On average, if a lead actor is over 40 years of age, movie revenue is \$8.7 million less than those movies with a lead actor no more than 40 years of age. The interaction variable *FemXOver40* isn't significant (p-value is 0.206), so movie revenue doesn't appear to be affected by having a lead character who is both female and over the age 40.

. regress grossbox_mil budget_mil Female Over40 FemXOver40

Source	SS	df	MS		
				Number of obs = 580	
				F (4,575) = 142.50	
Model	1526285.01	4	381571.252	Prob > F = 0.0000	
Residual	1539689.91	575	2677.72159	R-squared = 0.4978	
				Adj R-squared = 0.4943	
Total	3065974.92	579	5295.29347	Root MSE = 51.747	

grossbox_mil	Coef.	Std. Err.	t	P>|t|	[95% Conf. Interval]	
budget_mil	1.140345	.0482678	23.63	0.000	1.045542	1.235147
Female	-1.619308	5.639364	-0.29	0.774	-12.69557	9.456956
Over40	-8.679181	5.168211	-1.68	0.094	-18.83006	1.471693
FemXOver40	14.48555	11.44924	1.27	0.206	-8.001877	36.97298
_cons	12.49282	4.030037	3.10	0.002	4.57743	20.40821

Figure 9-10: STATA regression output using two interacted dummy variables.

Segregate and Integrate: Testing for Significance

When using $J - 1$ dummy variables to represent a qualitative characteristic that has multiple possible outcomes (as discussed in the earlier section "Juggling multiple characteristics with dummy variables"), you have to take into account the collective significance of those variables. Their effect can be collectively significant even if they are individually insignificant (I discuss the difference between individual and joint significance in Chapter 7). In the following sections you find out two ways to determine whether your dummy variables have joint significance.

Revisiting the F-test for joint significance

Testing the joint significance of a group of dummy variables in a regression model is accomplished by generalizing the F-test of overall significance to

$$F = \frac{\dfrac{RSS_r - RSS_{ur}}{q}}{\dfrac{RSS_{ur}}{n - p - 1}}$$

where RSS_r is the residual sum of squares for the *restricted* model (the model excluding the dummy variables), RSS_{ur} is the residual sum of squares for the *unrestricted* model (the model including the dummy variables), n is the number of sample measurements, p is the number of independent variables in the unrestricted model, and q is the number of dummy variables variables added in your unrestricted model that are not contained in your restricted model.

Figure 9-11 contains STATA output where I estimate a movie revenue model with independent variables that include two quantitative variables (budget and viewer ratings), a dummy variable identifying whether the lead actor is female, a dummy variable indicating whether the lead actor is over 40 years of age, and three dummy variables identifying the movie's genre (action/horror, drama, and romantic comedy, with the comedy genre used as the reference group).

The results in Figure 9-11 suggest that every additional dollar in the movie's budget is associated with an additional $1.08 in revenue, holding other factors constant. Viewer ratings *(crit)* also have a positive effect on revenue, holding other factors constant. The actor's gender (p-value = 0.407) and age (p-value = 0.178) don't appear to have a statistically significant effect. When the qualitative characteristics for genre are considered, only the drama genre has an individually significant effect, whereas horror and romance have insignificant p-values. However, the F-test suggests that genre, overall, is highly statistically significant (p-value = 0.0000, which is less than 0.01 or 1 percent).

Revisiting the Chow test

If you suspect that the parameters of your model vary depending on the group (or type of observations) being analyzed, you can test the hypothesis that the structure is stable using the Chow test, which I introduce you to in Chapter 8.

Using a dummy variable and interaction terms, a test of joint significance can be equivalent to performing a Chow test. The dummy variable approach to a Chow test is conducted by applying the following steps:

1. **Create a dummy variable (*D*) that identifies any two groups suspected of a structural break.**

   For example, $D = 1$ if the observation belongs to group A and $D = 0$ if the observation belongs to group B.

2. **Create interaction variables with your dummy variable and every other variable in your model.**

3. **Estimate the regression model that includes the quantitative, dummy, and interaction variables.**

4. **Test the joint significance of the dummy variable identifying the two groups and all the interaction terms that include this dummy variable.**

```
. regress grossbox_mil budget_mil crit Female Over40 Act_Horr drama romcom
```

Source	SS	df	MS	Number of obs	=	580
				F (7,572)	=	95.07
Model	1648794.39	7	235542.056	Prob > F	=	0.0000
Residual	1417180.53	572	2477.58833	R-squared	=	0.5378
				Adj R-squared	=	0.5321
Total	3065974.92	579	5295.29347	Root MSE	=	49.775

grossbox_mil	Coef.	Std. Err.	t	P>|t|	[95% Conf.	Interval]
budget_mil	1.087884	.0488551	22.27	0.000	.9919264	1.183841
crit	.5681215	.0838044	6.78	0.000	.4035196	.7327233
Female	4.160335	5.017842	0.83	0.407	-5.69531	14.01598
Over40	-6.013934	4.455514	-1.35	0.178	-14.7651	2.73723
Act_Horr	-6.442873	5.924532	-1.09	0.277	-18.07936	5.193619
drama	-25.80312	6.401043	-4.03	0.000	-38.37554	-13.23071
romcom	-1.487109	8.179554	-0.18	0.856	-17.55273	14.57852
_cons	-3.043735	6.224471	-0.49	0.625	-15.26934	9.181872

```
. test Act_Horr drama romcom

 ( 1) Act_Horr = 0
 ( 2) drama = 0
 ( 3) romcom = 0

 F(3,572) = 7.20
 Prob > F = 0.0001
```

Figure 9-11: STATA regression output with *F*-test of significance for a group of dummy variables capturing one qualitative characteristic.

In order to illustrate the equivalence of the Chow test and the dummy variable approach to testing for a structural break, begin with

$$Y_i = \beta_0 + \beta_1 X_i + \varepsilon_i$$

where Y is the movie revenue (in millions of dollars) and X is movie budget (also in millions of dollars), using all observations to estimate the model (the restricted model). Then estimate the model separately for movies with a female lead and those with a male lead (two unrestricted models). Use these regression results to calculate the Chow *F*-test.

Figure 9-12 contains the STATA output needed for performing a Chow test — the restricted regression with all movies and the two unrestricted regressions (one using the sample of movies with female leads and one using the sample of movies with male leads).

. regress grossbox_mil budget_mil

Source	SS	df	MS	Number of obs	=	580
				F (1,578)	=	565.99
Model	1516888.19	1	1516888.19	Prob > F	=	0.0000
Residual	1549086.73	578	2680.08085	R-squared	=	0.4947
				Adj R-squared	=	0.4939
Total	3065974.92	579	5295.29347	Root MSE	=	51.769

grossbox_mil	Coef.	Std. Err.	t	P>|t|	[95% Conf. Interval]	
budget_mil	1.128824	.0474486	23.79	0.000	1.035631	1.222016
_cons	10.35808	3.096278	3.35	0.001	4.27675	16.4394

. regress grossbox_mil budget_mil if Female==1

Source	SS	df	MS	Number of obs	=	162
				F (1,160)	=	56.89
Model	106999.894	1	106999.894	Prob > F	=	0.0000
Residual	300953.136	160	1880.9571	R-squared	=	0.2623
				Adj R-squared	=	0.2577
Total	407953.03	161	2533.86975	Root MSE	=	43.37

grossbox_mil	Coef.	Std. Err.	t	P>|t|	[95% Conf. Interval]	
budget_mil	.8394756	.1113027	7.54	0.000	.6196636	1.059288
_cons	22.45376	5.148585	4.36	0.000	12.28581	32.62171

. regress grossbox_mil budget_mil if Female==0

Source	SS	df	MS	Number of obs	=	418
				F (1,416)	=	470.92
Model	1394654.86	1	1394654.86	Prob > F	=	0.0000
Residual	1232014.52	416	2961.57336	R-squared	=	0.5310
				Adj R-squared	=	0.5298
Total	2626669.38	417	6298.96734	Root MSE	=	54.42

grossbox_mil	Coef.	Std. Err.	t	P>|t|	[95% Conf. Interval]	
budget_mil	1.178223	.0542944	21.70	0.000	1.071497	1.284948
_cons	7.003623	3.869529	1.81	0.071	-.6026435	14.60989

Figure 9-12: STATA regression output of restricted regression (all observations) and two unrestricted regressions (female sample and male sample).

The results can be used to produce the following F-statistic:

$$F = \frac{\dfrac{RSS_r - \left(RSS_{ur,A} + RSS_{ur,B}\right)}{p+1}}{\dfrac{RSS_{ur,A} + RSS_{ur,B}}{n-2p-2}} = \frac{\dfrac{1{,}549{,}086.73 - \left(300{,}953.14 + 1{,}232{,}014.52\right)}{(1+1)}}{\dfrac{300{,}953.14 + 1{,}232{,}014.52}{580 - (2)(1) - 2}} = \frac{8{,}059.54}{2{,}661.40} = 3.03$$

Note: The specific components of the F-statistic for the Chow test are discussed in Chapter 8.

Figure 9-13 contains the STATA output with the dummy variable approach to the Chow test. Notice that the F-statistic for joint significance of the dummy variable identifying female leads and its interaction with the other variable in the model (budget) is identical to the F-statistic from the Chow test. In this case, the evidence points to rejecting the hypothesis of structural stability.

Figure 9-13: STATA regression output of dummy variable interacted model with F-test of joint significance.

grossbox_mil	Coef.	Std. Err.	t	P>|t|	[95% Conf.	Interval]
budget_mil	1.178223	.0514694	22.89	0.000	1.077132	1.279313
Female	15.45014	7.138782	2.16	0.031	1.428921	29.47135
budgetXFemale	-.3387471	.1420477	-2.38	0.017	-.6177416	-.0597525
_cons	7.003623	3.668192	1.91	0.057	-.2010404	14.20829

```
. test Female budgetXFemale

( 1) Female = 0
( 2) budgetXFemale = 0

F(2,576) = 3.03
Prob > F = 0.0492
```

The advantage of the dummy variable approach to testing for structural stability is that it allows you to identify the source of the difference between the groups. In other words, the F-test (covered in the preceding section) allows you to identify an overall structural break, but the significance of the individual coefficients allows you to identify whether the difference is primarily in the intercept, slope, or both. The disadvantage of the dummy variable approach is that it may not be practical if you're working with numerous independent variables.

Part IV
Violations of Classical Regression Model Assumptions

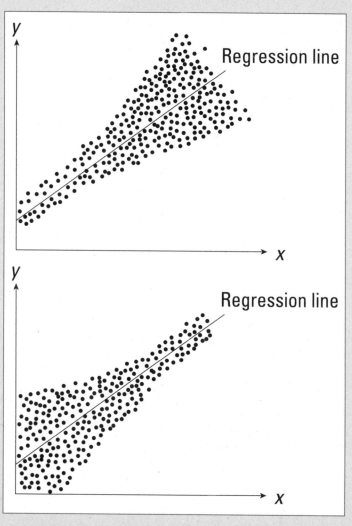

For a veritable crash course in econometrics basics, including an easily absorbed rundown of the three most common estimation problems, access this book's e-Cheat Sheet at www.dummies.com/extras/econometrics.

In this part . . .

- ✔ Understand the nature of the most commonly violated assumptions of the classical linear regression model (CLRM): multicollinearity, heteroskedasticity, and autocorrelation.

- ✔ Use standard procedures to evaluate the severity of assumption violations in your model.

- ✔ Evaluate the consequences of common estimation problems.

- ✔ Apply remedies to address multicollinearity, heteroskedasticity, and autocorrelation.

Chapter 10

Multicollinearity

● ●

In This Chapter
▶ Defining multicollinearity and describing its consequences
▶ Discovering multicollinearity issues in your regressions
▶ Fixing multicollinearity problems
● ●

*M*ulticollinearity arises when a linear relationship exists between two or more independent variables in a regression model. In practice, you rarely encounter perfect multicollinearity, but high multicollinearity is quite common and can cause substantial problems for your regression analysis. Never fear, though. In this chapter, I help you identify when multicollinearity becomes harmful and the options available to address the problem.

Distinguishing between the Types of Multicollinearity

Two types of multicollinearity exist:

✔ **Perfect multicollinearity** occurs when two or more independent variables in a regression model exhibit a *deterministic* (perfectly predictable or containing no randomness) linear relationship. When perfectly collinear variables are included as independent variables, you can't use the OLS technique to estimate the value of the parameters (*β*s). Perfect multicollinearity therefore violates one of the classical linear regression model (CLRM) assumptions that I tell you all about in Chapter 6.

✔ **High multicollinearity** results from a linear relationship between your independent variables with a high degree of correlation but aren't completely deterministic (in other words, they don't have perfect correlation). It's much more common than its perfect counterpart and can be equally problematic when it comes to estimating an econometric model.

In practice, perfect multicollinearity is uncommon and can be avoided with careful attention to the model's independent variables. However, high multicollinearity is quite common and can create severe estimation problems. For this reason, when econometricians point to a multicollinearity issue, they're typically referring to *high* multicollinearity rather than *perfect* multicollinearity.

The following sections further illustrate the differences between perfect and high multicollinearity so that you can readily spot them — and prevent them.

Pinpointing perfect multicollinearity

Getting a grasp on perfect multicollinearity is easier if you can picture an econometric model that uses two independent variables, such as the following:

$$Y_i = \beta_0 + \beta_1 X_{i1} + \beta_2 X_{i2} + \varepsilon_i$$

Suppose that, in this model,

$$X_{i2} = \alpha_0 + \alpha_1 X_{i1}$$

where the αs are constants. By substitution, you obtain

$$Y_i = \beta_0 + \beta_1 X_{i1} + \beta_2 (\alpha_0 + \alpha_1 X_{i1}) + \varepsilon_i$$

which indicates that the model collapses and can't be estimated as originally specified.

The result of perfect multicollinearity is that you can't obtain any structural inferences about the original model using sample data for estimation. In a model with perfect multicollinearity, your regression coefficients are indeterminate and their standard errors are infinite.

Perfect multicollinearity usually occurs when data has been constructed or manipulated by the researcher. For example, you have perfect multicollinearity if you include a dummy variable for every possible group or category of a qualitative characteristic instead of including a variable for all but one of the groups (I illustrate how to use dummy variables in Chapter 9).

In Figure 10-1, I use STATA to create a variable that is a linear combination of another variable. Then I plot the graph of the two variables and include both of them as independent variables in a regression model. Notice, however, that the results do not contain parameter estimates for both variables. Obtaining individual regression coefficients for every variable is impossible if you have perfect multicollinearity.

```
. des

Contains data from /Research/Econometrics for Dummies/ExampleData/hamburgers-data.dta
```

obs:	5			
vars:	2		5 Oct 2004 14:05	
size:	40			

variable name	storage type	display format	value label	variable label
y	float	%9.0g		
x	float	%9.0g		

```
Sorted by:
. gen w = 2*x
. twoway (connected w x)
```

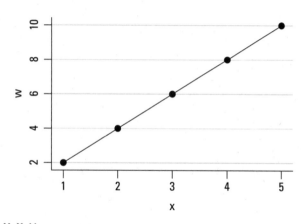

```
. regress y x w
note: x omitted because of collinearity
```

Source	SS	df	MS			
Model	3724.9	1	3724.9	Number of obs	=	5
Residual	13.9	3	4.63333333	F (1,3)	=	803.94
				Prob > F	=	0.0001
				R-squared	=	0.9963
Total	3738.8	4	934.7	Adj R-squared	=	0.9950
				Root MSE	=	2.1525

y	Coef.	Std. Err.	t	P>|t|	[95% Conf. Interval]	
x	0	(omitted)				
w	−9.65	.340343	−28.35	0.000	−10.73312	−8.566877
_cons	119.7	2.25758	53.02	0.000	112.5154	126.8846

Figure 10-1: STATA estimation in the presence of perfect multicollinearity.

Most econometric software programs identify perfect multicollinearity and drop one (or more) variables prior to providing the estimation results, taking care of the problem for you. The good news is that you can avoid perfect multicollinearity by exhibiting some care in creating variables and carefully choosing which ones to include as independent variables.

Zeroing in on high multicollinearity

You can describe an approximate linear relationship, which characterizes high multicollinearity, as follows:

$$X_{i2} = \alpha_0 + \alpha_1 X_{i1} + u_i$$

where the Xs are independent variables in a regression model and u represents a random error term (which is the component that differentiates high multicollinearity from perfect multicollinearity). Therefore, the difference between perfect and high multicollinearity is that some variation in the independent variable is not explained by variation in the other independent variable(s).

The stronger the relationship between the independent variables, the more likely you are to have estimation problems with your model.

Strong linear relationships resulting in high multicollinearity can sometimes catch you by surprise, but these three situations tend to be particularly problematic:

- ✔ **You use variables that are lagged values of one another.** For example, one independent variable is an individual's income in the current year, and another independent variable measures an individual's income in the previous year. These values may be completely different for some observations, but for most observations the two are closely related.

- ✔ **You use variables that share a common time trend component.** For example, you use yearly values for GDP (gross domestic product) and the DJIA (Dow Jones Industrial Average) as independent variables in a regression model. The value for these measurements tends to increase (with occasional decreases) and generally move in the same direction over time.

- ✔ **You use variables that capture similar phenomena.** For example, your independent variables to explain crime across cities may be unemployment rates, average income, and poverty rates. These variables aren't likely to be perfectly correlated, but they're probably highly correlated.

Technically, the presence of high multicollinearity doesn't violate any CLRM assumptions. Consequently, OLS estimates can be obtained and are BLUE (best linear unbiased estimators) with high multicollinearity.

Although OLS estimators remain BLUE in the presence of high multicollinearity, it reinforces a desirable *repeated sampling* property. In practice, you probably don't have an opportunity to utilize multiple samples, so you want *any given sample* to produce sensible and reliable results. With high multicollinearity, the OLS estimates still have the smallest variance, but *smallest* is a relative concept and doesn't ensure that the variances are actually small. In fact, the larger variances (and standard errors) of the OLS estimators are the main reason to avoid high multicollinearity.

The typical consequences of high multicollinearity include the following:

- **Larger standard errors and insignificant *t*-statistics:** The estimated variance of a coefficient in a multiple regression is

$$\sigma^2_{\hat{\beta}_k} = \frac{\hat{\sigma}^2_\varepsilon}{\sum\left(X_{ik} - \bar{X}_k\right)^2\left(1 - R_k^2\right)}$$

where $\hat{\sigma}^2_\varepsilon$ is the mean squared error (MSE) and R_k^2 is the R-squared value from regressing X_k on the other Xs. Higher multicollinearity results in a larger R_k^2, which increases the standard error of the coefficient. Figure 10-2 illustrates the effect of multicollinearity on the variance (or standard error) of a coefficient.

  Because the *t*-statistic associated with a coefficient is the ratio of the estimated coefficient to the standard error ($t_k = \frac{\hat{\beta}_k}{\hat{\sigma}_{\hat{\beta}_k}}$), high multicollinearity also tends to result in insignificant *t*-statistics.

- **Coefficient estimates that are sensitive to changes in specification:** If the independent variables are highly collinear, the estimates must emphasize small differences in the variables in order to assign an independent effect to each of them. Adding or removing variables from the model can change the nature of the small differences and drastically change your coefficient estimates. In other words, your results aren't robust (a topic that you can learn about in Chapter 8).

- **Nonsensical coefficient signs and magnitudes:** With higher multicollinearity, the variance of the estimated coefficients increases, which in turn increases the chances of obtaining coefficient estimates with extreme values. Consequently, these estimates may have unbelievably large magnitudes and/or signs that counter the expected relationship between the independent and dependent variables. Figure 10-3 illustrates how the sampling distribution of the estimated coefficients is affected by multicollinearity.

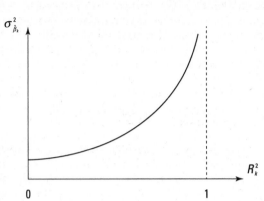

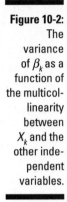

Figure 10-2: The variance of β_k as a function of the multicollinearity between X_k and the other independent variables.

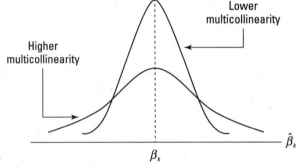

Figure 10-3: Effect of multicollinearity on variance of estimated coefficients.

When two (or more) variables exhibit high multicollinearity, there's more uncertainty as to which variable should be credited with explaining variation in the dependent variable. For this reason, a high R-squared value combined with many statistically insignificant coefficients is a common consequence of high multicollinearity.

Rules of Thumb for Identifying Multicollinearity

Because high multicollinearity doesn't violate a CLRM assumption and is a sample-specific issue, researchers typically choose from a couple popular alternatives to measure the degree or severity of multicollinearity.

You don't use formal statistical tests to detect multicollinearity. Instead, you use one or two sample measurements as indicators of a potential multicollinearity problem. The two most common are pairwise correlation coefficients and variance inflation factors, and I explain how to use them in the following sections.

Pairwise correlation coefficients

One way in which you can check for multicollinearity is by calculating the *pairwise correlation coefficient,* which is the value of sample correlation (something you can review in Chapter 2), for every pair of independent variables.

The sample correlation coefficient measures the linear association between any two independent variables, X_k and X_j. You calculate a sample correlation coefficient with this equation:

$$r_{kj} = \frac{\dfrac{\sum \left(X_{ik} - \bar{X}_k\right)\left(X_{ij} - \bar{X}_j\right)}{n-1}}{\left(\sqrt{\dfrac{\sum \left(X_{ik} - \bar{X}_k\right)^2}{n-1}}\right)\left(\sqrt{\dfrac{\sum \left(X_{ij} - \bar{X}_j\right)^2}{n-1}}\right)} = \frac{s_{kj}}{s_k s_j}$$

where $\bar{X}_k$ is the sample mean of X_k, $\bar{X}_j$ is the sample mean of X_j, s_{kj} is the covariance between X_k and X_j, s_k is the sample standard deviation of X_k, and s_j is the sample standard deviation of X_j.

As a rule of thumb, correlation coefficients around 0.8 or above may signal a multicollinearity problem.

To see how to calculate pairwise correlation coefficients, you can start with data from Major League Baseball players. Say you estimate a model with the natural log of the player's contract value as the dependent variable and several player characteristics as independent variables. The independent variables include three-year averages for the player's weighted measure of singles, doubles, triples, and home runs known as slugging percentage *(slg_3_avg);* their ability to get on base by any means, including walks, known as on-base-percentage *(obp_3_avg);* the frequency with which they help their teammates score runs known as runs-batted-in *(rbi_3_avg);* stolen bases *(sb_3_avg);* at-bats *(ab_3_avg);* errors *(e_3_avg);* the player's age; and the player's tenure (years) with the current team. Figure 10-4 shows STATA's regression output and the *correlation matrix* of the independent variables. The correlation matrix contains the correlation coefficients for each pair of independent variables.

```
. regress ln_real_con_val slg_3_avg obp_3_avg rbi_3_avg sb_3_avg ab_3_avg e_3_avg age tenure
```

Source	SS	df	MS		Number of obs	=	316
					F (8,307)	=	71.06
Model	438.617744	8	54.827218		Prob > F	=	0.0000
Residual	236.854147	307	.771511879		R-squared	=	0.6494
					Adj R-squared	=	0.6402
Total	675.47189	315	2.14435521		Root MSE	=	.87836

ln_real_co~1	Coef.	Std. Err.	t	P>|t|	[95% Conf. Interval]	
slg_3_avg	2.271693	1.428701	1.59	0.113	-.5395931	5.082978
obp_3_avg	2.032833	1.929276	1.05	0.293	-1.763444	5.82911
rbi_3_avg	.0300793	.0059807	5.03	0.00	.018311	.0418475
sb_3_avg	.0537857	.0086797	6.20	0.000	.0367066	.0708649
ab_3_avg	-.000552	.0009772	-0.56	0.573	-.0024748	.0013708
e_3_avg	.0218453	.0139624	1.56	0.119	-.0056289	.0493194
age	-.0912189	.014834	-6.15	0.000	-.120408	-.0620298
tenure	-.0145044	.0251371	-0.58	0.564	-.0639673	.0349585
_cons	14.81168	.627699	23.60	0.000	13.57654	16.04681

Figure 10-4:
STATA
regression
output and
correlation
matrix for
independent
variables.

```
. corr slg_3_avg obp_3_avg rbi_3_avg sb_3_avg ab_3_avg e_3_avg age tenure
(obs=316)
```

	slg_3_~g	ogp_3_~g	rbi_e_~g	sb_3_avg	ab_3_avg	e_3_avg	age	tenure
slg_3_avg	1.0000							
obp_3_avg	0.7454	1.0000						
rbi_3_avg	0.6610	0.4110	1.0000					
sb_3_avg	0.0964	0.1749	0.2280	1.0000				
ab_3_avg	0.4184	0.3201	0.8668	0.4670	1.0000			
e_3_avg	0.1346	0.0453	0.4114	0.2230	0.5118	1.0000		
age	-0.0280	0.1108	-0.1782	-0.1981	-0.2018	-0.2156	1.0000	
tenure	-0.0729	-0.0579	-0.0164	-0.0650	0.0187	0.0169	0.0223	1.0000

The correlation between slugging percentage and on-base-percentage and between runs-batted-in and at-bats are both near the 0.8 rule of thumb value. Additionally, the correlation between slugging percentage and runs-batted-in is also quite high.

Of course, before you officially determine that you have a multicollinearity problem due to a correlation coefficient near 0.8 or above, you should check your results for evidence of multicollinearity (insignificant *t*-statistics, sensitive coefficient estimates, and nonsensical coefficient signs and values). Also, keep in mind that low pairwise correlation coefficients don't necessarily indicate that you're clear of multicollinearity issues. The value of your independent variable could be determined by a linear combination of several other independent variables. The pairwise correlation coefficients only identify the linear relationship of a variable with one other variable.

Auxiliary regression and the variance inflation factor (VIF)

Calculating the variance inflation factor (VIF) for every independent variable is another way to check for multicollinearity. VIF measures the linear association between an independent variable and all the other independent variables.

A VIF for any given independent variable is calculated by

$$VIF_k = \frac{1}{1 - R_k^2}$$

where R_k^2 is the R-squared value obtained by regressing independent variable X_k on all the other independent variables in the model.

Most econometric software programs have a command that you can execute after estimating a regression to obtain the VIFs for each independent variable. However, if you need to calculate the VIFs individually, just follow these steps:

1. **Determine the econometric model and obtain the OLS estimates.**

    For example, your model may be something like:
    $$Y_i = \beta_0 + \beta_1 X_{i1} + \beta_2 X_{i2} + \beta_3 X_{i3} + \varepsilon_i$$

2. **Estimate auxiliary regressions by regressing each independent variable on the other independent variables and obtain the R-squared of each auxiliary regression.**

    For example, using the model in Step 1, you estimate the auxiliary regressions
    $$X_{i1} = \alpha_0 + \alpha_1 X_{i2} + \alpha_2 X_{i3} + u_{i1}$$
    $$X_{i2} = \delta_0 + \delta_1 X_{i1} + \delta_2 X_{i3} + u_{i3}$$
    $$X_{i3} = \gamma_0 + \gamma_1 X_{i1} + \gamma_2 X_{i2} + u_{i3}$$

    to obtain R_1^2, R_2^2, and R_3^2.

3. **Obtain the VIF for each independent variable with the formula**
    $$VIF_k = \frac{1}{1 - R_k^2}$$

As a rule of thumb, VIFs greater than 10 signal a highly likely multicollinearity problem, and VIFs between 5 and 10 signal a somewhat likely multicollinearity issue.

Time to put VIFs into practice. Using the same example from the last section, say you estimate a model with the natural log of an MLB player's contract value as the dependent variable and several player characteristics as independent variables. Again, use three-year averages for the player's slugging percentage *(slg_3_avg)*, on-base-percentage *(obp_3_avg)*, runs-batted-in *(rbi_3_avg)*, stolen bases *(sb_3_avg)*, at-bats *(ab_3_avg)*, errors *(e_3_avg)*, the player's age, and the player's tenure with the current team as independent variables. Figure 10-5 shows STATA's regression output followed by a table of VIFs. STATA internally calculates the auxiliary regressions and produces the VIF for every independent variable in the model.

```
. regress ln_real_con_val slg_3_avg obp_3_avg rbi_3_avg sb_3_avg ab_3_avg e_3_avg age tenure
```

Source	SS	df	MS		Number of obs	=	316
					F (8,307)	=	71.06
Model	438.617744	8	54.827218		Prob > F	=	0.0000
Residual	236.854147	307	.771511879		R-squared	=	0.6494
					Adj R-squared	=	0.6402
Total	675.47189	315	2.14435521		Root MSE	=	.87836

ln_real_co~1	Coef.	Std. Err.	t	P>|t|	[95% Conf. Interval]	
slg_3_avg	2.271693	1.428701	1.59	0.113	-.5395931	5.082978
obp_3_avg	2.032833	1.929276	1.05	0.293	-1.763444	5.82911
rbi_3_avg	.0300793	.0059807	5.03	0.00	.018311	.0418475
sb_3_avg	.0537857	.0086797	6.20	0.000	.0367066	.0708649
ab_3_avg	-.000552	.0009772	-0.56	0.573	-.0024748	.0013708
e_3_avg	.0218453	.0139624	1.56	0.119	-.0056289	.0493194
age	-.0912189	.014834	-6.15	0.000	-.120408	-.0620298
tenure	-.0145044	.0251371	-0.58	0.564	-.0639673	.0349585
_cons	14.81168	.627699	23.60	0.000	13.57654	16.04681

```
. estat vif
```

Variable	VIF	1/VIF
rbi_3_avg	9.75	0.102581
ab_3_avg	8.50	0.117661
slg_3_avg	4.64	0.215735
obp_3_avg	2.70	0.370700
sb_3_avg	1.66	0.602691
e_3_avg	1.41	0.709348
age	1.14	0.878131
tenure	1.02	0.979347
Mean VIF	3.85	

Figure 10-5: STATA regression output and variance inflations factors (VIFs).

The VIF for runs-batted-in (VIF = 9.75) suggests a very good chance of a multicollinearity problem. This suspicion is complemented by the surprising result that slugging percentage and on-base-percentage (two characteristics that are important in measuring the offensive contributions of a baseball player and should have a positive impact on their salary) are statistically insignificant. The high VIF, combined with this unexpected result, should lead you to suspect that high multicollinearity is problematic.

Before announcing to the world that you have a multicollinearity problem due to a high VIF, be sure to check your results for evidence of multicollinearity (insignificant *t*-statistics, sensitive or nonsensical coefficient estimates, and nonsensical coefficient signs and values). A high VIF is only an indicator of potential multicollinearity, but it may not result in a large variance for the estimator if the variance of the independent variable is also large.

Knowing When and How to Resolve Multicollinearity Issues

Resolving high multicollinearity may only fix issues that are unique to a specific sample. In other words, mitigating high multicollinearity in one case doesn't necessarily lead to a solution in another similar case. Furthermore, you need to be careful that your efforts to resolve high multicollinearity don't lead to other serious problems (violations of CLRM assumptions).

Your success in resolving high multicollinearity depends on its complexity and severity in the sample you're using for econometric analysis. A successful resolution to high multicollinearity likely requires some experimentation with a few different potential solutions while keeping in mind that the solutions to multicollinearity can cause more severe problems in other areas.

But how do you know when to proceed with pursuing a resolution? Well, follow these guidelines:

- ✔ If the primary purpose of your study is to estimate a model for prediction or forecasting, then the best solution may be to do nothing.

- ✔ If you want to obtain reliable estimates of the individual parameters in the model, you need to be more concerned with multicollinearity. (But you shouldn't modify your model if the *t*-statistics of the suspect variable(s) are greater than 2 *and* the coefficient signs and magnitudes make economic sense.)

When considering various resolutions to multicollinearity, I advise taking a holistic approach that considers the benefits of eliminating high correlation between the independent variables against the costs of addressing an issue that's specific to the sample you're using rather than the population of interest. If you've done this and decided that resolving the multicollinearity issue is your best option, then you have a few ways of proceeding. You can

✔ Acquire more data.

✔ Apply a new model.

✔ Cut the problem variable loose.

I discuss these options in the following sections.

Get more data

Gathering additional data can not only improve the efficiency (in other words, reduce the variance) of your estimates but also help with multicollinearity issues. How so? Well, high multicollinearity may be unique to your sample, so the acquisition of additional data is a potential solution. Additional data can be compiled by acquiring more observations for an existing sample or by appending the data with a new sample.

If you're using cross-sectional data (covered in Chapter 4), you may be able to obtain more data by returning to your population of interest immediately or after a period of time (thereby creating a pooled cross section). Another way to increase the number of observations with cross-sectional or panel data is to reduce the level of aggregation. For example, rather than using country-level data, you could consider state-, county-, city-, household-, or individual-level data.

If you're working with time-series data (also covered in Chapter 4), you can increase the number of observations by increasing the frequency of the data. For example, instead of using yearly data, you could consider quarterly, monthly, daily, or even hourly data. Of course, you have to consider whether increasing the frequency is appropriate or possible. In the United States, for example, employment data is tabulated on a monthly basis, so obtaining these figures on an hourly basis is impossible.

The collection of additional data may be costly or could inadvertently result in a change of your population, so don't automatically assume a "more is better" mentality when building your database.

Use a new model

In some cases, you may be able to rethink your theoretical model or the way in which you expect your independent variables to influence your dependent variable in order to address a multicollinearity issue.

Respecifying the econometric model can address a multicollinearity issue by transforming highly correlated independent variables. The most common ways of accomplishing it are through log transformations, reciprocal functions, first-differencing, and combining collinear independent variables.

In Chapter 8, I discuss various forms of log transformations (log-log, log-linear, and linear-log) and reciprocal functions. Because those transformations are nonlinear, independent variables that exhibited a linear relationship may no longer do so after respecification. I address the other two options in the next sections.

In some cases, high multicollinearity may persist even after respecifying the model. However, a more serious concern is resolving a multicollinearity issue with an increased chance of committing specification bias.

First-differencing

First-differencing is a technique that can be used with data that has a time component. In other words, its use is limited to models utilizing time-series or panel data. For instance, suppose you observe each cross-sectional unit i (a country, or state, or household, or whatever) in more than one time period (t). A basic econometric model would have the form

$$Y_{it} = \beta_0 + \beta_1 X_{it1} + \beta_2 X_{it2} + \ldots + \beta_p X_{itp} + \varepsilon_{it}$$

where the i and t subscripts represent the cross-sectional unit and time period, respectively. If you subtract the previous period's values of your variables from the values in the current period for each cross-sectional unit, you'd have

$$Y_{it} - Y_{i(t-1)} = \alpha_0 + \beta_1\left(X_{it1} - X_{i(t-1)1}\right) + \beta_2\left(X_{it2} - X_{i(t-1)2}\right) + \ldots + \beta_p\left(X_{itp} - X_{i(t-1)p}\right) + \left(\varepsilon_{it} - \varepsilon_{i(t-1)}\right)$$

or

$$\Delta Y_i = \alpha_0 + \beta_1 \Delta X_{i1} + \beta_2 \Delta X_{i2} + \ldots + \beta_p \Delta X_{ip} + u_i$$

where Δ represents the change from period $t-1$ to period t. This equation is called the *first-differenced equation,* and when you obtain estimates for the βs using OLS, they're called *first-differenced estimators.*

If you're planning to use first-differencing, make sure your variables have variation over time. If not, $\Delta X_{ik} = 0$ and you can't estimate the model using OLS.

The first-differencing technique has its costs:

- **Losing observations:** In order to calculate the change in a variable, you need to sacrifice one time period.

- **Losing variation in your independent variables:** This loss in variation can result in insignificant coefficients, even with the multicollinearity issues resolved.

- **Changing the specification (possibly resulting in misspecification bias):** Modeling wage levels, for example, isn't the same as modeling changes in wages.

The composite index variable

You can create a composite index variable by combining collinear variables that measure similar characteristics. Suppose you have two highly collinear and related variables X_1 and X_2. You can create an index variable (X_3) with a linear combination of related variables such as $X_{i3} = aX_{i1} + bX_{i2}$ where a and b are constants. If the index variable is a weighted average of X_1 and X_2, then $a + b = 1$.

The consumer price index (CPI) is an example of a composite index variable. Applied econometricians often include the CPI as an independent variable in a model rather than numerous variables measuring prices of various goods. This avoids the high multicollinearity that would be likely if prices of goods were included as separate variables.

When you combine variables into an index, their association should make sense. For example, in a model using independent variables measured at the city-level, unemployment rates and poverty rates can be combined into an "economic conditions" variable. This type of procedure consolidates the collinear variables and creates a more parsimonious model.

Never combine variables into an index that would, individually, be expected to have opposite signs. Doing so makes interpretation difficult, if not impossible. It could even make the coefficient insignificant as the variables end up working against each other.

Expel the problem variable (s)

Dropping highly collinear independent variables from your model is one way to address high multicollinearity. Of course, anytime you drop a variable from an econometric model, you run the risk of committing a specification error. If variables are redundant, however, then dropping a variable improves an *overspecified* model.

In cases of severely high multicollinearity (correlation coefficients greater than 0.9), you don't have to follow any statistical rationale for choosing to drop one variable over another. If you're using VIFs to detect multicollinearity, a variable with a VIF greater than 10 is usually the most likely to be dropped. In either case, however, you should try to retain the variable(s) with the strongest theoretical justification.

If it's not clear which variable should be dropped or if the severity of multicollinearity is questionable, then you need to weigh the cost and benefit of dropping a variable from the model.

The cost of dropping a variable is that you're effectively forcing the coefficient of the variable to be zero. If the effect of the variable isn't actually zero and the variable isn't completely redundant, you've created a specification bias. I discuss specification issues and the amount of bias created by omitting a relevant variable in Chapter 8.

In some cases, the benefit of reduced variability in the other coefficients more than compensates for any bias that's been introduced by dropping a variable. You can evaluate it by examining the mean square error (MSE). A smaller MSE usually signals that the statistical benefits of dropping the variable exceed the costs of specification bias.

The most practical advice I can provide about dropping a variable to resolve a multicollinearity issue is to save it as a last resort and place theoretical considerations above purely statistical justifications.

To see the effects of dropping a variable, consider the results from a model of baseball player salaries (refer to Figure 10-5). The VIF for runs-batted-in is quite high, and theoretically important variables are statistically insignificant. For example, slugging percentage, on-base-percentage, and at-bats (characteristics that are important in measuring the offensive contributions of a baseball player and should have a positive impact on their salary) are statistically insignificant. The high VIFs, combined with unexpected results, would lead any econometrician to suspect that the model may be overspecified and therefore may benefit from dropping a variable.

In Figure 10-6, I re-estimate the model of baseball player salaries after dropping the variable with the highest VIF (runs-batted-in). In comparison to Figure 10-5, the results in Figure 10-6 make much more sense. Slugging percentage and at-bats now have the expected significance and the appropriate (positive) magnitude. On-base-percentage remains statistically insignificant, but the VIFs don't show any indication that the lack of statistical significance is due to high multicollinearity. The model now simply identifies the relevant variables in baseball salary determination with more accuracy.

The main takeaway here is that

✔ The results no longer contain unreasonably large coefficients that are statistically insignificant. Some coefficients remain insignificant, but they also have small magnitudes.

✔ The variable believed to be one of the most important performance measures in baseball (slugging percentage) is significant after the high multicollinearity is addressed. This is another sensible outcome.

✔ My original results in Figure 10-5 didn't contain coefficients with strange signs, even though it's definitely possible with high multicollinearity.

```
. regress ln_real_con_val slg_3_avg obp_3_avg sb_3_avg ab_3_avg e_3_avg age tenure
```

Source	SS	df	MS		Number of obs	=	316
					F (7,308)	=	71.93
Model	419.102366	7	59.8717665		Prob > F	=	0.0000
Residual	256.369525	308	.832368587		R-squared	=	0.6205
					Adj R-squared	=	0.6118
Total	675.47189	315	2.14435521		Root MSE	=	.91234

ln_real_co~1	Coef.	Std. Err.	t	P>|t|	[95% Conf. Interval]	
slg_3_avg	7.011411	1.115358	6.29	0.000	4.816727	9.206096
obp_3_avg	-.8580737	1.912916	-0.45	0.654	-4.622111	2.905963
sb_3_avg	.0359449	.0082282	4.37	0.000	.0197543	.0521355
ab_3_avg	.0037372	.0004955	7.54	0.000	.0027622	.0047122
e_3_avg	.0168912	.0144665	1.17	0.244	-.0115745	.0453568
age	-.0961308	.0153745	-6.25	0.000	-.1263831	-.0658785
tenure	-.0213462	.0260715	-8.82	0.414	-.072647	.0299545
_cons	14.00995	.6306109	22.22	0.000	12.7691	15.2508

```
. estat vif
```

Figure 10-6: STATA regression output with VIF values for each independent variable.

Variable	VIF	1/VIF
slg_3_avg	2.62	0.381898
obp_3_avg	2.46	0.406811
ab_3_avg	2.03	0.493721
e_3_avg	1.40	0.712896
sb_3_avg	1.38	0.723543
age	1.13	0.881954
tenure	1.02	0.982224
Mean VIF	1.72	

Chapter 11

Heteroskedasticity

● ●

● ●

As I explain in Chapter 6, a critical assumption of the classical linear regression model is homoskedasticity — that the variance of the error term is constant over various values of the independent variables. However, this assumption may not always hold. When it doesn't happen, you have heteroskedasticity. This chapter shows you how to determine whether you have heteroskedasticity in a particular application and what you can do to remedy it if you do.

Distinguishing between Homoskedastic and Heteroskedastic Disturbances

The error term is the most important component of the classical linear regression model (CLRM). Most of the CLRM assumptions that allow econometricians to prove the desirable properties of the OLS estimators (the Gauss-Markov theorem) directly involve characteristics about the error term (or disturbances). One of the CLRM assumptions deals with the conditional variance of the error term; namely, that the variance of the error term is constant (homoskedastic). In the following sections, I describe the difference between homoskedasticity and heteroskedasticity and illustrate the consequences of heteroskedasticity on OLS.

Homoskedastic error versus heteroskedastic error

CLRM relies on the error term variance being constant. Enter the term *homoske-dasticity,* which refers to a situation where the error has the same variance regardless of the value(s) taken by the independent variable(s). Econometricians usually express homoskedasticity as $Var(\varepsilon \mid \mathbf{X}_i) = \sigma_\varepsilon^2 = $ a constant for all i ($i = 1,2,...,N$), where $\mathbf{X}_i$ represents a vector of values for each individual and for all the independent variables.

As you can see in Figure 11-1, when the error term is homoskedastic, the dispersion of the error remains the same over the range of observations and regardless of functional form.

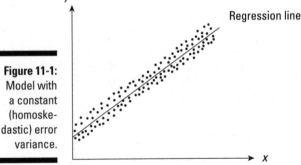

Figure 11-1: Model with a constant (homoske-dastic) error variance.

In many situations, however, the error term doesn't have a constant variance, leading to *heteroskedasticity* — when the variance of the error term changes in response to a change in the value(s) of the independent variable(s). Econometricians typically express heteroskedasticity as $Var(\varepsilon \mid \mathbf{X}_i) = \sigma_{i\varepsilon}^2$ ($i = 1,2,...,N$).

If the error term is heteroskedastic, the dispersion of the error changes over the range of observations, as shown in Figure 11-2. The heteroskedasticity patterns depicted in Figure 11-2 are only a couple among many possible patterns. Any error variance that doesn't resemble that in Figure 11-1 is likely to be heteroskedastic.

If you recall that *homogeneous* means uniform or identical, whereas *heterogeneous* is defined as assorted or different, you may have an easier time remembering the concept of heteroskedasticity forever. Lucky you!

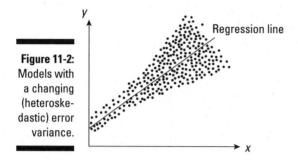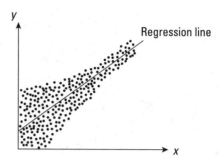

The consequences of heteroskedasticity

Heteroskedasticity violates one of the CLRM assumptions. When an assumption of the CLRM is violated, the OLS estimators may no longer be BLUE (best linear unbiased estimators).

Specifically, in the presence of heteroskedasticity, the OLS estimators may not be efficient (achieve the smallest variance). In addition, the estimated standard errors of the coefficients will be biased, which results in unreliable hypothesis tests (*t*-statistics). The OLS estimates, however, remain unbiased.

Under the assumption of homoskedasticity, in a model with one independent variable ($Y_i = \beta_0 + \beta_1 X_i + \varepsilon_i$), the variance of the estimated slope coefficient is

$$Var\left(\hat{\beta}_1\right) = \frac{\sigma_\varepsilon^2}{TSS_X}$$

where σ_ε^2 is the homoskedastic variance of the error and $TSS_X = \sum\left(X_i - \bar{X}\right)^2$.

However, without the homoskedasticity assumption, the variance of β_1 is

$$Var\left(\hat{\beta}_1\right) = \frac{\sum\left(X_i - \bar{X}\right)^2 \sigma_{i\varepsilon}^2}{TSS_X^2}$$

where $\sigma_{i\varepsilon}^2$ is the heteroskedastic variance of the error.

Therefore, if you fail to appropriately account for heteroskedasticity in its presence, you improperly calculate the variances and standard errors of the coefficients. The *t*-statistic for coefficients is calculated with

$$t = \frac{estimated\ \beta - hypothesized\ \beta}{std\ error}$$

Therefore, any bias in the calculation of the standard errors is passed on to your *t*-statistics and conclusions about statistical significance.

Heteroskedasticity is a common problem for OLS regression estimation, especially with cross-sectional and panel data. (I tell you all about these two types of data in Chapter 4.) However, you usually have no way to know in advance if it's going to be present, and theory is rarely useful in anticipating its presence.

Detecting Heteroskedasticity with Residual Analysis

The challenge to identifying heteroskedasticity is that you can only know $\sigma^2_{i\varepsilon}$ if you have the entire population corresponding to the chosen independent variables (*X*s). In practice, you'll be using a sample with only a limited number of observations for a particular *X*. Consequently, in applied situations the detection of heteroskedasticity relies on your intuition, prior empirical work, educated guesswork, or even sheer speculation.

Fortunately, a number of well-established techniques can guide you through the detection process. They involve both visual inspections and formal statistical tests, as you discover in the next sections.

Examining the residuals in graph form

An informal way of checking for heteroskedasticity is with a graphical examination of the residuals.

If you want to use graphs for an examination of heteroskedasticity, you first choose an independent variable that's likely to be responsible for the heteroskedasticity. Then you can construct a scatter diagram with the chosen independent variable and the squared residuals from your OLS regression.

Figure 11-3 illustrates the typical pattern of the residuals if the error term is homoskedastic.

Figure 11-4 exhibits the potential existence of heteroskedasticity with various relationships between the residual variance (squared residuals) and the values of the independent variable *X*. Each graph represents a specific example, but the possible heteroskedasticity patterns are limitless because the core problem in this case is the changing of the residual variances as the value of the independent variable X changes.

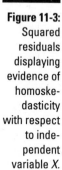

Figure 11-3: Squared residuals displaying evidence of homoskedasticity with respect to independent variable X.

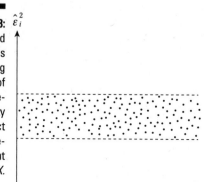

Figure 11-4: Squared residual suggesting heteroskedasticity with various patterns.

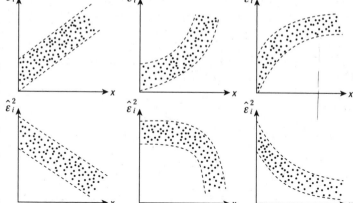

Graphical examinations don't provide evidence of homoskedasticity or heteroskedasticity. They merely suggest independent variables that may be related to the variability of the error term.

You can use the graphical result comparing the squared residuals to an independent variable to set up additional (formal) tests of heteroskedasticity.

Brushing up on the Breusch-Pagan test

The Breusch-Pagan (BP) test is one of the most common tests for heteroskedasticity. It begins by allowing the heteroskedasticity process to be a function of one or more of your independent variables, and it's usually applied by assuming that heteroskedasticity may be a linear function of all the independent variables in the model. This assumption can be expressed as $\varepsilon_i^2 = \alpha_0 + \alpha_1 X_{i1} + \ldots + \alpha_p X_{ip} + u_i$.

The values for ε_i^2 aren't known in practice, so the $\hat{\varepsilon}_i^2$ are calculated from the residuals and used as proxies for ε_i^2. Generally, the BP test is based on the estimation of $\hat{\varepsilon}_i^2 = \alpha_0 + \alpha_1 X_{i1} + \ldots + \alpha_p X_{ip} + u_i$.

Alternatively, a BP test can be performed by estimating $\hat{\varepsilon}_i^2 = \delta_0 + \delta_1 \hat{Y}_i$ where $\hat{Y}$ represents the predicted values from $\hat{Y}_i = \hat{\beta}_0 + \hat{\beta}_1 X_{i1} + \ldots + \hat{\beta}_p X_{ip}$.

Here's how to perform a BP test:

1. **Estimate your model, $Y_i = \beta_0 + \beta_1 X_{i1} + \ldots + \beta_p X_{ip} + \varepsilon_i$, using OLS.**

2. **Obtain the predicted Y values ($\hat{Y}_i$) after estimating the model.**

3. **Estimate the auxiliary regression, $\hat{\varepsilon}_i^2 = \delta_0 + \delta_1 \hat{Y}_i$, using OLS.**

4. **Retain the R-squared value $R_{\hat{\varepsilon}^2}^2$ from this auxiliary regression.**

5. **Calculate the F-statistic, $F = \dfrac{\dfrac{R_{\hat{\varepsilon}^2}^2}{1}}{\dfrac{\left(1 - R_{\hat{\varepsilon}^2}^2\right)}{n-2}}$, or the chi-squared statistic,**

   $\chi^2 = n R_{\hat{\varepsilon}^2}^2$.

The degrees of freedom for the F-test are equal to 1 in the numerator and $n-2$ in the denominator. The degrees of freedom for the chi-squared test are equal to 1. If either of these test statistics is significant, then you have evidence of heteroskedasticity. If not, you fail to reject the null hypothesis of homoskedasticity.

To show you how the BP test works, I use some data about Major League Baseball players. First, I estimate a model with the natural log of the player's contract value as the dependent variable and several player characteristics as independent variables, including three-year averages for the player's slugging percentage and at-bats, the player's age, and the player's tenure with the current team. Then I run the BP test in STATA, which retains the predicted Y values, estimates the auxiliary regression internally, and reports the chi-squared test. I can also request that STATA conduct the F-test version of the test. In Figure 11-5, I show both results, and they're consistent in rejecting the null hypothesis of homoskedasticity. Therefore, the statistical evidence implies that heteroskedasticity is present.

. regress ln_real_con_val slg_3_avg ab_3_avg tenure age

Source	SS	df	MS			
Model	428.083421	4	107.020855			
Residual	291.18819	325	.895963662			
Total	719.271611	329	2.1862359			

				Number of obs =	330
				F(4, 325) =	119.45
				Prob > F =	0.0000
				R-squared =	0.5952
				Adj R-squared =	0.5902
				Root MSE =	.94655

ln_real_co~l	Coef.	Std. Err.	t	P>|t|	[95% Conf.	Interval]
slg_3_avg	6.209006	.7695022	8.07	0.000	4.695172	7.72284
ab_3_avg	.0049325	.0004016	12.28	0.000	.0041425	.0057225
tenure	-.0376795	.0268191	-1.40	0.161	-.0904404	.0150813
age	-.1050854	.0146173	-7.19	0.000	-.1338419	-.0763289
_cons	14.29176	.5891517	24.26	0.000	13.13273	15.45079

. estat hettest

Figure 11-5:
STATA output of OLS regression followed by a Breusch-Pagan test for heteroskedasticity.

Breusch-Pagan / Cook-Weisberg test for heteroskedasticity
    Ho: Constant variance
    Variables: fitted values of ln_real_con_val

    chi2(1)   =   8.00
    Prob > chi2 = 0.0047

. estat hettest, fstat

Breusch-Pagan / Cook-Weisberg test for heteroskedasticity
    Ho: Constant variance
    Variables: fitted values of ln_real_con_val

    F(1 , 328) =   6.26
    Prob > F   = 0.0128

WARNING!

A weakness of the BP test is that it assumes the heteroskedasticity is a linear function of the independent variables. Failing to find evidence of heteroskedasticity with the BP doesn't rule out a nonlinear relationship between the independent variable(s) and the error variance. Additionally, the BP test isn't useful for determining how to correct or adjust the model for heteroskedasticity.

Getting acquainted with the White test

Another extremely common test for heteroskedasticity is the White test, which begins by allowing the heteroskedasticity process to be a function of one or more of your independent variables. It's similar to the Breusch-Pagan test (see the preceding section), but the White test allows the independent variable to have a nonlinear and interactive effect on the error variance.

REMEMBER

Typically, you apply the White test by assuming that heteroskedasticity may be a linear function of all the independent variables, a function of their squared values, and a function of their cross products ($X_k X_j$ for $k \neq j$).

TECHNICAL STUFF

As in the Breusch-Pagan test, because the values for ε_i^2 aren't known in practice, the $\hat{\varepsilon}_i^2$ are calculated from the residuals and used as proxies for ε_i^2. The White test is based on the estimation of the following:

$$\widehat{\varepsilon}_i^2 = \alpha_0 + \alpha_1 X_{i1} + \ldots + \alpha_p X_{ip} + \alpha_{p+1} X_{i1}^2 + \ldots \alpha_{2p} X_{ip}^2 + \alpha_{2p+1}\left(X_{i1} X_{i2}\right) + \ldots + u_i$$

Alternatively, a White test can be performed by estimating $\widehat{\varepsilon}_i^2 = \delta_0 + \delta_1 \widehat{Y}_i + \delta_2 \widehat{Y}_i^2$ where $\widehat{Y}_i$ represents the predicted values from $\widehat{Y}_i = \widehat{\beta}_0 + \widehat{\beta}_1 X_{i1} + \ldots + \widehat{\beta}_p X_{ip}$. Follow these five steps to perform a White test:

1. **Estimate your model, $Y_i = \beta_0 + \beta_1 X_{i1} + \ldots + \beta_p X_{ip} + \varepsilon_i$, using OLS.**

2. **Obtain the predicted Y values $(\widehat{Y}_i)$ after estimating your model.**

3. **Estimate the model $\widehat{\varepsilon}_i^2 = \delta_0 + \delta_1 \widehat{Y}_i + \delta_2 \widehat{Y}_i^2$ using OLS.**

4. **Retain the R-squared value $(R_{\widehat{\varepsilon}^2}^2)$ from this regression.**

5. **Calculate the F-statistic, $F = \dfrac{\dfrac{R_{\widehat{\varepsilon}^2}^2}{2}}{\dfrac{\left(1 - R_{\widehat{\varepsilon}^2}^2\right)}{n-3}}$, or the chi-squared statistic,**

$\chi^2 = nR_{\widehat{\varepsilon}^2}^2.$

The degrees of freedom for the F-test are equal to 2 in the numerator and $n-3$ in the denominator. The degrees of freedom for the chi-squared test are 2. If either of these test statistics is significant, then you have evidence of heteroskedasticity. If not, you fail to reject the null hypothesis of homoskedasticity.

Imagine that you're estimating a model with the natural log of Major League Baseball players' contract value as the dependent variable and several player characteristics as independent variables. (See the preceding section for more detail.) When you plug this information into STATA (which lets you run a White test via a specialized command), the program retains the predicted Y values, estimates the auxiliary regression internally, and reports the chi-squared test. Figure 11-6 shows the resulting output, which suggests you should reject the homoskedasticity hypothesis.

Although the White test provides a flexible functional form that's useful for identifying nearly any pattern of heteroskedasticity, it's not useful for determining how to correct or adjust the model for heteroskedasticity.

. regress ln_real_con_val slg_3_avg ab_3_avg tenure age

Source	SS	df	MS
Model	428.083421	4	107.020855
Residual	291.18819	325	.895963662
Total	719.271611	329	2.1862359

Number of obs = 330
F(4, 325) = 119.45
Prob > F = 0.0000
R-squared = 0.5952
Adj R-squared = 0.5902
Root MSE = .94655

ln_real_co~l	Coef.	Std. Err.	t	P>|t|	[95% Conf.	Interval]
slg_3_avg	6.209006	.7695022	8.07	0.000	4.695172	7.72284
ab_3_avg	.0049325	.0004016	12.28	0.000	.0041425	.0057225
tenure	-.0376795	.0268191	-1.40	0.161	-.0904404	.0150813
age	-.1050854	.0146173	-7.19	0.000	-.1338419	-.0763289
_cons	14.29176	.5891517	24.26	0.000	13.13273	15.45079

Figure 11-6: STATA output of OLS regression followed by a White test for heteroskedasticity.

. estat imtest, white

White's test for Ho: homoskedasticity
against Ha: unrestricted heteroskedasticity

chi2(14) = 112.93
Prob > chi2 = 0.0000

Trying out the Goldfeld-Quandt test

The Goldfeld-Quandt (GQ) test begins by assuming that a defining point exists and can be used to differentiate the variance of the error term. Sample observations are divided into two groups, and evidence of heteroskedasticity is based on a comparison of the residual sum of squares (*RSS*) using the *F*-statistic.

The assumption is that the researcher can determine the appropriate criteria to separate the sample. Typically, a predetermined value for one of the independent variables is used as a threshold, which places some observations in Group A and the other observations in Group B.

Most econometrics software doesn't let you perform a GQ test automatically, but you can use software to conduct this test by taking these simple steps:

1. **Estimate your model separately for each group and obtain the residual sum of squares for Group A (RSS_A) and the residual sum of squares for Group B (RSS_B).**

2. **Compute the *F*-statistic by**

$$F = \frac{\dfrac{RSS_A}{n-p-1}}{\dfrac{RSS_B}{n-p-1}}$$

The null hypothesis for the GQ test is homoskedasticity. The larger the *F*-statistic, the more evidence you'll have against the homoskedasticity assumption and the more likely you have heteroskedasticity (different variance for the two groups).

Assume for a moment that you're estimating a model with the natural log of Major League Baseball players' contract value as the dependent variable and several player characteristics as independent variables. Three-year averages for slugging percentages *(slg_3_avg)* and at-bats *(ab_3_avg)*, age, and tenure (the number of years a player has been with his current team) are the independent variables. You can arbitrarily divide the sample by the average number of at-bats. Players in Group A have below-average at-bats, and players in Group B have above-average at-bats. The *F*-statistic in Figure 11-7, which shows the process of performing a GQ test in STATA, suggests that the difference in the *RSS* for the two groups is marginally significant in a one-tailed test (*p*-value = 0.0730).

```
. regress ln_real_con_val slg_3_avg ab_3_avg tenure age
```

Source	SS	df	MS				Number of obs =	330
							F(4, 325) =	119.45
Model	428.083421	4	107.020855				Prob > F =	0.0000
Residual	291.18819	325	.895963662				R-squared =	0.5952
							Adj R-squared =	0.5902
Total	719.271611	329	2.1862359				Root MSE =	.94655

ln_real_co~l	Coef.	Std. Err.	t	P>|t|	[95% Conf.	Interval]
slg_3_avg	6.209006	.7695022	8.07	0.000	4.695172	7.72284
ab_3_avg	.0049325	.0004016	12.28	0.000	.0041425	.0057225
tenure	-.0376795	.0268191	-1.40	0.161	-.0904404	.0150813
age	-.1050854	.0146173	-7.19	0.000	-.1338419	-.0763289
_cons	14.29176	.5891517	24.26	0.000	13.13273	15.45079

```
. predict uhat, resid
(66 missing values generated)

. estat sum ab_3_avg

  Estimation sample regress          Number of obs =      330
```

Variable	Mean	Std. Dev.	Min	Max
ab_3_avg	322.8843	146.7064	5	677.667

```
. gen groupA=ab_3_avg<323

. sdtest uhatsq, by(groupA)

Variance ratio test
```

Group	Obs	Mean	Std. Err.	Std. Dev.	[95% Conf.	Interval]
0	161	1.081988	.1045421	1.326491	.8755279	1.288449
1	169	.6922372	.1143666	1.486766	.4664564	.918018
combined	330	.8823885	.0782874	1.422161	.7283814	1.036396

```
    ratio = sd(0) / sd(1)                                  f =   0.7960
Ho: ratio = 1                               degrees of freedom =  160, 168

Ha: ratio < 1              Ha: ratio != 1                  Ha: ratio > 1
Pr(F < f) = 0.0730      2*Pr(F < f) = 0.1460           Pr(F > f) = 0.9270
```

Figure 11-7: STATA output of OLS regression followed by a Goldfeld-Quandt test for heteroskedasticity.

A weakness of the GQ test is that the result is dependent on the criteria chosen for separating the sample measurements into their respective groups. This process is often quite arbitrary, so failing to find evidence of heteroskedasticity in one test doesn't rule it out with different criteria used for separating the sample. Consequently, the GQ test doesn't provide any guidance for correcting or adjusting the model for heteroskedasticity, which is one reason why applied econometricians typically don't rely on it in order to test for heteroskedasticity.

Conducting the Park test

The Park test begins by assuming a specific model of the heteroskedastic process. Specifically, it assumes that the heteroskedasticity may be proportional to some power of an independent variable (X_k) in the model. This assumption can be expressed as $\sigma_{i\varepsilon}^2 = \sigma_\varepsilon^2 X_{ik}^\alpha$.

You can obtain a linearized version of the Park model by using a log transformation:

$$\ln\sigma_{i\varepsilon}^2 = \ln\sigma_\varepsilon^2 + \alpha\ln X_{ik} + u_i$$

Because the values for $\sigma_{i\varepsilon}^2$ aren't known in practice, your $\hat{\varepsilon}_i^2$ are calculated from the residuals and used as proxies for $\sigma_{i\varepsilon}^2$.

Most econometrics software programs don't have commands that allow you to automatically perform a Park test. However, you can perform the test by following these steps:

1. **Estimate the model $Y_i = \beta_0 + \beta_1 X_{i1} + \ldots + \beta_p X_{ip} + \varepsilon_i$ using OLS.**

2. **Obtain the squared residuals, $\hat{\varepsilon}_i^2$, after estimating your model.**

3. **Estimate the model $\ln\hat{\varepsilon}_i^2 = \gamma + \alpha\ln X_{ik} + u_i$ using OLS.**

4. **Examine the statistical significance of α using the t-statistic: $t = \dfrac{\hat{\alpha}}{\hat{\sigma}_{\hat{\alpha}}}$.**

The value of γ from estimating the regression $\ln\hat{\varepsilon}_i^2 = \gamma + \alpha\ln X_{ik} + u_i$ is an estimate of the constant (homoskedastic) portion of the error variance. Consequently, if the estimate of the α coefficient is statistically significant, then you have evidence of heteroskedasticity. If not, you fail to reject the null hypothesis of homoskedasticity.

Using data from Major League Baseball players once again, you can estimate a model with the natural log of the player's contract value as the dependent variable and several player characteristics as independent variables. The independent variables include three-year averages for the player's slugging percentage *(slg_3_avg)* and at-bats *(ab_3_avg)*, the player's age, and the player's tenure *(years)* with the current team. In Figure 11-8, I illustrate the step-by-step process of performing a Park test in STATA. My assumption is that if there's heteroskedasticity, then *at-bats* is the variable responsible for it. In this case, the coefficient for the variable *lnabavg* (using the natural log of *ab_3_avg* as specified by the Park test) is statistically significant with a *p*-value of 0.03. Therefore, I'd reject the hypothesis of homoskedasticity.

```
. regress ln_real_con_val slg_3_avg ab_3_avg tenure age
```

Source	SS	df	MS
Model	428.083421	4	107.020855
Residual	291.18819	325	.895963662
Total	719.271611	329	2.1862359

```
Number of obs =    330
F( 4,  325) = 119.45
Prob > F      = 0.0000
R-squared     = 0.5952
Adj R-squared = 0.5902
Root MSE      = .94655
```

ln_real_co~l	Coef.	Std. Err.	t	P>|t|	[95% Conf.	Interval]
slg_3_avg	6.209006	.7695022	8.07	0.000	4.695172	7.72284
ab_3_avg	.0049325	.0004016	12.28	0.000	.0041425	.0057225
tenure	-.0376795	.0268191	-1.40	0.161	-.0904404	.0150813
age	-.1050854	.0146173	-7.19	0.000	-.1338419	-.0763289
_cons	14.29176	.5891517	24.26	0.000	13.13273	15.45079

```
. predict uhat, resid
(66 missing values generated)

. gen uhatsq = uhat^2
(66 missing values generated)

. gen lnuhatsq = log(uhatsq)
(66 missing values generated)

. gen lnabavg = log(ab_3_avg)

. regress lnuhatsq lnabavg
```

Figure 11-8:
STATA output of OLS regression followed by a Park test for heteroskedasticity.

Source	SS	df	MS
Model	19.0093778	1	19.0093778
Residual	1366.6488	328	4.1666122
Total	1385.65818	329	4.21172699

```
Number of obs =    330
F( 1,  328) =   4.56
Prob > F      = 0.0334
R-squared     = 0.0137
Adj R-squared = 0.0107
Root MSE      = 2.0412
```

lnuhatsq	Coef.	Std. Err.	t	P>|t|	[95% Conf.	Interval]
lnabavg	.409902	.1919056	2.14	0.033	.0323809	.7874232
_cons	-3.627648	1.088863	-3.33	0.001	-5.769685	-1.485611

The Park test's weakness is that it assumes the heteroskedasticity has a particular functional form. Furthermore, identifying heteroskedasticity with one independent variable doesn't rule out the fact that other variables may also play a role.

Although discussions of the Park test are still common in many econometrics textbooks, applied econometricians typically rely on other alternatives to test for heteroskedasticity, such as the Breusch-Pagan or White tests.

Correcting Your Regression Model for the Presence of Heteroskedasticity

After you determine that heteroskedasticity is likely, you can modify the estimation of your econometric model to obtain accurate standard errors. The two most common solutions to heteroskedasticity are weighted least squares and robust standard errors. I tell you all about both solutions in the following sections.

Weighted least squares (WLS)

The *weighted least squares* (WLS) technique transforms the original (heteroskedastic) model into a homoskedastic one by using information about the nature of the heteroskedasticity. The goal of the WLS transformation is to make the error term in the original econometric model homoskedastic. First, you assume that the heteroskedasticity is determined proportionally from some function of the independent variables. Then you use knowledge of this relationship to divide both sides of the original model by the component of heteroskedasticity that give the error term a constant variance.

Suppose your original model takes the form $Y_i = \beta_0 + \beta_1 X_{i1} + \ldots + \beta_p X_{ip} + \varepsilon_i$ and that the variance of the error term is defined by $Var(\varepsilon \mid \mathbf{X}_i) = \sigma_\varepsilon^2 h(\mathbf{X}_i)$, where $\mathbf{X}_i$ is a vector of some or all of the independent variables and $h(\mathbf{X}_i)$ represents the portion of the error variance that's unique to each observation and is some function of the independent variables. Notice that this violates the assumption of homoskedasticity because the error isn't constant and depends on the value of $h(\mathbf{X}_i)$, which changes as the value of any independent variable changes.

Because the variance of the error is $\sigma_\varepsilon^2 h(\mathbf{X}_i)$, you can generate a homoskedastic variance by dividing both sides of the original model by $\sqrt{h(\mathbf{X}_i)}$. This results in

$$\frac{Y_i}{\sqrt{h(\mathbf{X}_i)}} = \frac{\beta_0}{\sqrt{h(\mathbf{X}_i)}} + \beta_1 \frac{X_{i1}}{\sqrt{h(\mathbf{X}_i)}} + \ldots + \beta_p \frac{X_{ip}}{\sqrt{h(\mathbf{X}_i)}} + \frac{\varepsilon_i}{\sqrt{h(\mathbf{X}_i)}}$$

$$Y_i^* = \beta_0^* + \beta_1^* X_{i1}^* + \ldots + \beta_p^* X_{ip}^* + \varepsilon_i^*$$

which satisfies the homoskedasticity assumption because

$$Var(\varepsilon_i^*) = Var\left(\frac{\varepsilon_i}{\sqrt{h(\mathbf{X}_i)}}\right) = \frac{1}{h(\mathbf{X}_i)} Var(\varepsilon_i) = \sigma_\varepsilon^2$$

The β's are the WLS estimators and are a specific type of *generalized least squares* (GLS) estimator (In this case, the GLS estimator is used to correct for heteroskedasticity, but you can also use a GLS estimator to address autocorrelation issues, as I explain in Chapter 12).

The objective of OLS is $\min \sum \left(Y_i - \hat{\beta}_0 - \hat{\beta}_1 X_{i1} - \dots - \hat{\beta}_p X_{ip} \right)^2$. However, for WLS, the objective is $\min \sum \dfrac{\left(Y_i - \hat{\beta}_0 - \hat{\beta}_1 X_{i1} - \dots - \hat{\beta}_p X_{ip} \right)^2}{h(\mathbf{X}_i)}$ so $h_i = h(\mathbf{X}_i)$ are the weights.

In practice, knowing the exact functional form of $h(\mathbf{X}_i)$ is impossible. In applied settings, you can assume a functional form and estimate each h_i. That is, you use $\hat{h}_i$ values for weighting in the GLS transformation instead of h_i. Estimators using this procedure are known as *feasible generalized least squares* (FGLS) estimators.

The exponential function is the most common approach to modeling heteroskedasticity. This approach assumes that

$$Var\left(\varepsilon \mid \mathbf{X}_i \right) = \sigma_\varepsilon^2 \exp\left(\alpha_0 + \alpha_1 X_{i1} + \dots + \alpha_p X_{ip} \right)$$

which implies

$$\varepsilon_i^2 = \sigma_\varepsilon^2 \exp\left(\alpha_0 + \alpha_1 X_{i1} + \dots + \alpha_p X_{ip} \right) u_i$$

and

$$\ln \varepsilon_i^2 = \gamma + \delta_1 X_{i1} + \dots + \delta_p X_{ip} + v_i$$

In practice, you replace the unobserved error, ε, with the OLS residual.

You can use WLS with a FGLS procedure by applying the following steps:

1. **Estimate the original model, $Y_i = \beta_0 + \beta_1 X_{i1} + \dots + \beta_p X_{ip} + \varepsilon_i$, and obtain the residuals, $\hat{\varepsilon}_i$.**

2. **Square the residuals and take their natural log to generate $\ln \hat{\varepsilon}_i^2$.**

3. **Estimate the regression $\ln \hat{\varepsilon}_i^2 = \gamma + \delta_1 X_{i1} + \dots + \delta_p X_{ip} + v_i$ or $\ln \hat{\varepsilon}_i^2 = \gamma + \phi_1 \hat{Y}_i + \phi_2 \hat{Y}_i^2 + u_i$ and obtain the fitted values: $\hat{g}_i = \hat{\gamma} + \hat{\phi}_1 \hat{Y}_i + \hat{\phi}_2 \hat{Y}_i^2$.**

4. **Take the inverse natural log of the fitted residuals $\exp\left(\hat{g}_i \right)$ to obtain $\hat{h}_i$.**

5. **Estimate the regression $Y_i = \beta_0 + \beta_1 X_{i1} + \ldots + \beta_p X_{ip} + \varepsilon_i$ by WLS using $\hat{h}_i$ as weights.**

If the proposed model of heteroskedasticity, $h_i = h(\mathbf{X}_i)$, is misspecified, then WLS may not be more efficient than OLS. The problem is that misspecification of the heteroskedasticity is difficult to identify.

Using data from Major League Baseball players, you can estimate a model using the natural log of the player's contract value as the dependent variable and several player characteristics as independent variables, including 3-year averages for slugging percentages and at-bats, player age, and player tenure on his current team. You can use STATA to perform WLS by using a standard FGLS procedure. Figure 11-9 shows the resulting output. As you can see, the WLS estimates are similar to the OLS estimates, but they're not identical. All the coefficients have the same sign before and after the heteroskedasticity correction. In this example, all the coefficients that were statistically significant with OLS remain significant with WLS. However, the effect of tenure is marginally significant with WLS but wasn't significant with OLS.

If your WLS coefficients are drastically different from the OLS coefficients, you should be concerned that the primary issue isn't heteroskedasticity. A large difference between OLS and WLS coefficients is more likely to imply that the model suffers from functional form specification bias (you can turn to Chapter 8 for more details about this type of bias).

Robust standard errors (also known as White-corrected standard errors)

The calculation of *robust standard errors* is the most popular remedy for heteroskedasticity. It uses the OLS coefficient estimates but adjusts the OLS standard errors for heteroskedasticity without transforming the model being estimated. The *robust standard errors* are also known as *White-corrected standard errors* and *heteroskedasticity-corrected standard errors.* The strength of this method is that it's able to deal with heteroskedasticity without making assumptions about the functional form of heteroskedasticity.

```
. regress ln_real_con_val slg_3_avg ab_3_avg tenure age
```

Source	SS	df	MS
Model	428.083421	4	107.020855
Residual	291.18819	325	.895963662
Total	719.271611	329	2.1862359

Number of obs = 330
F(4, 325) = 119.45
Prob > F = 0.0000
R-squared = 0.5952
Adj R-squared = 0.5902
Root MSE = .94655

ln_real_co~l	Coef.	Std. Err.	t	P>|t|	[95% Conf.	Interval]
slg_3_avg	6.209006	.7695022	8.07	0.000	4.695172	7.72284
ab_3_avg	.0049325	.0004016	12.28	0.000	.0041425	.0057225
tenure	-.0376795	.0268191	-1.40	0.161	-.0904404	.0150813
age	-.1050854	.0146173	-7.19	0.000	-.1338419	-.0763289
_cons	14.29176	.5891517	24.26	0.000	13.13273	15.45079

```
. predict uhat, resid
(66 missing values generated)

. gen uhatsq = uhat^2
(66 missing values generated)

. gen lnuhatsq = log(uhatsq)
(66 missing values generated)

. regress lnuhatsq slg_3_avg ab_3_avg tenure age
```

Source	SS	df	MS
Model	77.9804547	4	19.4951137
Residual	1307.67772	325	4.02362377
Total	1385.65818	329	4.21172699

Number of obs = 330
F(4, 325) = 4.85
Prob > F = 0.0008
R-squared = 0.0563
Adj R-squared = 0.0447
Root MSE = 2.0059

lnuhatsq	Coef.	Std. Err.	t	P>|t|	[95% Conf.	Interval]
slg_3_avg	2.539347	1.630697	1.56	0.120	-.6687073	5.747401
ab_3_avg	.000987	.000851	1.16	0.247	-.0006872	.0026612
tenure	-.0334463	.0568338	-0.59	0.557	-.145255	.0783623
age	-.0973393	.0309764	-3.14	0.002	-.1582789	-.0363997
_cons	.7058304	1.248506	0.57	0.572	-1.750343	3.162004

```
. predict ghat, xb
(59 missing values generated)

. gen hhat = exp(ghat)
(59 missing values generated)

. regress ln_real_con_val slg_3_avg ab_3_avg tenure age [aweight = 1/hhat]
(sum of wgt is   1.3768e+03)
```

Figure 11-9:
Using
STATA to
produce
weighted
least
squares
(WLS)
estimates.

Source	SS	df	MS
Model	274.340707	4	68.5851767
Residual	232.509416	325	.715413587
Total	506.850123	329	1.54057788

Number of obs = 330
F(4, 325) = 95.87
Prob > F = 0.0000
R-squared = 0.5413
Adj R-squared = 0.5356
Root MSE = .84582

ln_real_co~l	Coef.	Std. Err.	t	P>|t|	[95% Conf.	Interval]
slg_3_avg	4.752839	.7103876	6.69	0.000	3.3553	6.150377
ab_3_avg	.0046397	.0003822	12.14	0.000	.0038879	.0053916
tenure	-.0364669	.0197548	-1.85	0.066	-.0753302	.0023964
age	-.0817186	.0125148	-6.53	0.000	-.1063388	-.0570984
_cons	14.15933	.4957018	28.56	0.000	13.18414	15.13451

In a model with one independent variable and homoskedasticity, the variance of the estimator can be reduced to $Var\left(\hat{\beta}_1\right) = \sigma_\varepsilon^2 \sum c_i^2$. However, with heteroskedasticity, the variance of the estimator is $Var\left(\hat{\beta}_1\right) = \sum c_i^2 \sigma_{i\varepsilon}^2$.

In the real world, the $\sigma_{i\varepsilon}^2$ terms aren't directly observable. In applied settings, the squared residuals $(\hat{\varepsilon}_i^2)$ are used as estimates of $\sigma_{i\varepsilon}^2$. Using these values to estimate standard errors of the OLS estimators produces the robust standard errors.

In a model with one independent variable, the robust standard error is

$$se\left(\hat{\beta}_1\right)_{HC} = \sqrt{\frac{\sum\left(X_i - \bar{X}\right)\hat{\varepsilon}_i^2}{\left(\sum\left(X_i - \bar{X}\right)^2\right)^2}}$$

Generalizing this result to a multiple regression model, the robust standard error is

$$se\left(\hat{\beta}_k\right)_{HC} = \sqrt{\frac{\sum \hat{w}_{ik}^2 \hat{\varepsilon}_i^2}{\left(\sum \hat{w}_{ik}^2\right)^2}}$$

where the $\hat{w}_{ik}^2$ are the residuals obtained from the auxiliary regression of X_j on all the other independent variables.

Here's how to calculate robust standard errors:

1. **Estimate your original multivariate model,** $Y_i = \beta_0 + \beta_1 X_{i1} + \ldots + \beta_p X_{ip} + \varepsilon_i$, **and obtain the squared residuals,** $\hat{\varepsilon}_i^2$.

2. **Estimate p auxiliary regressions of each independent variable on all the other independent variables and retain all p squared residuals** $(\hat{w}_{ik}^2)$.

3. **For any independent variable, calculate the robust standard errors:**

$$se\left(\hat{\beta}_k\right)_{HC} = \sqrt{\frac{\sum \hat{w}_{ik}^2 \hat{\varepsilon}_i^2}{\left(\sum \hat{w}_{ik}^2\right)^2}}$$

Most econometrics software programs allow you to produce the robust standard errors with a simple command that instantaneously performs all the preceding steps.

The use of robust standard errors to compute t-statistics, confidence intervals, and p-values relies on asymptotic properties. That is, the reliability of hypothesis testing using robust standard errors improves with larger sample sizes.

To see what I mean, imagine that you're working again with the same data for MLB players. (See the preceding sections for more detail.) Using STATA to obtain robust standard errors, you simply need to utilize the "robust" option with the basic "regress" command.

Figure 11-10 shows the standard results along with the robust standard errors. Notice that both sets of results have identical coefficients. However, the robust standard errors change the t-statistics, confidence intervals, and p-values for the coefficients. Some of the standard errors increase with the heteroskedasticity correction and others decrease. In this example, all the coefficients that were originally significant remain significant with the heteroskedasticity correction. However, the effect of *tenure* was originally insignificant, but is marginally significant using the robust standard error. *Note:* The goal isn't to make all coefficients statistically significant, but to obtain more accurate standard errors in the presence of heteroskedasticity. If some standard errors increase to the point of making some coefficients insignificant that were previously significant, then you should accept this as part of your correction and more legitimate results.

. regress ln_real_con_val slg_3_avg ab_3_avg tenure age

Source	SS	df	MS
Model	428.083421	4	107.020855
Residual	291.18819	325	.895963662
Total	719.271611	329	2.1862359

Number of obs = 330
F(4, 325) = 119.45
Prob > F = 0.0000
R-squared = 0.5952
Adj R-squared = 0.5902
Root MSE = .94655

ln_real_co~l	Coef.	Std. Err.	t	P>|t|	[95% Conf.	Interval]
slg_3_avg	6.209006	.7695022	8.07	0.000	4.695172	7.72284
ab_3_avg	.0049325	.0004016	12.28	0.000	.0041425	.0057225
tenure	-.0376795	.0268191	-1.40	0.161	-.0904484	.0150813
age	-.1050854	.0146173	-7.19	0.000	-.1338419	-.0763289
_cons	14.29176	.5891517	24.26	0.000	13.13273	15.45079

. regress ln_real_con_val slg_3_avg ab_3_avg tenure age, robust

Linear regression

Number of obs = 330
F(4, 325) = 126.92
Prob > F = 0.0000
R-squared = 0.5952
Root MSE = .94655

ln_real_co~l	Coef.	Robust Std. Err.	t	P>|t|	[95% Conf.	Interval]
slg_3_avg	6.209006	1.091458	5.69	0.000	4.061791	8.356221
ab_3_avg	.0049325	.0004039	12.21	0.000	.0041379	.0057271
tenure	-.0376795	.0205547	-1.83	0.068	-.0781167	.0027576
age	-.1050854	.0174495	-6.02	0.000	-.1394137	-.0707571
_cons	14.29176	.8939651	15.99	0.000	12.53307	16.05045

Figure 11-10: Using STATA to produce robust (heteroske-dasticity-corrected) standard errors.

Numerous versions of robust standard errors exist for the purpose of improving the statistical properties of the heteroskedasticity correction. Applied econometricians usually rely on any version calculated by their econometrics software, though, because no form of robust standard error is preferred above all others.

Chapter 12

Autocorrelation

- -

In This Chapter

▶ Examining autocorrelation patterns

▶ Revealing the consequences of autocorrelation

▶ Testing for autocorrelation

▶ Correcting econometric models when autocorrelation is present

- -

*A*utocorrelation, also known as *serial correlation,* may exist in a regression model when the order of the observations in the data is relevant or important. In other words, with time-series (and sometimes panel or logitudinal) data, autocorrelation is a concern. When a regression model is estimated using data of this nature, the value of the error in one period may be related to the value of the error in another period (autocorrelation), which results in a violation of a classical linear regression model (CLRM) assumption. (I tell you all about these in Chapter 6.)

In this chapter, you discover exactly why autocorrelation is problematic, how to identify different autocorrelation patterns, and how to modify a standard regression model in the presence of autocorrelation.

Examining Patterns of Autocorrelation

As I explain in Chapter 6, most of the CLRM assumptions that allow econometricians to prove the desirable properties of the OLS estimators (the Gauss-Markov theorem) directly involve characteristics of the error term. One of the CLRM assumptions deals with the relationship between values of the error term. Specifically, the CLRM assumes there's no autocorrelation. *No autocorrelation* refers to a situation in which no identifiable relationship exists between the values of the error term. Econometricians express no autocorrelation as $Cov(\varepsilon_t, \varepsilon_s) = 0$ or $Corr(\varepsilon_t, \varepsilon_s) = 0$ for all $t \neq s$.

Figure 12-1 shows the regression of a model satisfying the CLRM assumption of no autocorrelation. As you can see, when the error term exhibits no autocorrelation, the positive and negative error values are random.

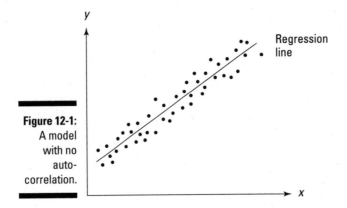

Figure 12-1: A model with no auto-correlation.

When autocorrelation does occur, it takes either positive or negative form. Of course, autocorrelation can be incorrectly identified as well. The following sections explain how to distinguish between positive and negative correlation as well as how to avoid falsely stating that autocorrelation exists.

Positive versus negative autocorrelation

If autocorrelation is present, positive autocorrelation is the most likely outcome. *Positive autocorrelation* occurs when an error of a given sign tends to be followed by an error of the same sign. For example, positive errors are usually followed by positive errors, and negative errors are usually followed by negative errors.

Positive autocorrelation is expressed as $Corr(\varepsilon_t, \varepsilon_s) > 0$ for all $t \neq s$.

The positive autocorrelation depicted in Figure 12-2 is only one among several possible patterns. An error term with a sequencing of positive and negative error values usually indicates positive autocorrelation. *Sequencing* refers to a situation where most positive errors are followed or preceded by additional positive errors or when negative errors are followed or preceded by other negative errors.

Although unlikely, negative autocorrelation is also possible. *Negative autocorrelation* occurs when an error of a given sign tends to be followed by an error of the opposite sign. For instance, positive errors are usually followed by negative errors and negative errors are usually followed by positive errors.

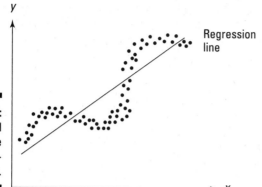

Negative autocorrelation is expressed as $Corr(\varepsilon_t, \varepsilon_s) < 0$ for all $t \neq s$.

Figure 12-3 illustrates the typical pattern of negative autocorrelation. An error term with a *switching* of positive and negative error values usually indicates negative autocorrelation. A switching pattern is the opposite of sequencing, so most positive errors tend to be followed or preceded by negative errors and vice versa.

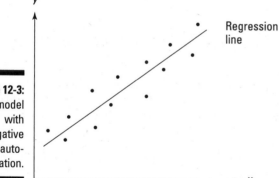

Whether you have positive or negative autocorrelation, in the presence of autocorrelation, the OLS estimators may not be efficient (that is, they may not achieve the smallest variance). In addition, the estimated standard errors of the coefficients are biased, which results in unreliable hypothesis tests (*t*-statistics). The OLS estimates, however, remain unbiased.

Misspecification and autocorrelation

When you're drawing conclusions about autocorrelation using the error pattern, all other CLRM assumptions must hold, especially the assumption that the model is correctly specified. If a model isn't correctly specified, you may mistakenly identify the model as suffering from autocorrelation.

To see what I mean, take a look at Figure 12-4, which illustrates a scenario where the model has been inappropriately specified as linear when the relationship is nonlinear. The misspecification shown here would end up producing an error pattern that resembles positive autocorrelation.

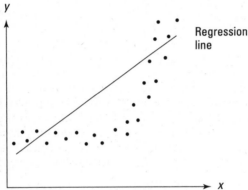

Figure 12-4: A misspecified model can have a residual pattern that gives the appearance of autocorrelation.

I advise you to perform misspecification checks (like the ones covered in Chapter 8) if there's evidence of autocorrelation and you're uncertain about the accuracy of the specification. Misspecification is a more serious issue than autocorrelation because you can't prove the OLS estimators to be unbiased if the model isn't correctly specified.

Illustrating the Effect of Autoregressive Errors

You tend to encounter autocorrelated errors in time-series models where the goal is to describe the path of a variable Y in terms of contemporaneous (and/or lagged) factors X. A time-series model has the form

$$Y_t = \beta_0 + \beta_1 X_{t1} + \ldots + \beta_p X_{tp} + \varepsilon_t$$

where ε_t represents a random shock that occurs at time t. It's entirely plausible that individuals (or firms, or households, or what have you) don't react to that shock completely in the period in which it occurs. In this case, the error term is correlated such that $Corr(\varepsilon_t, \varepsilon_s) \neq 0$.

Knowledge that the error term is correlated is too general to be of any use. In order to determine the precise consequences of autocorrelation, a more specific pattern to the autocorrelation must be assumed. Typically, autocorrelation is assumed to be represented by a *first-order autoregression;* also known as an AR(1). In general, an autoregressive process occurs any time the value for a variable in one period can be modeled as a function of values of the same variable in previous periods. In the specific case of autocorrelation, the random variable displaying this characteristic is the error term.

In an AR(1), the model $Y_t = \beta_0 + \beta_1 X_{t1} + ... + \beta_p X_{tp} + \varepsilon_t$ has an error term of the form

$$\varepsilon_t = \rho\varepsilon_{t-1} + u_t$$

where ρ represents the relationship between the error terms in period t and $t-1$ and u_t is a random error that satisfies the CLRM assumptions; namely $E(u_t \mid \varepsilon_{t-1}) = 0$, $Var(u_t \mid \varepsilon_{t-1}) = \sigma_u^2$, and $Cov(u_t, u_s) = 0$ for all $t \neq s$. This equation also assumes that $-1 < \rho < 1$, which is known as the *stationarity assumption* (I explain the importance of this assumption in the next section). If $\rho = 0$, there's no autocorrelation and the original model satisfies the CLRM assumption.

Autocorrelation processes can be more elaborate than an AR(1); for example, an AR(2), AR(3), or AR(4) is possible with quarterly time series, and an AR(12) can be observed with monthly data. The number inside the parentheses represents the number of lags of the error term that are correlated with the current value. These patterns, however, are far less common than an AR(1) and don't change the fundamental point that autocorrelated errors cause bias in the standard errors and *t*-statistics.

You can prove the zero conditional mean for an AR(1) error by repetitive substitution into $\varepsilon_t = \rho\varepsilon_{t-1} + u_t$ as follows:

$$\varepsilon_t = \rho(\rho\varepsilon_{t-2} + u_{t-1}) + u_t = \rho^2\varepsilon_{t-2} + \rho u_{t-1} + u_t$$

$$\varepsilon_t = \rho^2(\rho\varepsilon_{t-3} + u_{t-2}) + \rho u_{t-1} + u_t = \rho^3\varepsilon_{t-3} + \rho^2 u_{t-2} + \rho u_{t-1} + u_t$$

By continuing to substitute the autoregressive process and organizing the right-hand side in ascending order of the power of u, you obtain

$$\varepsilon_t = u_t + \rho u_{t-1} + \rho^2 u_{t-2} + \rho^3 u_{t-3} + ...$$

Since $E(u_t) = 0$, then $E(\varepsilon_t) = 0$.

The variance of an AR(1) error depends on the relationship between the error in period t and the error in period $t-1$. OLS doesn't appropriately account for this, so the resulting standard errors will be biased.

After repetitive substitution, you can express the variance properties of an AR(1) error term as

$$Var(\varepsilon_t) = \sigma_u^2 + \rho^2\sigma_u^2 + \rho^4\sigma_u^2 + \rho^6\sigma_u^2 + \ldots$$

The stationarity assumption ($|\rho| < 1$) is necessary to constrain the variance from becoming an infinite value.

The stationary assumption implies that $Var(\varepsilon_t) = Var(\varepsilon_{t-1}) = \sigma_\varepsilon^2$, because $\rho^s \to 0$ as $s \to \infty$. Using the result that $Var(\varepsilon_t) = Var(\varepsilon_{t-1}) = \sigma_\varepsilon^2$ allows you to form the following simple expression for the variance of ε_t:

$$Var(\varepsilon_t) = \rho^2 Var(\varepsilon_{t-1}) + Var(\varepsilon_t) + 2\rho Cov(\varepsilon_{t-1}, u_t)$$

Using the CLRM assumptions for u_t allows you to reduce the variance of ε_t to

$$\sigma_\varepsilon^2 = \rho^2\sigma_\varepsilon^2 + \sigma_u^2 + 0$$

$$\sigma_\varepsilon^2 = \frac{\sigma_u^2}{1-\rho^2}$$

OLS assumes no autocorrelation; that is, $\rho = 0$ in the expression $\sigma_\varepsilon^2 = \frac{\sigma_u^2}{1-\rho^2}$.

Consequently, in the presence of autocorrelation, the estimated variances and standard errors from OLS are underestimated.

Analyzing Residuals to Test for Autocorrelation

Serial correlation in the error term (autocorrelation) is a common problem for OLS regression estimation, especially with time-series and panel data. However, you usually have no way of knowing in advance if it's going to be present, and theory doesn't usually help you anticipate its presence. Consequently, you have to inspect your residuals to determine if they're characterized by autocorrelation. You can either inspect your residuals visually or conduct one of three special tests, which I explain in the following sections.

Taking the visual route: Graphical inspection of residuals

Looking over your residuals visually is an easy, informal way of checking for autocorrelation, but it should only be used as a complement, and not a substitute, for formal statistical tests of autocorrelation. Graphical examinations of residuals don't provide conclusive evidence of the existence or nonexistence of autocorrelation. If you truly suspect autocorrelation, consider conducting one of the more formal statistical tests covered in the following three sections.

Using graphs for an examination of autocorrelation requires that you retain your OLS residuals and sort the data chronologically. Then you construct a scatter diagram, with the variable capturing your units of time on the horizontal axis and the residual values from your OLS regression along the vertical axis.

Figure 12-5a illustrates the typical pattern of the residuals if the error term isn't plagued by autocorrelation, Figure 12-5b exhibits the potential existence of positive autocorrelation, and Figure 12-5c displays negative autocorrelation.

Using the normal distribution to identify residual sequences: The run test

The *run test,* also known as the *Geary test,* uses the sequences of positive and negative residuals to test the hypothesis of no autocorrelation. You want to use the run test if you're uncertain about the nature of the autoregressive process, because no assumptions about the number of lags or fixed parameters (ρ values) describing the autocorrelation are necessary to perform the test.

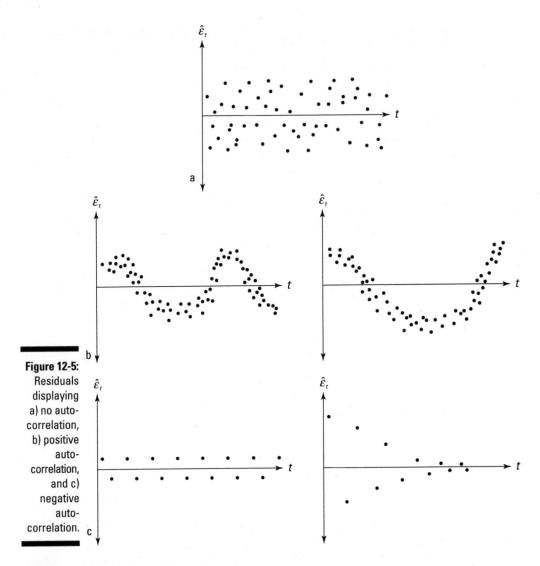

Figure 12-5:
Residuals
displaying
a) no auto-
correlation,
b) positive
auto-
correlation,
and c)
negative
auto-
correlation.

A *run* is defined as a sequence of positive or negative residuals. The hypothesis of no autocorrelation isn't sustainable if the residuals have too many or too few runs.

The most common version of the test assumes that runs are distributed normally. If the assumption of no autocorrelation is sustainable, with 95 percent confidence, then the number of runs should be between

$$\mu_r \pm 1.96\sigma_r$$

where μ_r is the expected number of runs and σ_r is the standard deviation. These values are calculated by

$$\mu = \frac{2T_1T_2}{T_1+T_2} + 1$$

and

$$\sigma_r = \sqrt{\frac{2T_1T_2\left(2T_1T_2 - T_1 - T_2\right)}{\left(T_1+T_2\right)^2\left(T_1+T_2-1\right)}}$$

where r is the number of observed runs (sequences of residuals with one given sign, positive or negative), T_1 is the number of positive residuals, T_2 is the number of negative residuals, and T is the total number of observations.

To put the run test to work, suppose you have a dataset with 32 observations sorted chronologically and, after estimating your model using OLS, the signs of the residuals from the first to the last observation are as follows (note that each run is enclosed in parentheses):

$$[(-------)(+ + + + + + + + + + + + + +)(-)(+)(---------)]$$

So you have $T = 32$, $T_1 = 14$, $T_2 = 18$, and $r = 5$. Using that information, you can calculate

$$\mu_r = \frac{2(14)(18)}{14+18} + 1 = 16.75$$

and

$$\sigma_r = \sqrt{\frac{2(14)(18)\left[2(14)(18)-14-18\right]}{(14+18)^2(14+18-1)}} = 2.74$$

The 95 percent confidence interval is $16.75 \pm (1.96)(2.74)$, which implies that you can expect the number of runs to be somewhere between 11 and 22. Because the number of runs observed ($r = 5$) is outside the interval $[11, 22]$, it's unlikely to be a random pattern and the hypothesis of no autocorrelation is rejected. More specifically, in this example, the number of observed runs is less than the lower bound of the confidence interval, so there's evidence of positive autocorrelation.

If the number of observed runs is below the expected interval, it's evidence of positive autocorrelation. On the other hand, if the number of runs exceeds the upper bound of the expected interval, it provides evidence of negative autocorrelation.

In Figure 12-6, I illustrate the step-by-step process of performing a run test in STATA, using yearly sales and inventory data from 1950 to 1991. Prior to performing any time-series operation, I specify which variable captures the time component using the "tsset" command. (Doing so keeps the data organized internally and allows me to perform operations that rely on the order of the data.)

The results in Figure 12-6 place the 95 percent confidence interval for the number of runs in between 16 and 26. Because I have only 11 runs ($r = 11$), the null hypothesis of no autocorrelation is rejected in favor of positive autocorrelation because 11 is less than the lower limit of 16 here. The calculated Z-statistic is less than -1.96, so it's consistent with the confidence interval result.

```
. tsset year
        time variable:  year, 1950 to 1991
                delta:  1 unit

. regress inventories sales

      Source |       SS      df       MS          Number of obs =      42
-------------+------------------------------      F (1,40)      = 49518.79
       Model | 2.7511e+12     1   2.7511e+12      Prob > F      =   0.0000
    Residual | 2.2222e+09    40   55556036.6      R-squared     =   0.9992
-------------+------------------------------      Adj R-squared =   0.9992
       Total | 2.7533e+12    41   6.7153e+10      Root MSE      =   7453.6

------------------------------------------------------------------------------
  inventories |      Coef.   Std. Err.      t    P>|t|     [95% Conf. Interval]
-------------+----------------------------------------------------------------
       sales |   1.554329   .0069849   222.53   0.000     1.540213    1.568446
       _cons |   1668.669   1806.696     0.92   0.361    -1982.799    5320.138
------------------------------------------------------------------------------
```

Figure 12-6:
STATA
output with
a run test
for auto-
correlation.

```
. predict ehat, resid

. runtest ehat, mean
  N(ehat <= -.0000145321800595) = 26
  N(ehat >  -.0000145321800595) = 16
          obs = 42
     N(runs) = 11
           z = -3.25
    Prob>|z| = 0
```

The strength of the run test is that it doesn't impose restrictions on the process generating autocorrelation; AR(1), AR(2), and so on are all possible. This strength, however, is also a weakness. Detection of autocorrelation without any indication of the process doesn't provide any guidance to correct the problem.

Detecting autocorrelation of an AR (1) process: The Durbin-Watson test

The Durbin-Watson (DW) test begins by assuming that if autocorrelation is present, then it can be described by an AR(1) process. Consequently, you use the DW test if the autoregressive process is such that the value of the error in period t depends on its value in period $t - 1$.

In a model such as $Y_t = \beta_0 + \beta_1 X_{t1} + ... + \beta_p X_{tp} + \varepsilon_t$, an AR(1) error term is described by $\varepsilon_t = \rho \varepsilon_{t-1} + u_t$. The actual value of ρ isn't known, so the DW test uses the estimated correlation between the residual in period t and the residual in period $t - 1$ to test for autocorrelation. The value produced by the DW test is called a d statistic and is calculated as follows:

$$d = \frac{\sum_{t=2}^{T}\left(\hat{\varepsilon}_t - \hat{\varepsilon}_{t-1}\right)^2}{\sum_{t=1}^{T}\hat{\varepsilon}_t^2}$$

where T represents the last observation in the time series.

Unlike other statistical tests (Z, t, χ^2, or F), the DW test has no unique critical value defining the point at which you reject the null hypothesis of no auto-correlation. However, it does have a zone of indecision defined by a lower bound (d_l) and upper bound (d_u) that depend on the number of observations in the sample and the number of estimated coefficients ($p + 1$) in the original model. Figure 12-7 illustrates how you can use the calculated d statistic to draw conclusions about autocorrelation.

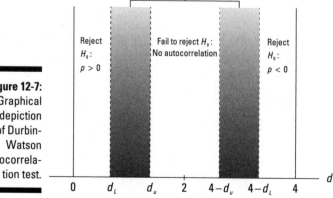

Figure 12-7:
Graphical
depiction
of Durbin-
Watson
autocorrela-
tion test.

The closer d is to 2, the stronger the evidence of no autocorrelation. However, the closer d is to 0, the more likely it is that no autocorrelation is rejected in favor of positive autocorrelation. If d is closer to 4, then no autocorrelation is rejected in favor of negative autocorrelation.

Imagine you have some yearly sales and inventory data from 1950 to 1991 that you want to analyze in STATA by using the DW d test. (Remember to use the "tsset" command to help you keep the data organized.) The d statistic of 1.4 in Figure 12-8 must be compared to the d_L and d_U or $4 - d_U$ and $4 - d_L$ values. Using the DW d-statistic table in the appendix, where the number of coefficients is 2 and the number of observations is 42, you can see that the approximate values for d_L and d_U are 1.391 and 1.600. This implies that the calculated d-statistic (from STATA output $d = 1.37$) rejects no autocorrelation in favor of positive autocorrelation, but it's on the border of the indecision zone.

Meet the AR(1) autocorrelation detector extraordinaire: The DW d statistic

In order to show why the DW d statistic is reasonable for detecting AR(1) autocorrelation, take the formula for the d statistic and expand the equation to

$$d = \frac{\sum_{t=2}^{T}\hat{\varepsilon}_t^2}{\sum_{t=1}^{T}\hat{\varepsilon}_t^2} + \frac{\sum_{t=2}^{T}\hat{\varepsilon}_{t-1}^2}{\sum_{t=1}^{T}\hat{\varepsilon}_t^2} - \frac{2\sum_{t=2}^{T}\hat{\varepsilon}_t\hat{\varepsilon}_{t-1}}{\sum_{t=1}^{T}\hat{\varepsilon}_t^2}$$

If you focus on the last term, you can see that it's the ratio of the covariance to the variance. If you work with the covariance term, you can redefine the numerator as

$$Cov\left(\hat{\varepsilon}_t,\hat{\varepsilon}_{t-1}\right)=\frac{\hat{\rho}\hat{\sigma}_u^2}{1-\hat{\rho}^2}$$

The variance of ε is

$$Var\left(\hat{\varepsilon}_t\right)=\frac{\hat{\sigma}_u^2}{1-\hat{\rho}^2}$$

Consequently, by substituting this into the last term with the appropriate sample estimates and reducing the first two terms, you can rewrite the d statistic as

$$d \approx 1+1-\frac{2\left(\frac{\hat{\rho}\hat{\sigma}_u^2}{1-\hat{\rho}^2}\right)}{\frac{\hat{\sigma}_u^2}{1-\hat{\rho}^2}} \approx 2(1-\hat{\rho})$$

This approximation holds because the first two terms differ from 1 through the exclusion of $\hat{\varepsilon}_1^2$ and $\hat{\varepsilon}_T^2$ from the first and second numerator summations, respectively. If there's no autocorrelation, $\hat{\rho}=0$ and $d\approx 2$.

```
. tsset year
        time variable:  year, 1950 to 1991
              delta:  1 unit

. regress inventories sales
```

Figure 12-8:
STATA
time-series
OLS output
followed by
the calcula-
tion of the
Durbin-
Watson *d*
statistic.

Source	SS	df	MS		Number of obs =	42
					F (1,40) =	49518.79
Model	2.7511e+12	1	2.7511e+12		Prob > F =	0.0000
Residual	2.2222e+09	40	55556036.6		R-squared =	0.9992
					Adj R-squared =	0.9992
Total	2.7533e+12	41	6.7153e+10		Root MSE =	7453.6

inventories	Coef.	Std. Err.	t	P>|t|	[95% Conf. Interval]
sales	1.554329	.0069849	222.53	0.000	1.540213 1.568446
_cons	1668.669	1806.696	0.92	0.361	-1982.799 5320.138

```
. estat dwatson

Durbin-Watson d-statistic(2,42) = 1.374673
```

WARNING! The DW *d*-statistic is the most popular test for autocorrelation, but it's limited to identifying AR(1) autocorrelation. It's a good initial test, but additional testing may be required to rule out other forms of autocorrelation. Furthermore, a *d*-statistic that ends up in the indecision zone requires an alternative test to achieve a more conclusive result.

Detecting autocorrelation of an AR (q) process: The Breusch-Godfrey test

The Breusch-Godfrey (BG) test begins by assuming that if autocorrelation is present, then it can be described by an AR(q) process. You want to use a BG test if the autoregressive process is such that the value of the error in period t depends on its value in period $t-1$, through $t-q$, where q is some number greater than or equal to 1 and less than the total number of periods in your data (a special case of this test with $q = 1$ is known as *Durbin's alternative statistic*).

REMEMBER In a model such as $Y_t = \beta_0 + \beta_1 X_{t1} + ... + \beta_p X_{tp} + \varepsilon_t$, AR($q$) autocorrelation is described by $\varepsilon_t = \rho_1 \varepsilon_{t-1} + \rho_2 \varepsilon_{t-2} + ... \rho_q \varepsilon_{t-q} + u_t$, where $1 \leq q < T$. The BG test uses the estimated correlation between the residual in period t with the residuals in periods $t-1$ through $t-q$ to test for autocorrelation.

Generally, the BG test is based on the estimation of $\varepsilon_t = \alpha_0 + \alpha_1 X_{t1} + \ldots$ $+ \alpha_p X_{tp} + \rho_1 \varepsilon_{t-1} + \rho_2 \varepsilon_{t-2} + \ldots \rho_q \varepsilon_{t-q} + u_t$.

You can perform a BG test by following these steps:

1. **Estimate the model** $Y_t = \beta_0 + \beta_1 X_{t1} + \ldots + \beta_p X_{tp} + \varepsilon_t$ **using OLS.**

2. **Obtain the residual values,** $\hat{\varepsilon}_t$, **after estimating your model.**

3. **Estimate the auxiliary regression** $\hat{\varepsilon}_t = \alpha_0 + \alpha_1 X_{t1} + \ldots + \alpha_p X_{pt} + \rho_1 \hat{\varepsilon}_{t-1}$ $+ \ldots + \rho_q \hat{\varepsilon}_{t-q} + u_t$ **using OLS.**

4. **Retain the R-squared value,** $R_{\hat{\varepsilon}}^2$, **from this regression.**

5. **Calculate the F-statistic for joint significance of** $\hat{\rho}_1, \hat{\rho}_2, \ldots,$ **and** $\hat{\rho}_q$ **or the chi-squared statistic** $\chi^2 = (n-q) R_{\hat{\varepsilon}}^2$ **with** q **degrees of freedom.**

If the F or chi-squared test statistics are significant, then you have evidence of autocorrelation. If not, you fail to reject the null hypothesis of no autocorrelation, which is $H_0 : \rho_1 = \rho_2 = \ldots = \rho_q = 0$.

Figure 12-9 illustrates the step-by-step process of performing a BG test in STATA using yearly sales and inventory data from 1950 to 1991. The results in Figure 12-11 show the results of my BG test for AR(1) and AR(2) autocorrelation. Any autoregressive order can be tested using the *lags* option and each is tested separately. In this case, the outcome rejects no autocorrelation in favor of an AR(1) but not an AR(2).

```
. tsset year
        time variable:  year, 1950 to 1991
                delta:  1 unit

. regress inventories sales
```

Source	SS	df	MS		
Model	2.7511e+12	1	2.7511e+12		
Residual	2.2222e+09	40	55556036.6		
Total	2.7533e+12	41	6.7153e+10		

```
                                    Number of obs =      42
                                    F (1,40)      = 49518.79
                                    Prob > F      =   0.0000
                                    R-squared     =   0.9992
                                    Adj R-squared =   0.9992
                                    Root MSE      =   7453.6
```

inventories	Coef.	Std. Err.	t	P>|t|	[95% Conf. Interval]
sales	1.554329	.0069849	222.53	0.000	1.540213 1.568446
_cons	1668.669	1806.696	0.92	0.361	-1982.799 5320.138

```
. estat bgodfrey, lags(1 2)

Breusch-Godfrey LM test for autocorrelation
```

lags(p)	chi2	df	Prob > chi2
1	4.046	1	0.0443
2	4.310	2	0.1159

```
                    H0: no serial correlation
```

Figure 12-9: STATA time-series OLS output and the Breusch-Godfrey (BG) test.

Remedying Harmful Autocorrelation

After you determine that autocorrelation is likely, you need to modify the estimation of your econometric model to obtain accurate results. The two most common solutions to autocorrelation are *feasible generalized least squares* (FGLS) and *serial correlation robust standard errors*.

Feasible generalized least squares (FGLS)

FGLS estimation has several names, depending on the precise method used to modify the estimation of the econometric model. The two FGLS techniques used to address AR(1) autocorrelation are:

- ✔ The Cochrane-Orcutt (CO) transformation
- ✔ The Prais-Winsten (PW) transformation

For other forms of FGLS estimation used to address heteroskedasticity, see Chapter 11.

The CO and PW techniques transform the original model with autocorrelation into one without autocorrelation. So the goal of the CO and PW transformations is to make the error term in the original econometric model uncorrelated. First, you assume that the autocorrelation is determined by an AR(1) process. Then you use knowledge of this relationship to perform a *quasi-differencing* that results in an uncorrelated error term. Quasi-differencing subtracts the previous value of each variable scaled by the autocorrelation parameter, ρ (as opposed to differencing, discussed in Chapter 17, where the subtraction merely differences the previous from the current value).

If the proposed AR(1) model of autocorrelation, $\varepsilon_t = \rho\varepsilon_{t-1} + u_t$, isn't correct, then you have no guarantee of getting more accurate standard errors with FGLS than OLS. Here's how to apply either the CO or PW technique:

1. **Estimate your original model, $Y_t = \beta_0 + \beta_1 X_{t1} + \ldots + \beta_p X_{tp} + \varepsilon_t$, and obtain the residuals $\hat{\varepsilon}_t$.**

2. **Use the residuals to estimate ρ by performing one of the following calculations:**

$$\bullet \; \hat{\rho} = \frac{\sum_{t=2}^{T} \hat{\varepsilon}_t \hat{\varepsilon}_{t-1}}{\sum_{t=1}^{T} \hat{\varepsilon}_t^2}$$

This calculation can be used in large samples but may have significant error in smaller samples.

- $\hat{\rho} = 1 - \dfrac{d}{2}$

  This calculation, known as *Thiel's estimator,* can be used with smaller samples.

- **Estimate $\hat{\varepsilon}_t = \rho\hat{\varepsilon}_{t-1} + u_t$ and obtain $\hat{\rho}$ from the regression.**

  This method is the most common for estimating ρ but is recommended only with larger samples.

In practice, knowing the exact value of ρ is impossible. In applied settings, you use the estimated value for ρ (that is, $\hat{\rho}$) to transform the model.

3. **Estimate the quasi-differenced CO or PW regression using $\hat{\rho}$ in place of ρ.**

Now that you know the basic steps, try applying them to first find the CO transformation. Suppose your original model takes the form

$$Y_t = \beta_0 + \beta_1 X_{t1} + \dots + \beta_p X_{tp} + \varepsilon_t$$

and that the error term is defined by

$$\varepsilon_t = \rho\varepsilon_{t-1} + u_t$$

where u_t satisfies the CLRM assumptions such that $E(u_t \mid \varepsilon_{t-1}) = 0$, $Var(u_t \mid \varepsilon_{t-1}) = \sigma_u^2$, and $Cov(u_t, u_s) = 0$. Notice that the model for Y violates the assumption of no autocorrelation because the errors in period t and $t-1$ are correlated.

If the model for Y holds true in period t, it should also hold in $t-1$, so

$$Y_{t-1} = \beta_0 + \beta_1 X_{(t-1)1} + \dots + \beta_p X_{(t-1)p} + \varepsilon_{t-1}$$

Multiply both sides of Y_{t-1} by ρ and subtract from the original model to obtain the quasi-differenced model:

$$Y_t - \rho Y_{t-1} = \beta_0(1-\rho) + \beta_1\left(X_{t1} - \rho X_{(t-1)1}\right) + \dots + \beta_p\left(X_{tp} - \rho X_{(t-1)p}\right) + \left(\varepsilon_t - \rho\varepsilon_{t-1}\right)$$

Because $\varepsilon_t = \rho\varepsilon_{t-1} + u_t$, you can substitute for ε_t and get

$$Y_t - \rho Y_{t-1} = \beta_0(1-\rho) + \beta_1\left(X_{t1} - \rho X_{(t-1)1}\right) + \dots + \beta_p\left(X_{tp} - \rho X_{(t-1)p}\right) + \left(\rho\varepsilon_{t-1} + u_t - \rho\varepsilon_{t-1}\right)$$

$$Y_t - \rho Y_{t-1} = \beta_0(1-\rho) + \beta_1\left(X_{t1} - \rho X_{(t-1)1}\right) + \dots + \beta_p\left(X_{tp} - \rho X_{(t-1)p}\right) + u_t$$

$$Y_t^* = \beta_0^* + \beta_1^* X_{t1}^* + \dots + \beta_p^* X_{tp}^* + \varepsilon_t^*$$

The β's are the CO estimators. $\varepsilon_t^* = u_t$, so this model satisfies all of the CLRM assumptions. Notice, however, that one observation is lost because the first observation doesn't have an antecedent.

The PW transformation maintains the CO structure with the exception of the first observation. In order to avoid the loss of the first observation, you can transform the Y, X, and ε values as follows:

$$Y_1^* = \left(\sqrt{1-\rho^2}\right)Y_1$$

$$X_1^* = \left(\sqrt{1-\rho^2}\right)X_1$$

$$\varepsilon_1^* = \left(\sqrt{1-\rho^2}\right)\varepsilon_1$$

You can show that the error term in the first period also satisfies the CLRM assumptions, because

$$E\left(\varepsilon_1^*\right) = E\left(\left(\sqrt{1-\rho^2}\right)\varepsilon_1\right) = \left(\sqrt{1-\rho^2}\right)E\left(\varepsilon_1\right) = 0$$

and

$$Var\left(\varepsilon_1^*\right) = Var\left(\left(\sqrt{1-\rho^2}\right)\varepsilon_1\right) = \left(1-\rho^2\right)Var\left(\varepsilon_1\right) = \left(1-\rho^2\right)\left(\frac{\sigma_u^2}{1-\rho^2}\right) = \sigma_u^2$$

In large samples, the difference between the CO and PW estimates is usually small. In small samples, however, the difference between CO and PW estimates can be significant.

Most econometrics software programs allow you to perform FGLS to correct for autocorrelation by utilizing a specialized command. In STATA, you specify which variable captures the time component by using the "tsset" command in order to keep the data internally organized so you can perform operations that rely on the order of the data. Figure 12-10a illustrates how to use STATA to estimate a CO transformation using yearly sales and inventory data; Figure 12-10b shows the PW results. (**Note:** The PW is the standard AR(1) transformation in STATA, but the CO transformation can be utilized as an option to the "prais" command.) The CO and PW results are similar but not identical. The difference is due to the use of all 42 observations in the PW estimation compared to the loss of the first observation ($T = 41$) in the CO estimation. Both results can be compared to the OLS results (in Figure 12-9), which underestimate the standard errors and lead to larger t-statistics and higher levels of statistical significance.

Serial correlation robust standard errors

Estimating the model using OLS and adjusting the standard errors for autocorrelation has become more popular than other correction methods. There are two reasons for this: (1) The serial correlation robust standard errors can adjust the results in the presence of a basic AR(1) process or a more complex AR(q) process, and (2) only the biased portion of the results (the standard errors) are adjusted, while the unbiased estimates (the coefficients) are untouched, so no model transformation is required.

```
. tsset year
        time variable:  year, 1950 to 1991
                delta:  1 unit

. prais inventories sales, corc

Iteration 0: rho = 0.0000
Iteration 1: rho = 0.3110
Iteration 2: rho = 0.3126
Iteration 3: rho = 0.3126
Iteration 4: rho = 0.3126

Cochrane-Orcutt AR(1) regression - iterated estimates
```

Source	SS	df	MS	Number of obs =	41
				F (1,39) =	25649.40
Model	1.3178e+12	1	1.3178e+12	Prob > F =	0.0000
Residual	2.0037e+09	39	51376912.9	R-squared =	0.9985
				Adj R-squared =	0.9984
Total	1.3198e+12	40	3.2995e+10	Root MSE =	7167.8

inventories	Coef.	Std. Err.	t	P>|t|	[95% Conf. Interval]	
sales	1.552833	.0096959	160.15	0.000	1.533221	1.572445
_cons	2010.464	2598.927	0.77	0.444	-3246.362	7267.29
rho	.3126123					

```
Durbin-Watson statistic (original)    1.374673
Durbin-Watson statistic (transformed) 2.047804
```

a

```
. tsset year
        time variable:  year, 1950 to 1991
                delta:  1 unit

. prais inventories sales

Iteration 0: rho = 0.0000
Iteration 1: rho = 0.3110
Iteration 2: rho = 0.3120
Iteration 3: rho = 0.3120
Iteration 4: rho = 0.3120

Paris-Winsten AR(1) regression - iterated estimates
```

Source	SS	df	MS	Number of obs =	42
				F (1,40) =	26850.77
Model	1.3475e+12	1	1.3475e+12	Prob > F =	0.0000
Residual	2.0074e+09	40	50185275.8	R-squared =	0.9985
				Adj R-squared =	0.9985
Total	1.3495e+12	41	3.2915e+10	Root MSE =	7084.2

inventories	Coef.	Std. Err.	t	P>|t|	[95% Conf. Interval]	
sales	1.553381	.009363	165.91	0.000	1.534458	1.572305
_cons	1805.825	2454.323	0.74	0.466	-3154.546	6766.196
rho	.3119815					

Figure 12-10:
a) STATA time-series Cochrane-Orcutt (CO) FGLS estimates and b) STATA time-series Prais-Winsten (PW) FGLS estimates.

```
Durbin-Watson statistic (original)    1.374673
Durbin-Watson statistic (transformed) 2.049700
```

b

Adjusting the OLS standard errors for autocorrelation produces *serial correlation robust standard errors*. These are also referred to as *Newey-West (NW) standard errors*. The strength of this method is that it's able to simultaneously deal with higher-order autocorrelation (AR(q)) and heteroskedasticity.

The variances and covariances of the errors can be shown in a matrix known as the *error covariance matrix*. This can be expressed as

$$Cov(\varepsilon_t, \varepsilon_s) = \begin{bmatrix} \sigma_1^2 & \sigma_{12} & \cdots & \sigma_{1T} \\ \sigma_{21} & \sigma_2^2 & \cdots & \sigma_{2T} \\ \vdots & \vdots & \ddots & \vdots \\ \sigma_{T1} & \sigma_{T2} & \cdots & \sigma_T^2 \end{bmatrix}$$

The diagonals represent the error variance, and the off-diagonals are the covariance values. Under the assumption of homoskedasticity, the diagonals have the same value; if there's no autocorrelation, then the off-diagonals are all zero.

The serial correlation robust standard errors can be calculated by applying the following steps:

1. **Estimate your original model** $Y_t = \beta_0 + \beta_1 X_{t1} + \ldots + \beta_p X_{tp} + \varepsilon_t$ **and obtain the residuals:** $\hat{\varepsilon}_t$.

2. **Estimate the auxiliary regression** $X_{t1} = \alpha_0 + \alpha_2 X_{t2} + \ldots + \alpha_p X_{tp} + r_t$ **and retain the residuals:** $\hat{r}_t$.

3. **Find the intermediate adjustment factor,** $\hat{a}_t = \hat{r}_t \hat{\varepsilon}_t$, **and decide how much serial correlation (the number of lags) you're going to allow.**

   A Breusch-Godfrey test (see the earlier related section) can be useful in making this determination.

4. **Obtain the error variance adjustment factor,** $\hat{v} = \sum_{t=1}^{T} \hat{a}_t^2 + 2 \sum_{h=1}^{g} \left[1 - \dfrac{h}{(g+1)} \right]$ $\left(\sum_{t=h+1}^{T} \hat{a}_t \hat{a}_{t-h} \right)$, **where** g **represents the number of lags determined in Step 3.**

5. **Calculate the serial correlation robust standard error.**

   It's also known as the *heteroskedasticity-autocorrelation-corrected* (HAC) standard error because the calculation simultaneously adjusts the standard error for heteroskedasticity (covered in Chapter 11) and autocorrelation. For variable X_1,

$$se\left(\hat{\beta}_I\right)_{HAC} = \left(\frac{se\left(\hat{\beta}_I\right)}{\hat{\sigma}_\varepsilon}\right)^2 \sqrt{\hat{v}}$$

6. Repeat Steps 2 through 5 for independent variables X_2 through X_p.

Fortunately, most econometrics software programs allow you to obtain serial correlation robust standard errors with a specialized command that instantaneously performs all the steps. The command that achieves this function in STATA is the "tsset" command combined with the "newey" option of "regress". In Figure 12-11, I illustrate how you estimate the OLS coefficients with the serial correlation robust standard errors using yearly sales and inventory data. The figure shows the standard OLS results along with the robust standard errors. Notice that both sets of results have identical coefficients. However, the serial correlation robust (NW) standard errors change the *t*-statistics, confidence intervals, and *p*-values for the coefficients.

```
. tsset year
        time variable:  year, 1950 to 1991
               delta:  1 unit

. regress inventories sales
```

Source	SS	df	MS		
Model	2.7511e+12	1	2.7511e+12		
Residual	2.2222e+09	40	55556036.6		
Total	2.7533e+12	41	6.7153e+10		

```
                                          Number of obs =      42
                                          F (1,40)      = 49518.79
                                          Prob > F      =  0.0000
                                          R-squared     =  0.9992
                                          Adj R-squared =  0.9992
                                          Root MSE      =  4753.6
```

inventories	Coef.	Std. Err.	t	P>|t|	[95% Conf. Interval]	
sales	1.554329	.0069849	222.53	0.000	1.540213	1.568446
_cons	1668.669	1806.696	0.92	0.361	-1982.799	5320.138

```
. newey inventories sales, lag(1)

Regression with Newey-West standard errors        Number of obs =      42
maximum lag: 1                                     F (1,40)      = 40363.47
                                                   Prob > F      =  0.0000
```

inventories	Newey-West Coef.	Std. Err.	t	P>|t|	[95% Conf. Interval]	
sales	1.554329	.007366	200.91	0.000	1.538693	1.569966
_cons	1668.669	1051.258	1.59	0.120	-456.0015	3793.34

Figure 12-11: Using STATA to estimate a time-series model with serial correlation robust (Newey-West) standard errors.

Part V

Discrete and Restricted Dependent Variables in Econometrics

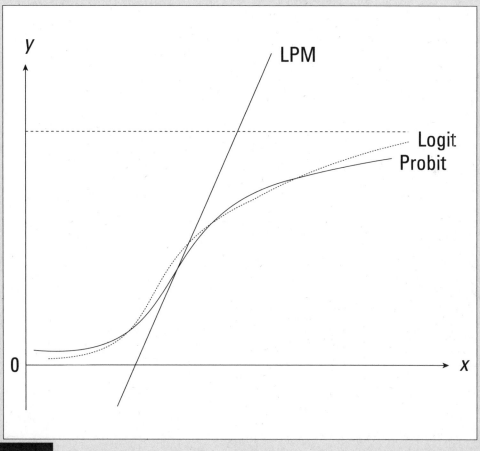

Check out www.dummies.com/extras/econometrics for a refresher of how discrete and restricted dependent variables work before heading into your next exam.

In this part . . .

✔ Model economic outcomes that are qualitative or have limited
  values to address questions such as "What distinguishes a job
  applicant who gets hired from one who doesn't?"

✔ Discover how to use maximum likelihood (ML) estimation as an
  alternative to the OLS technique so you can choose values for
  your estimated parameter(s) that maximize the probability of
  observing the values contained in your data sample.

✔ Deal with limited dependent variables, namely censored
  dependent variables and truncated dependent variables, to
  prevent one or more of the traditional regression model
  assumptions from failing.

✔ Find out how to implement econometric techniques to modify
  traditional regression analysis in the presence of limited dependent variables with the help of econometric software.

Chapter 13

Qualitative Dependent Variables

· ·

· ·

*W*hat distinguishes a job applicant who gets hired from one who doesn't? What influences whether an individual's loan application gets approved or rejected? How does a commuter decide between using a car and using some alternative form of transportation to reach work? These questions all concern qualitative outcomes that either occur or do not occur. The outcomes are dichotomous (meaning only two outcomes are possible) and not continuous or normally distributed. For this reason, these models are also known as *dummy dependent variable models.* If you want to model qualitative outcomes of this nature and use regression analysis, you can use traditional ordinary least squares (OLS), but you'll likely need special econometric techniques to properly model the outcome of interest.

In this chapter, I show you the econometric techniques most commonly used when the dependent variable is qualitative. These techniques can be quantitatively burdensome and practically impossible without a computer, so I focus on explaining the structure of the models and interpretation of the computer output.

Modeling Discrete Outcomes with the Linear Probability Model (LPM)

If your outcome of interest is dichotomous (can take only two possible outcomes rather than an infinite number of possibilities), then you can create a dummy variable to capture the qualitative characteristic. Using the ordinary least squares (OLS) technique to estimate a model with a dummy dependent variable is known as creating a *linear probability model,* or LPM.

In Figure 13-1, I illustrate the concept of fitting a line with a qualitative dependent variable. Fitting the relationship between Y and X when Y is a dummy variable produces the conditional probability that $Y = 1$. I tell you about conditional probabilities and how to interpret the results of estimating LPM with OLS in the following sections.

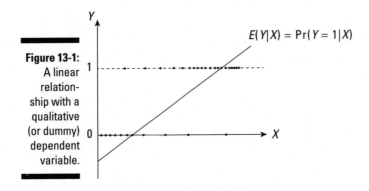

Figure 13-1:
A linear relationship with a qualitative (or dummy) dependent variable.

Estimating LPM with OLS

A basic LPM can be expressed as

$$Y_i = \beta_0 + \beta_1 X_i + \varepsilon_i$$

where Y, the dependent variable, is a dummy variable that is equal to 1 if a particular outcome is observed and 0 otherwise (in Chapter 9 I discuss how dummy variables can be defined, but that chapter focuses on their use as independent variables). Additionally, X is the independent variable, and ε represents that random error term. Without the error term, the left-hand side of a linear model is the conditional mean. However, because the conditional mean in an LPM can only take one of two possible values, the resulting binomial probability distribution is shown in Table 13-1 (notice that summing the probabilities of each outcome is equal to 1, as $1 - P_i + P_i = 1$).

Table 13-1	Binomial Probability Distribution for the Dependent Variable
Y	**f(Y)**
0	$1 - P_i$
1	P_i

Using the possible values for the dependent variable and the probabilities that they occur gives you the expected value of Y as follows:

$$E(Y) = 0(1 - P_i) + 1(P_i) = P_i = \Pr(Y = 1)$$

The unconditional mean of the dependent variable is the fraction of times (or probability) that the outcome is observed.

If the dependent variable is assumed to be a function of X such that $E(Y \mid X) = \beta_0 + \beta_1 X_i$, then the $E(Y \mid X)$ represents the *conditional probability* of observing the outcome given the value of the independent variable; in other words, $E(Y \mid X) = \Pr(Y = 1 \mid X)$.

In Figure 13-2, I illustrate how the regression line can be used to obtain the conditional probability that the outcome of interest is observed.

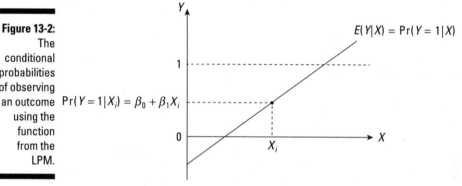

Figure 13-2: The conditional probabilities of observing an outcome using the function from the LPM.

With sample data, you can estimate the function using OLS. The predicted values of the dependent variable $\hat{Y}_i = \hat{P}_i$ from the regression are estimates of the conditional probabilities $E(Y \mid X_i) = \Pr(Y = 1 \mid X_i)$.

Time for an example that uses some real-life data. Say you have data from 20 Major League Baseball (MLB) players to estimate an LPM. The dependent variable captures whether a player was released or retained by his team at the end of the season. The dependent variable Y *(plexit)* is 1 if the player was released and 0 if the player was retained. The independent variable X is the player's three-year slugging average *(slg_3_avg)*. Figure 13-3 shows the STATA results. Notice that the results in Figure 13-3 are obtained by using the standard "regress" command in STATA. In other words, the OLS technique is used with the dependent variable representing a qualitative outcome measured with a dummy variable rather than a continuous quantitative variable. The same command that's used to obtain the predicted values of the dependent variable ("predict") can be used to calculate the predicted probabilities.

```
. regress plexit slg_3_avg
```

Source	SS	df	MS
Model	1.38742347	1	1.38742347
Residual	3.41257653	18	.189587585
Total	4.8	19	.252631579

Number of obs =	20
F(1, 18) =	7.32
Prob > F =	0.0145
R-squared =	0.2890
Adj R-squared =	0.2495
Root MSE =	.43542

plexit	Coef.	Std. Err.	t	P>|t|	[95% Conf. Interval]	
slg_3_avg	-3.128688	1.156546	-2.71	0.014	-5.5585	-.6988764
_cons	1.575665	.4453668	3.54	0.002	.6399841	2.511346

```
. predict lpmpr, xb

. twoway (scatter lpmpr slg_3_avg)
```

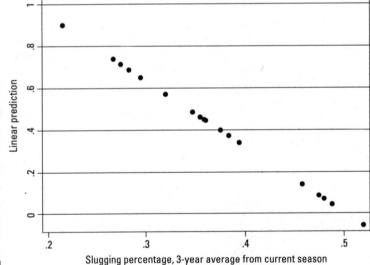

Figure 13-3:
STATA
estimation
of a linear
probability
model (LPM)
with the
predicted
probabilities.

Slugging percentage, 3-year average from current season

Interpreting your results

In the LPM, like any model estimated using OLS, the regression coefficients represent the effect of the independent variable(s) on the dependent variable.

The $\hat{\beta}$ terms in an LPM estimate the impact on the predicted probability for a unit-change in the independent variable(s). The predicted probability is the chance of observing the outcome defined with a value of 1 in the dichotomous dependent variable.

Using the results in Figure 13-3, you can write the estimated LPM equation as $\hat{P}_i = 1.6 - 3.1X_i$. This equation implies that if a player's slugging percentage increases by 0.1, the probability of his being fired by his team decreases by 0.31 ($3.1 \times 0.1 = 0.31$ or 31 percent).

Although OLS estimation always produces the typical R-squared measure of fit, its interpretation is less meaningful when all the values of the dependent variable are at 0 or 1. The R-squared value may be low even if the model predicts very accurate probabilities. You can obtain more appropriate measures of fit for an LPM by comparing the model's predicted probabilities to the observed Y values. In the case of an LPM (or any model where the dependent variable is dichotomous), more appropriate measures of fit capture the fraction of times the model predicts accurately.

Before you can calculate a measure of fit, you first need to determine what can be considered an accurate prediction from the model. Then you need a rule for aggregating the accurate predictions to provide an overall goodness-of-fit measure.

Because no measure of fit is universally accepted, I can best demonstrate these steps using the results from the model estimated in Figure 13-3 to calculate the percentage accurately predicted using four different methodologies. Figure 13-4 lists the actual Y values and the predicted probabilities from estimating the LPM illustrated in Figure 13-3.

. list plexit lpmpr

	plexit	lpmpr
1.	0	.0444273
2.	0	.4632384
3.	0	.7168095
4.	1	.4874257
5.	1	.6524824
6.	0	.1401361
7.	0	-.0548616
8.	0	.4005708
9.	0	.0692596
10.	1	.9052319
11.	1	.6906267
12.	0	.4478419
13.	1	.0858135
14.	0	.3735235
15.	0	.398946
16.	0	.3403419
17.	0	.0723431
18.	1	.4516147
19.	1	.7413482
20.	1	.5728803

Figure 13-4: The observed Y values and LPM predicted probabilities.

Using the LPM predictions in Figure 13-4, you can estimate the following four measures of fit, which are the four most common approaches. How they're applied varies, but typically (when working independently on a project or research paper) you should report at least two of these measures.

✔ If you use these two criteria:

- Accurate prediction defined as (a) $\hat{P}_i \geq 0.5$ and $Y = 1$ or (b) $\hat{P}_i < 0.5$ and $Y = 0$ (that is, using a simple 50-50 chance as the cutoff)

- Accurate predictions aggregated by calculating the total number of accurate predictions as a percentage of the total number of observations

Then you obtain $\left(\frac{5+11}{20}\right)100\% = 80\%$. Note: From Figure 13-4, five observations satisfy the definition of an accurate prediction for category (a), and 11 observations are classified into category (b).

✔ Using these criteria:

- Accurate prediction defined as (a) $\hat{P}_i \geq \bar{Y} \geq 0.4$ and $Y = 1$ or (b) $\hat{P}_i < \bar{Y} < 0.4$ and $Y = 0$ (that is, using the average value of the dependent variable, in this case 0.4, as the cutoff point)

- Accurate predictions aggregated by calculating the total number of accurate predictions as a percentage of the total number of observations

You obtain $\left(\frac{7+8}{20}\right)100\% = 75\%$. Note: From Figure 13-4, seven observations satisfy the definition of an accurate prediction for category (a), and eight observations are classified into category (b).

✔ Using these criteria:

- Accurate prediction defined as $\hat{P}_i \geq 0.5$ and $Y = 1$ or $\hat{P}_i < 0.5$ and $Y = 0$ (that is, using a simple 50-50 chance as the cutoff)

- Accurate predictions aggregated by calculating the percent of accurate predictions in each group (for $Y = 0$ and $Y = 1$) and weighting the percent of observations in each group

You obtain $\left(\frac{5}{8}\right)(40\%) + \left(\frac{11}{12}\right)(60\%) = 80\%$. Note: From Figure 13-4, five out of eight observations satisfy the definition of an accurate prediction for category (a), but they're given a 40 percent weight because $Y = 1$ for 40 percent of the total observations. Similarly, 11 out of 12 observations are classified into category (b), but they're given a 60 percent weight because $Y = 0$ for 60 percent of the total observations.

✔ Using these criteria:

- Accurate prediction defined as $\hat{P}_i \geq \bar{Y} \geq 0.4$ and $Y = 1$ or $\hat{P}_i < \bar{Y} < 0.4$ and $Y = 0$ (that is, using the average value of the dependent variable, in this case 0.4, as the cutoff point)

- Accurate predictions aggregated by calculating the percent of accurate predictions in each group (for $Y = 0$ and $Y = 1$) and weighting the percent of observations in each group

You obtain $\left(\dfrac{7}{8}\right)(40\%) + \left(\dfrac{8}{12}\right)(60\%) = 75\%$. Note: From Figure 13-4, seven out of eight observations satisfy the definition of an accurate prediction for category (a), but they're given a 40 percent weight because $Y = 1$ for 40 percent of the total observations. Similarly, 8 out of 12 observations are classified into category (b), but these are given a 60 percent weight because $Y = 0$ for 60 percent of the total observations.

All four of these methods of obtaining the fraction of accurate predictions provide a reasonable alternative to the R-squared value with qualitative dependent variable models.

Presenting the Three Main LPM Problems

LPMs aren't perfect. Three specific problems can arise:

✔ Non-normality of the error term

✔ Heteroskedastic errors

✔ Potentially nonsensical predictions

The following sections describe how these problems arise — as well as their consequences — in detail.

Non-normality of the error term

The assumption that the error is normally distributed is critical for performing hypothesis tests after estimating your econometric model. (I discuss the normality assumption and its role in OLS estimation in Chapter 7).

The error term of an LPM has a binomial distribution instead of a normal distribution. It implies that the traditional t-tests for individual significance and F-tests for overall significance are invalid.

As you can see in Figure 13-5, the error term in an LPM has one of two possible values for a given X value. One possible value for the error (if $Y = 1$) is given by A, and the other possible value for the error (if $Y = 0$) is given by B. Consequently, it's impossible for the error term to have a normal distribution.

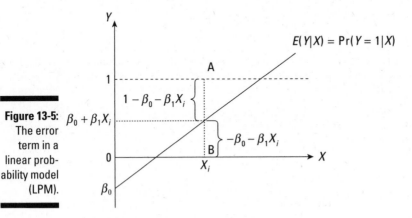

Figure 13-5: The error term in a linear probability model (LPM).

Heteroskedasticity

The classical linear regression model (CLRM) assumes that the error term is homoskedastic. The assumption of homoskedasticity is required to prove that the OLS estimators are efficient (or best). The proof that OLS estimators are efficient is an important component of the Gauss-Markov theorem (which I show in Chapter 6). The presence of heteroskedasticity can cause the Gauss-Markov theorem to be violated and lead to other undesirable characteristics for the OLS estimators.

The error term in an LPM is heteroskedastic because the variance isn't constant. Instead, the variance of an LPM error term depends on the value of the independent variable(s).

Using the structure of the LPM, I can characterize the variance of its error term as follows

$$Var(\varepsilon) = E\left(\varepsilon_i^2\right) = \left(1 - \beta_0 - \beta_1 X_i\right)^2 \left(P_i\right) + \left(-\beta_0 - \beta_1 X_i\right)^2 \left(1 - P_i\right)$$

$$Var(\varepsilon) = \left(1 - \beta_0 - \beta_1 X_i\right)\left(1 - \beta_0 - \beta_1 X_i\right)\left(P_i\right) + \left(-\beta_0 - \beta_1 X_i\right)\left(-\beta_0 - \beta_1 X_i\right)\left(1 - P_i\right)$$

$$Var(\varepsilon) = \left(1 - P_i\right)\left(1 - P_i\right)\left(P_i\right) + \left(-P_i\right)\left(-P_i\right)\left(1 - P_i\right)$$

$$Var(\varepsilon) = P_i\left(1 - P_i\right)$$

$$Var(\varepsilon) = \left(\beta_0 + \beta_1 X_i\right)\left(1 - \beta_0 - \beta_1 X_i\right)$$

Because the variance of the error depends on the value of X, it exhibits heteroskedasticity rather than homoskedasticity. (For more on the problems with heteroskedasticity, see Chapter 11.)

Unbounded predicted probabilities

The most basic probability law states that the probability of an event occurring must be contained within the interval [0,1]. But the nature of an LPM is such that it doesn't ensure this fundamental law of probability is satisfied. Although most of the predicted probabilities from an LPM have sensible values (between 0 and 1), some predicted probabilities may have nonsensical values that are less than 0 or greater than 1.

To see what I mean, take a look at Figure 13-6 and focus your attention on the segments of the regression line where the conditional probability is greater than 1 or less than 0. When the dependent variable is continuous, you don't have to worry about unbounded values for the conditional means. However, dichotomous variables are problematic because the conditional means represent conditional probabilities. Interpreting probabilities that aren't bounded by 0 and 1 is difficult.

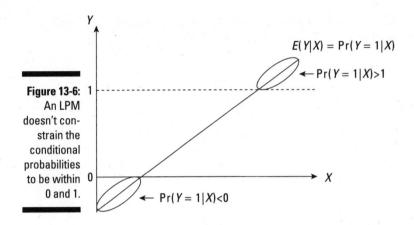

Figure 13-6:
An LPM
doesn't con-
strain the
conditional
probabilities
to be within
0 and 1.

You can see an example of this problem with actual data in Figure 13-4. Most of the estimated probabilities from my LPM estimation are contained within the [0,1] interval, but the predicted probability for the seventh observation is negative. Unfortunately, nothing in the estimation of an LPM ensures that all the predicted probabilities stay within reasonable values.

Specifying Appropriate Nonlinear Functions: The Probit and Logit Models

If your outcome of interest is qualitative, you use a dummy dependent variable and estimate the probability that the outcome ($Y = 1$) occurs using your econometric model. Although OLS can be used to estimate a model with a qualitative dependent variable, doing so would result in an error term that's heteroskedastic and isn't normally distributed. (See Chapter 7 for the scoop on the normality assumption and Chapter 11 for information on heteroskedasticity.)

The most obvious problem with estimating a dummy dependent variable model using OLS is that the predicted probabilities aren't guaranteed to be within the [0,1] interval. OLS can't be modified to fully address this issue because nonlinearity in parameters is required in order to guarantee that all predicted probabilities have sensible values. Consequently, an alternative specification must be used. Econometricians choose either the probit or the logit function.

With a probit or logit function, the conditional probabilities are nonlinearly related to the independent variable(s). Additionally, both functions have the characteristic of approaching 0 and 1 gradually (asymptotically), so the predicted probabilities are always sensible.

In Figure 13-7, I illustrate the conditional probabilities from an OLS (also known as the linear probability model LPM), a probit, and a logit model.

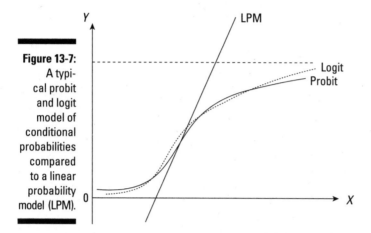

Working from the standard normal CDF: The probit model

The probit model is based on the standard normal cumulative density function (CDF), which is defined as

$$F(Z) = \int_{-\infty}^{Z} (2\pi)^{\frac{1}{2}} e^{\frac{-Z^2}{2}} dZ$$

where Z is a standardized normal variable (if you need to review standard normal variables, the topic is discussed in Chapter 3) and e is the base of the natural log (the value 2.71828 . . .).

In a probit model, the standard normal CDF replaces the linear function, so you estimate

$$E(Y \mid X_i) = \Pr(Y = 1 \mid X_i) = F(\beta_0 + \beta_1 X_i) = \int_{-\infty}^{\beta_0 + \beta_1 X_i} (2\pi)^{\frac{1}{2}} e^{\frac{\beta_0 + \beta_1 X_i}{2}} d(\beta_0 + \beta_1 X_i)$$

The β terms can't be estimated using OLS, so you need to use a technique known as *maximum likelihood* (ML). I explain the ML technique in the later "Using Maximum Likelihood (ML) Estimation" section.

For any given X, the probit model provides the Z value for the observation. The standard normal PDF or CDF can then be used to obtain the probability that $Y = 1$ for that observation.

Figure 13-8 shows how to go about finding the probability for any given observation.

Figure 13-8:
The standard normal probability density function (PDF) and cumulative density function (CDF) in a probit model.

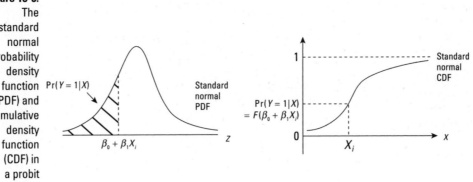

After estimating a probit model, most econometric software can calculate the predicted probabilities for all sample observations. Head to the later section "Interpreting Probit and Logit Estimates" for more on this topic.

Basing off of the logistic CDF: The logit model

The logit model is based on the logistic cumulative density function (CDF), defined as

$$F(G) = \frac{e^G}{1 + e^G}$$

where G is a logistic random variable and e is the base of the natural log (the value 2.71828 . . .).

The logistic distribution may be unfamiliar to you, but it's similar to a standard normal. However, it does have less density within one standard deviation of the mean than a standard normal distribution. Figure 13-9 illustrates the difference between the standard normal and the logistic distributions.

Figure 13-9:
The logistic
probability
density
function
(PDF) com-
pared to the
standard
normal
probability
density
function
(PDF).

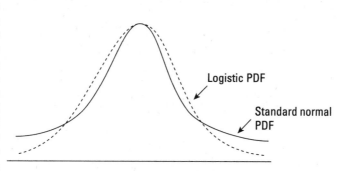

In a logit model, the logistic CDF replaces the linear function so that you estimate

$$E(Y \mid X_i) = \Pr(Y = 1 \mid X_i) = F(\beta_0 + \beta_1 X_i) = \frac{e^{\beta_0 + \beta_1 X_i}}{1 + e^{\beta_0 + \beta_1 X_i}}$$

Note: You can't use OLS to estimate the βs; instead, you have to use the maximum likelihood (ML) technique, which I tell you more about in the following section.

For any given X, the logit model provides the value for the observation that can be used with the logistic CDF to find the probability that $Y = 1$ for that observation.

In Figure 13-10, I illustrate how you find the probability for any given observation.

Figure 13-10:
The logistic
probability
density
function
(PDF) and
cumulative
density
function
(CDF) in a
logit model.

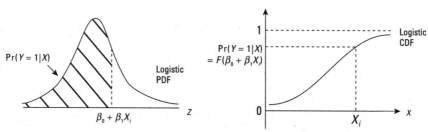

When you have your logit model estimated, you can use econometric software such as STATA to calculate the predicted probabilities for all your sample observations. I explain how in the later "Interpreting Probit and Logit Estimates" section.

Using Maximum Likelihood (ML) Estimation

Probit and logit functions are both nonlinear in parameters, so OLS can't be used to estimate the βs. Instead, you have to use a technique known as maximum likelihood (ML) estimation.

The objective of maximum likelihood (ML) estimation is to choose values for the estimated parameters (βs) that would maximize the probability of observing the Y values in the sample with the given X values. This probability is summarized in what is called the *likelihood function*. I explain how to construct this function — and how to make it more manageable — in the next sections.

Constructing the likelihood function

The likelihood function, which calculates the *joint probability* of observing all the values of the dependent variable, assumes that each observation is drawn randomly and independently from the population. If the values of the dependent variable are random and independent, then you can find the joint probability of observing all the values simultaneously by multiplying the individual density functions.

Assuming that each observed value of the dependent variable is random and independent, the likelihood function is

$$L = f(Y_1) \cdot f(Y_2) \cdot \ldots \cdot f(Y_n) = \prod_{i=1}^{n} f(Y_i)$$

where Π is the product (multiplication) operator. You can rewrite this equation as

$$L = \prod_{i=1}^{n} P_i^{Y_i} (1 - P_i)^{1-Y_i} = \prod_{i=1}^{n} F(\beta_0 + \beta_1 X_i)^{Y_i} \left[1 - F(\beta_0 + \beta_1 X_i) \right]^{1-Y_i}$$

where P represents the probability that $Y = 1$, $(1 - P)$ is the probability that $Y = 0$, and F can represent that standard normal or logistic CDF; in the probit and logit models, these are the assumed probability distributions.

The log transformation and ML estimates

In order to make the likelihood function more manageable, the optimization is performed using a *natural log transformation* of the likelihood function. You can justify it mathematically because log transformations are a type of monotonic transformation. In other words, for any function $f(X)$ and log transformation $g(X)$, $f(X_1) > f(X_2) \rightarrow g(X_1) > g(X_2)$. Therefore, the optimizing solution for the likelihood function is the same as the log likelihood function.

From the likelihood function L, using a natural log transformation I can write the estimated log likelihood function as

$$\ln \hat{L} = \sum_{i=1}^{n} \left[Y_i \ln F\left(\hat{\beta}_0 + \hat{\beta}_1 X_i\right) + (1 - Y_i) \ln\left(1 - F\left(\hat{\beta}_0 + \hat{\beta}_1 X_i\right)\right) \right]$$

where F denotes either the standard normal CDF (for the probit model) or the logistic CDF (for the logit model). Finding the optimal values for the $\hat{\beta}$ terms requires solving the following first-order conditions

$$\frac{\delta \ln \hat{L}}{\delta \hat{\beta}_0} = \sum_{i=1}^{n} \left[\frac{Y_i \cdot f\left(\hat{\beta}_0 + \hat{\beta}_1 X_i\right)}{F\left(\hat{\beta}_0 + \hat{\beta}_1 X_i\right)} + \frac{(1 - Y_i) \cdot -f\left(\hat{\beta}_0 + \hat{\beta}_1 X_i\right)}{\left(1 - F\left(\hat{\beta}_0 + \hat{\beta}_1 X_i\right)\right)} \right] = 0$$

$$\frac{\delta \ln \hat{L}}{\delta \hat{\beta}_1} = \sum_{i=1}^{n} \left[\frac{Y_i \cdot f\left(\hat{\beta}_0 + \hat{\beta}_1 X_i\right)}{F\left(\hat{\beta}_0 + \hat{\beta}_1 X_i\right)} + \frac{(1 - Y_i) \cdot -f\left(\hat{\beta}_0 + \hat{\beta}_1 X_i\right)}{\left(1 - F\left(\hat{\beta}_0 + \hat{\beta}_1 X_i\right)\right)} \right] (X_i) = 0$$

ML estimation is computationally intense because the first-order conditions for maximization don't have a simple algebraic representation. Econometric software relies on numerical optimization by searching for the values of the $\hat{\beta}$s that achieve the largest possible value of the log likelihood function, which means that a process of iteration (a repeated sequence of gradually improving solutions) is required to estimate the coefficients.

The econometric software searches (uses an iterative process) until it finds the values for all the $\hat{\beta}$s that simultaneously maximize the likelihood of obtaining the observed values of the dependent variable. I illustrate the software's optimization procedure for ML estimation in Figure 13-11.

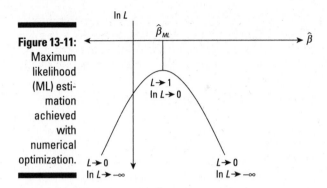

Figure 13-11:
Maximum
likelihood
(ML) esti-
mation
achieved
with
numerical
optimization.

Interpreting Probit and Logit Estimates

As you may expect, the nonlinearity of the probit and logit functions makes interpreting the results difficult.

- **Interpreting a probit model:** In a probit model, the value of $\hat{\beta}_0 + \hat{\beta}_1 X_i$ provides the estimated Z (standard normal) value for observation i. Sometimes the $\hat{\beta}_0 + \hat{\beta}_1 X_i$ values are referred to as *probability units* or *probits*. You can use these values to obtain the predicted probability for each observation (I explain how to convert these values into probabilities that you can review in the earlier section "Working from the standard normal CDF: The probit model"). Most econometric software calculates all of the predicted probabilities with a single command.

- **Interpreting a logit model:** In a logit model, the value of $\hat{\beta}_0 + \hat{\beta}_1 X_i$ provides the estimated G (logistic) value for observation i. Sometimes the $\hat{\beta}_0 + \hat{\beta}_1 X_i$ values are referred to as *logistic units* or *logits*. You can use these values to obtain the predicted probability for each observation (to see how to convert these values into probabilities, refer to the earlier "Basing off of the logistic CDF: The logit model" section of this chapter). As with the probit model, most econometric software also calculates predicted probabilities from a logit model with a simple command.

I used data from 20 Major League Baseball (MLB) players to estimate probit and logit models. The dependent variable captures whether a player was released or retained by his team at the end of the season. The dependent variable Y *(plexit)* = 1 if the player was released and Y *(plexit)* = 0 if the player was retained. The independent variable X is the player's 3-year slugging average *(slg_3_avg)*. Figures 13-12 and 13-13 show the STATA probit and logit results, respectively. The results in Figures 13-12 and 13-13 are obtained by using the "probit" and "logit" commands in STATA. The iterations in the output show how the ML technique is searching for the coefficient estimates that can maximize the log likelihood. You can use the "predict" command with the *p* option to obtain the predicted probabilities.

```
. probit plexit slg_3_avg

Iteration 0:    log likelihood = -13.460233
Iteration 1:    log likelihood = -10.250021
Iteration 2:    log likelihood =  -10.22414
Iteration 3:    log likelihood = -10.224106
Iteration 4:    log likelihood = -10.224106
```

Probit regression				Number of obs	=	20
				LR chi2(1)	=	6.47
				Prob > chi2	=	0.0110
Log likelihood = -10.224106				Pseudo R2	=	0.2404

plexit	Coef.	Std. Err.	z	P>|z|	[95% Conf. Interval]	
slg_3_avg	-9.909194	4.341084	-2.28	0.022	-18.41756	-1.400826
_cons	3.396796	1.614144	2.10	0.035	.2331309	6.560461

```
. predict probitpr, p
```

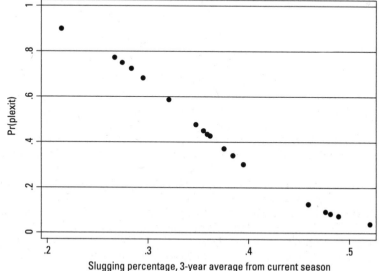

Figure 13-12:
STATA
probit
results and
predicted
probabilities.

```
. logit plexit slg_3_avg

Iteration 0:   log likelihood = -13.460233
Iteration 1:   log likelihood = -10.228237
Iteration 2:   log likelihood = -10.156101
Iteration 3:   log likelihood = -10.155964
Iteration 4:   log likelihood = -10.155964
```

```
Logistic regression                          Number of obs   =        20
                                             LR chi2(1)      =      6.61
                                             Prob > chi2     =    0.0101
Log likelihood = -10.155964                  Pseudo R2       =    0.2455
```

plexit	Coef.	Std. Err.	z	P>|z|	[95% Conf. Interval]	
slg_3_avg	-17.45519	8.47928	-2.06	0.040	-34.07428	-.8361081
_cons	5.95787	3.06312	1.95	0.052	-.0457343	11.96147

```
. predict logitpr, p
```

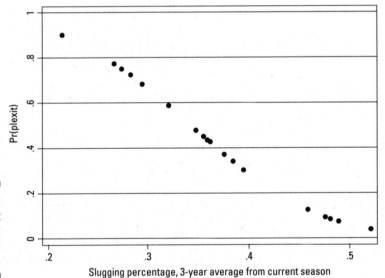

Figure 13-13:
STATA logit
results and
predicted
probabilities.

Slugging percentage, 3-year average from current season

Probit and logit estimation always produces a Pseudo R-squared measure of fit. It's calculated by $\tilde{R}^2 = 1 - \dfrac{\ln \hat{L}_{ur}}{\ln \hat{L}_0}$, where $\ln L_{ur}$ is the log likelihood for the estimated model and $\ln L_0$ is the log likelihood in the model with only an intercept. It's comparable to the R-squared value in OLS regression, but other measures are usually preferred for evaluating fit when the dependent variable is a dummy (dichotomous).

You can obtain more appropriate measures of fit for probit and logit models by comparing the model's predicted probabilities to the observed Y values. Appropriate measures of fit typically capture the fraction of times the model accurately predicts the outcome.

When you have to calculate a measure of fit using the predicted probabilities, start by determining how you define an accurate prediction from the model. Then set up a rule for aggregating the accurate predictions to provide an overall goodness-of-fit measure. No single measure of fit is universally accepted, but in the earlier section "Modeling Discrete Outcomes with the Linear Probability Model (LPM)" of this chapter, I use four different methodologies to calculate the percent accurately predicted. You can apply the same measures of fit used for the LPM to the probit and logit models. With a qualitative dependent variable, measures of the fraction of accurate predictions provide a reasonable alternative to the R-squared and Pseudo R-squared values. If you're not sure about which method (probit or logit) to use in a specific situation, you may want to compare these measures of fit to make your decision. Usually, however, the decision to go with one over the other is determined by norms in a particular area of research.

In the sections that follow, you continue working with output from probit and logit models. In particular, the coefficients from these models require special attention because the nonlinearity of the functions makes coefficient interpretation more complex.

Probit coefficients

When you estimate a probit function, keep in mind that the model is nonlinear and the coefficients can't be interpreted as partial-slope coefficients.

The coefficient(s) produced by estimating a probit model provide the change in the Z (standard normal) value for a unit change in the independent variable(s). Because the probit is derived from the standard normal distribution (a nonlinear function), you need calculus in order to obtain the impact of the independent variable(s) on the probability of observing the outcome. These influences are known as *marginal effects*.

You can see how marginal effects are calculated by looking at the probit specification. The standard probit model has the following form:

$$E(Y \mid X) = F(\beta_0 + \beta_1 X_i)$$

where F represents the standard normal CDF. Using calculus to obtain the slope (change in Y for a change in X), you get

$$\frac{\delta E(Y \mid X)}{\delta X} = f(\beta_0 + \beta_1 X_i) \cdot \beta_1$$

where f is the standard normal PDF.

You can estimate the marginal effect without calculus by using the estimated function and changing the value of X by unit. For example, suppose the estimated probit function is $\hat{P}_i = F(-3.2 + 0.4X_i)$ and $X = 10$. This becomes $F(0.8)$, so using the standard normal CDF, the predicted probability at $Z = 0.8$ is 0.79. If you increase the value of X by one unit to $X = 11$, the predicted probability becomes $F(1.2) = 0.88$. Therefore, the estimated marginal effect is $0.88 - 0.79 = 0.09$.

Even better than that trick is the fact that most econometric software that's equipped to estimate probit models can also calculate the marginal effects, as you can see in Figure 13-14, which uses the probit model from Figure 13-12 to illustrate how to obtain precise marginal effects. The results in Figure 13-14 are obtained by using the "probit" command in STATA followed by the "mfx" command. In other words, STATA uses the estimated coefficients and performs the calculus required to obtain the marginal effects. The results imply that if a player's slugging percentage increases by 0.1, the probability of that player being fired by his team decreases by 0.37 ($3.7 \times 0.1 = 0.37$).

```
. probit plexit slg_3_avg

Iteration 0:   log likelihood = -13.460233
Iteration 1:   log likelihood = -10.250021
Iteration 2:   log likelihood = -10.22414
Iteration 3:   log likelihood = -10.224106
Iteration 4:   log likelihood = -10.224106

Probit regression                                        Number of obs  =        20
                                                         LR chi2(1)     =      6.47
                                                         Prob > chi2    =    0.0110
Log likelihood = -10.224106                              Pseudo R2      =    0.2404
```

plexit	Coef.	Std. Err.	z	P>|z|	[95% Conf.	Interval]
slg_3_avg	-9.909194	4.341084	-2.28	0.022	-18.41756	-1.400826
_cons	3.396796	1.614144	2.10	0.035	.2331309	6.560461

```
. mfx

Marginal effects after probit
      y = Pr(plexit) (predict)
        = .37191895
```

variable	dy/dx	Std. Err.	z	P>|z|	[95% C.I.]	X
slg_3_~g	-3.747667	1.62937	-2.30	0.021	-6.94116 -.55417	.375769

Figure 13-14: STATA probit results with estimated marginal effects.

Keep in mind that estimating marginal effects using discrete unit changes is only an estimation and not perfectly precise. The reason for this is that the nonlinearity implies that the marginal effects change continuously along the estimated function.

Logit coefficients

You shouldn't interpret coefficients from your logit estimation as partial slope coefficients, because the model is nonlinear.

The coefficient(s) produced by estimating a logit model provide the change in the G (logistic) value for a unit change in the independent variable(s). Because the logit is derived from the logistic distribution (a nonlinear function), you have to use calculus to figure out the impact of the independent variable(s) on the probability of observing the outcome (that is, the marginal effects).

By beginning with the logit specification, I can show how the marginal effects are calculated. The standard logit model has the following form:

$$E(Y \mid X) = F(\beta_0 + \beta_1 X_i)$$

where F represents the logistic CDF. Using calculus to obtain the slope (change in Y for a change in X), I get

$$\frac{\delta E(Y \mid X)}{\delta X} = \frac{e^{\beta_0 + \beta_1 X_i} \beta_1}{1 + e^{\beta_0 + \beta_1 X_i}} \left(1 - \frac{e^{\beta_0 + \beta_1 X_i}}{1 + e^{\beta_0 + \beta_1 X_i}}\right) = \frac{e^{\beta_0 + \beta_1 X_i} \beta_1}{\left(1 + e^{\beta_0 + \beta_1 X_i}\right)^2}$$

where e is the base of the natural log (the value 2.71828 . . .).

To estimate the marginal effect *without* calculus, use the estimated function and change the value of X by one unit. For example, suppose the estimated logit function is

$$\hat{P}_i = F(-2.1 + 0.2 X_i) = \frac{e^{-2.1 + 0.2 X_i}}{1 + e^{-2.1 + 0.2 X_i}}$$

and $X = 18$. It becomes $F(-2.1 + 0.2(18)) = F(1.5)$, so using the logistic CDF, the predicted probability is

$$\hat{P}_i = F(1.5) = \frac{e^{1.5}}{1 + e^{1.5}} = \frac{4.4817}{5.4817} = 0.82$$

If you increase the value of X by one unit to $X = 19$, the predicted probability becomes

$$\hat{P}_i = F(1.7) = \frac{e^{1.7}}{1 + e^{1.7}} = \frac{5.4739}{6.4739} = 0.85$$

Therefore, the estimated marginal effect is $0.85 - 0.82 = 0.03$.

Using my logit model from Figure 13-13, in Figure 13-15 I show how you obtain precise marginal effects. I got the results in Figure 13-15 by using the "logit" command in STATA followed by the "mfx" command. In other words, STATA uses the estimated coefficients and performs the calculus required to obtain the marginal effects. The results imply that if a player's slugging percentage increases by 0.1, the probability of being released (fired) by his team decreases by 0.39 ($3.9 \times 0.1 = 0.39$).

```
. logit plexit slg_3_avg

Iteration 0:   log likelihood = -13.460233
Iteration 1:   log likelihood = -10.228237
Iteration 2:   log likelihood = -10.156101
Iteration 3:   log likelihood = -10.155964
Iteration 4:   log likelihood = -10.155964

Logistic regression                                          Number of obs  =      20
                                                             LR chi2(1)     =    6.61
                                                             Prob > chi2    =  0.0101
Log likelihood = -10.155964                                  Pseudo R2      =  0.2455
```

plexit	Coef.	Std. Err.	z	P>|z|	[95% Conf.	Interval]
slg_3_avg	-17.45519	8.47928	-2.06	0.040	-34.07428	-.8361081
_cons	5.95787	3.06312	1.95	0.052	-.0457343	11.96147

```
. mfx

Marginal effects after logit
      y  = Pr(plexit) (predict)
         = .35405636
```

variable	dy/dx	Std. Err.	z	P>|z|	[95% C.I.]	X
slg_3_~g	-3.99201	1.8509	-2.16	0.031	-7.6197 -.36432	.375769

Figure 13-15:
STATA logit
results with
estimated
marginal
effects.

Keep in mind that estimating marginal effects using discrete unit changes is only an estimation and not perfectly precise. The nonlinearity implies that the marginal effects change continuously along the estimated function.

Chapter 14

Limited Dependent Variable Models

. . . .

In This Chapter

▶ Exploring censored and truncated variables

▶ Understanding and dealing with selection issues

. . . .

*L*imited dependent variables are usually quantitative but have restricted values. You must pay particular attention to these types of situations because missing or constrained values for the dependent variable cause one or more traditional regression model assumptions to fail. Here are two examples of scenarios that result in limited dependent variables:

✔ You want to model the labor market using wages as the dependent variable, but only positive wages are observed, because when the wage is too low, individuals drop out of the labor force or the wage doesn't meet the legal minimum wage.

✔ You want to model demand for basketball games using ticket sales as the dependent variable, but sales reach a maximum at the arena's capacity (even if demand exceeds the sell-out capacity).

The restricted data available for outcomes makes using traditional regression analysis difficult. Fortunately, you can use econometric techniques to modify traditional regression analysis in the presence of limited dependent variables. In this chapter, get ready to see some practical examples, find out how to implement the techniques using STATA, and interpret your results.

The Nitty-Gritty of Limited Dependent Variables

Limited dependent variables arise when some minimum threshold value must be reached before the values of the dependent variable are observed and/or when some maximum threshold value restricts the observed values of the dependent variable.

A limited dependent variable causes the standard model to become

$$Y_i^* = \beta_0 + \beta_1 X_i + \varepsilon_i$$

where restricted values don't allow you to always observe Y^*. Specifically, you observe $Y_i^* = \max(Y_i^*, a)$ if the dependent variable is limited by a lower threshold and/or $Y_i^* = \min(Y_i^*, b)$ if the dependent variable is limited by an upper threshold. Because the ordinary least squares (OLS) technique estimates the model without accounting for the missing data or the values that are at the threshold (rather than their actual values), the resulting estimated coefficients are biased.

Situations where the dependent variable is *discrete* (meaning it has a finite number of possible outcomes) or where measurement of the dependent variable takes place while the process is still ongoing (like the amount of time unemployed) are also problematic for OLS estimation. A number of techniques (multinomial probit, multinomial logit, ordered probit, ordered logit, Poisson, negative binomial, and duration models) can be used for these scenarios, but treatment of these topics is usually reserved for advanced or graduate-level econometrics courses.

A limited dependent variable results in either a censored sample or a truncated sample. In other words, censored and truncated dependent variables are the two types of specific limited dependent variables you'll encounter.

Censored dependent variables

With a *censored dependent variable,* information is lost because some of the actual values for the dependent variable are limited to a minimum and/or maximum threshold value.

Typical examples of censored dependent variables include

- **The number of hours worked in a week:** Hours may be constrained by firms wanting to avoid payment of overtime rates even though employees may want to work more hours.
- **Income earned:** Income can be capped in survey data to maintain respondent confidentiality.
- **Sale of tickets to concerts and sporting events:** Ticket sales can be limited by stadium capacity.
- **Exam scores:** Exams scores may be limited to a range of 0 to 100, even though people receiving the minimum or maximum score aren't likely to be of exactly equal ability.

In Figure 14-1, I illustrate a situation with a censored dependent variable. The dots represent actual and observed values, and the asterisks represent values that would have corresponded to the observations but aren't actually observed. The empty circles indicate values that are observed but censored. Without censoring, their values would be at the * points.

Using data where the dependent variable captures a combination of actual values and values that are observed but limited to a threshold (censored), you can see a violation of the classical linear regression model (CLRM) assumption. Specifically, the conditional mean of the error isn't zero. In addition, the value of the error is correlated with the value of the independent variable.

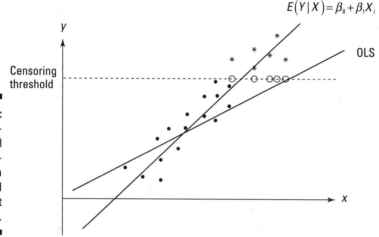

Figure 14-1: A regression model in the presence of a censored dependent variable.

Truncated dependent variables

With a *truncated dependent variable,* information is lost because some of the values for the variables are missing (meaning they aren't observed if they are above or below some threshold). Sometimes observations included in the sample have missing values for both the independent and dependent variables, and in other cases only the values for the dependent variable are missing.

A common scenario resulting in truncation is *nonrandom sample selection,* when some measurements from the population are less (or more) likely to be included in the sample than others. For example, researchers may be interested in the impact of a public program and only include individuals below the poverty line in the sample. The other typical scenario is when individual observations are included in a sample through *self-selection,* when the sample is essentially choosing itself rather than being determined by the researcher through randomization. For example, a dataset may include wages earned from work, but wages will be missing for people who have chosen to stay out of the labor force.

In Figure 14-2, I illustrate a situation with a truncated dependent variable. The dot indicates actual and observed values; the asterisk represents values that would have corresponded to the sample observations but aren't actually observed. Using the data where some values of the dependent variable aren't observed (truncated), you can see that the conditional mean of the error isn't zero (which violates a CLRM assumption). In addition, the value of the error is correlated with the value of the independent variable.

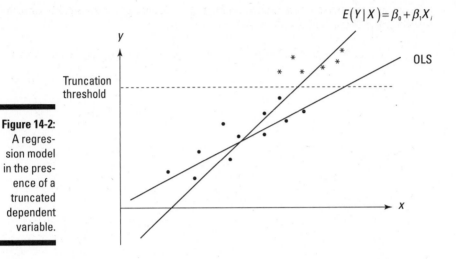

Figure 14-2:
A regres-
sion model
in the pres-
ence of a
truncated
dependent
variable.

The primary difference between a truncated and a censored variable is that the value of a truncated variable isn't observed at all. However, a value is observed for a censored variable, but it's suppressed for some observations at the threshold point.

Censored and truncated dependent variables lead to similar problems (biased coefficients), but the solution to the problem isn't the same in both scenarios. Properly identifying the dependent variable as censored or truncated helps you determine how to modify the estimation procedure in order to deal with the limited values of the dependent variable.

Modifying Regression Analysis for Limited Dependent Variables

Although you can deal with limited dependent variables in several ways depending on the nature of the data generating process, the most common are the *Tobit, truncated normal,* and *Heckman selection* models. I tell you all about these models in the following sections.

Tobin's Tobit

The Tobit model is best for when the dependent variable is censored (I give you the specifics on censored dependent variables in the earlier related section).

If you use OLS estimation with the observed data as if they're all uncensored values, you get biased coefficients. To avoid them, the estimation procedure must properly account for the censoring of the dependent variable. Maximum likelihood (ML) estimation does so.

Suppose you have the following model with upper-limit censoring (the most common type):

$$Y_i^* = \beta_0 + \beta_1 X_i + \varepsilon_i$$

$$\varepsilon \sim N\left(0, \sigma_\varepsilon^2\right)$$

$$Y_i = \begin{cases} Y_i^* & if\ Y_i^* < b \\ b & if\ Y_i^* \geq b \end{cases}$$

In the final equation, b is the maximum (censored) value of the dependent variable observed in the sample data. Using the probability of censorship, estimation is accomplished with ML rather than OLS. The log likelihood function that's maximized is

$$\ln L = \sum_{i=1}^{n} \left\{ \ln F\left(\frac{\beta_0 + \beta_1 X_i - b}{\sigma_\varepsilon}\right) + \ln\left[\frac{1}{\sigma_\varepsilon} f\left(\frac{Y_i - \beta_0 - \beta_1 X_i}{\sigma_\varepsilon}\right)\right] \right\}$$

where F denotes the standard normal CDF and f is the standard normal PDF (I cover the ML estimation technique in detail in Chapter 13). The coefficients estimated using this procedure represent the *marginal effects* (the impact on the dependent variable for a unit change in the independent variable) for the whole population. In that sense, ML estimation achieves the same outcome as OLS estimation. The difference, however, is that the ML technique can accommodate complex, nonlinear functions and produce estimates in situations where the solutions can't be expressed through simple algebraic formulas.

Most econometric software is equipped to estimate Tobit models. In Figure 14-3, I use data from a sample of workers (aged 18 – 64) to estimate how age affects the number of hours worked in a week. The sample contains censored observations because, although some individuals worked more than 40 hours in a week, 40 was the maximum workers could report. I got the results shown in Figure 14-3 by using the "tobit" command in STATA. (You can define the minimum and/or maximum threshold values at which the censoring occurs by using the options "ll" or "ul"). The bottom portion of the output (below the estimated coefficients) shows you how many observations have censored values.

Tobit estimation produces a likelihood ratio chi-squared statistic. It's analogous to the F-statistic in OLS, and it tests the null hypothesis that the estimated model doesn't produce a higher likelihood than a model with only a constant term.

You can interpret the resulting coefficients from Tobit estimation in the same manner as traditional marginal effects from OLS; an additional year of age increases the number of hours worked in a week by 0.299, on average.

```
. * Tobit with censored dependent variable

.tobit cenhrs age, ul(40)

Tobit regression                          Number of obs =   162148
                                          LR chi2(1)    =  3004.80
                                          Prob > chi2   =   0.0000
Log likelihood = -232649.08               Pseudo R2     =   0.0064
```

cenhrs	Coef.	Std. Err.	t	P>|t|	[95% Conf. Interval]	
age	.2987907	.00553	54.03	0.000	.2879519	.3096294
_cons	42.20982	.2346872	179.86	0.000	41.74983	42.6698
/sigma	21.65498	.09079			21.47704	21.83293

```
Obs. summary:        0   left-censored   observations
                 40161   uncensored      observations
                121987   right-censored  observations at cenhrs>=40
```

Figure 14-3:
```
. estat sum
```
STATA Estimation sample regress   Number of obs = 162148

Variable	Mean	Std. Dev.	Min	Max
cenhrs	36.52777	7.571247	1	40
age	41.40188	12.42228	18	64

Figure 14-3: STATA output from estimating a Tobit model.

In Figure 14-4, I estimate the same model that I use in Figure 14-3 but with OLS rather than the Tobit technique. If you ignore the censoring and estimate the model using OLS, the coefficients will be biased toward finding no relationship (smaller coefficients/effects). The p-values suggest that age is statistically significant, but the estimated effect is much smaller. The Tobit results (Figure 14-3) imply that an additional year of age increases the number of hours worked in a week by 0.299, on average. On the other hand, the OLS results (Figure 14-4) imply that hours worked increase by only 0.084 per week, on average.

```
. * OLS with censored dependent variable

. regress cenhrs age
```

Source	SS	df	MS		
Model	175260.436	1	175260.436		
Residual	9119619.51	162146	56.2432592		
Total	9294879.95	162147	57.3237861		

```
Number of obs =   162148
F (1,162146)  =  3116.11
Prob > F      =   0.0000
R-squared     =   0.0189
Adj R-squared =   0.0188
Root MSE      =   7.4996
```

cenhrs	Coef.	Std. Err.	t	P>|t|	[95% Conf. Interval]	
age	.0836924	.0014993	55.82	0.000	.0807539	.086631
_cons	33.06275	.0648064	510.18	0.000	32.93573	33.18977

Figure 14-4: STATA output using OLS to estimate a model that should be estimated with Tobit.

Truncated regression

Truncated regression applies the CLRM assumption of normality (which I tell you all about in Chapter 7), but it accounts for the drawing of observations from a restricted segment of the normal distribution. You can rely on it when the values for the dependent and independent variables are missing for part of the distribution (meaning they're above and/or below some threshold value).

When it comes to estimation, you can't apply OLS estimation to the observed data as if it's representative of the entire population. If you do, you'll wind up with biased coefficients. Instead, you need to use maximum likelihood (ML) estimation so you can properly account for the truncation by rescaling the normal distribution so that the cumulative probabilities add up to one over the restricted area. (For the full scoop on ML estimation, see Chapter 13.)

Imagine you have the following model with upper-limit truncation (the most common type of truncation you'll see):

$$Y_i^* = \beta_0 + \beta_1 X_i + \varepsilon_i$$

$$\varepsilon \sim N\left(0, \sigma_\varepsilon^2\right)$$

$$Y_i = \begin{cases} Y_i^* & \text{if } Y_i^* < b \\ \cdot & \text{if } Y_i^* \geq b \end{cases}$$

The dot ($\cdot$) represents a missing value at and above the truncation point. Using a rescaling of the normal distribution, estimation is accomplished with ML rather than OLS. The log likelihood function that's maximized is

$$\ln L = -\frac{n}{2} \ln\left(2\pi\sigma_\varepsilon^2\right) - \frac{1}{2\sigma_\varepsilon^2} \sum_{i=1}^{n} \left(Y_i - \beta_0 - \beta_1 X_i\right)^2 - \sum_{i=1}^{n} \ln F\left(\frac{b - \beta_0 - \beta_1 X_i}{\sigma_\varepsilon}\right)$$

where F denotes the standard normal CDF. The coefficients estimated using this procedure represent the *marginal effects* (the impact on the dependent variable for a unit change in the independent variable) for the whole population.

Figure 14-5 illustrates how to use STATA software to estimate a truncated normal regression model. In this case, I use data from a sample of workers to estimate how age affects the number of hours worked in a week. The sample is truncated because it includes only those individuals who worked full time (at least 35 hours in a week) and excludes those who worked part time. To get the results you see here, which show you how many observations are at the truncation point, I use the "truncreg" command in STATA. (To define the minimum and/or maximum threshold values at which the truncation occurs, you can use the "ll" or "ul" options.)

As with Tobit estimation, the resulting coefficients from the truncated normal estimation can be interpreted in the same manner as traditional marginal effects from OLS. In Figure 14-5, the estimated effect of an additional year of age is an increase of 0.243 hours worked per week, on average. Truncated normal estimation also produces a chi-squared statistic, which is like the F-statistic in OLS. It confirms or rejects the null hypothesis that the estimated model doesn't produce a higher likelihood than a model with only a constant term.

```
. * Truncated normal regression with truncated dependent variable

.truncreg trunhrs age, ll(35)
(note: 5710 obs. truncated)

Fitting full model:

Iteration 0: log likelihood = -410812.94
Iteration 1: log likelihood = -391182.99
Iteration 2: log likelihood = -390520.98
Iteration 3: log likelihood = -390442.95
Iteration 4: log likelihood = -390440.63
Iteration 5: log likelihood = -390440.62


Truncated regression
Limit:   lower =          35              Number of obs = 127528
         upper =        +inf             Wald chi2(1)  = 486.87
Log likelihood = -390440.62              Prob > chi2   = 0.0000
```

trunhrs	Coef.	Std. Err.	z	P>|t|	[95% Conf. Interval]
age	.2433834	.0110302	22.07	0.000	.2217646 .2650021
_cons	1.672696	1.07123	1.56	0.118	-.4268766 3.772269
/sigma	17.13738	.1882395	91.04	0.000	16.76844 17.50633

Figure 14-5:
STATA output from estimating a truncated normal model.

```
. estat sum

Estimation sample regress       Number of obs = 133238
```

Variable	Mean	Std. Dev.	Min	Max
trunhrs	42.61657	6.995591	35	98
age	42.18283	11.79904	18	64

Don't ignore the truncation and estimate the model using OLS or the coefficients will be biased toward finding no relationship (smaller coefficients/effects). I illustrate this in Figure 14-6, where I estimate the same model that I use in Figure 14-5 but using OLS instead of the truncated normal technique. Although age is statistically significant in both cases (p-values less than 0.10), notice that its estimated effect is much smaller in Figure 14-6 in comparison to Figure 14-5. The truncated normal regression results (Figure 14-5) imply that an additional year of age increases the number of hours worked in a week by 0.243, on average. On the other hand, the OLS results (Figure 14-6) imply that hours worked increase by only 0.044 per week, on average.

Oh, what the heck if I self select? Heckman's selection bias correction

Turn to the Heckman selection model when the dependent variable is truncated but the values for the independent variables are observed. (I describe truncated dependent variables in the earlier related section.)

Figure 14-6:
STATA
output using
OLS to
estimate a
model that
should be
estimated
using
truncated
normal
regression.

```
. * OLS with truncated dependent variable

. regress trunhrs age

    Source |       SS       df       MS              Number of obs =   133238
-----------+------------------------------           F (1,133236)  =   737.04
     Model | 35871.1329        1   35871.1329        Prob > F      =   0.0000
  Residual | 6484519.98133236     48.6694286         R-squared     =   0.0055
-----------+------------------------------           Adj R-squared =   0.0055
     Total | 6520391.12133237     48.9382913         Root MSE      =   6.9763

------------------------------------------------------------------------------
    cenhrs |      Coef.   Std. Err.      t    P>|t|     [95% Conf. Interval]
-----------+------------------------------------------------------------------
       age |   .0439758   .0016198    27.15   0.000     .0408009    .0471506
     _cons |   40.76154   .0709516   574.50   0.000     40.62248    40.90061
------------------------------------------------------------------------------
```

Again, assume you're working with the following model:

$$Y_i^* = \beta_0 + \beta_1 X_i + \varepsilon_i$$

$$\varepsilon \sim N\left(0, \sigma_\varepsilon^2\right)$$

with self-selection defined by

$$S_i = \gamma_0 + \gamma_1 W_{i1} + \gamma_2 W_{i2} + \dots + u_i$$

$$S_i = \begin{cases} 1 & \text{if } Y_i^* \text{ observed} \\ 0 & \text{if } Y_i^* \text{ not observed} \end{cases}$$

$$u \sim N\left(0,1\right)$$

$$Corr\left(\varepsilon, u\right) = \rho$$

Using the joint distribution of ε and u, you can accomplish the estimation required with the ML technique described in Chapter 13. (Why not use OLS estimation? Because that technique doesn't suitably account for the self-selection of observations into the estimation sample.)

The log likelihood function that's maximized is

$$\ln L = \sum_{i=1}^{n} \left\{ \ln F \left[\frac{\left(\left(\gamma_0 + \gamma_1 W_{i1} + \gamma_2 W_{i2} + \dots\right) + \left(Y_i^* - \beta_0 - \beta_1 X_i\right)\rho\right) / \sigma_\varepsilon}{\sqrt{1 - \rho^2}} \right] - \right.$$

$$\left. \frac{1}{2} \left(\frac{Y_i^* - \beta_0 - \beta_1 X_i}{\sigma_\varepsilon}\right)^2 - \ln\left(\sqrt{2\pi}\sigma_\varepsilon\right) + \ln F\left(-\gamma_0 - \gamma_1 W_{i1} - \gamma_2 W_{i2} - \dots\right) \right\}$$

where F denotes the standard normal CDF. In a Heckman model, the variables that influence truncation usually aren't identical to those that influence the value of the dependent variable (in contrast to the Tobit model, where they're assumed to be the same). The log likelihood function is also similar to the truncated normal, but values for the independent variables are observable (unlike the truncated normal). In other words, a Heckman model can improve your estimates over the truncated normal and Tobit techniques by using information from variables that influence whether or not your dependent variable is observed. The coefficients estimated using this procedure represent the *marginal effects* (the impact on the dependent variable for a unit change in the independent variable) for the whole population.

Although ML estimation is the most efficient way of estimating a selection model, the joint (bivariate normality) distributional assumptions are restrictive, and sometimes optimization of the likelihood function fails to converge.

An alternative to ML estimation of a selection model is to use the Heckit model. It can be accomplished by following these steps:

1. **Estimate the selection equation $S_i = \gamma_0 + \gamma_1 W_{i1} + \gamma_2 W_{i2} + \ldots + u_i$ with a probit model (I discuss the details of probit models in Chapter 13).**

2. **Compute the inverse Mills ratio:**

$$\hat{\lambda}_i = \frac{f\left(\hat{\gamma}_0 + \hat{\gamma}_1 W_{i1} + \hat{\gamma}_2 W_{i2} + \ldots\right)}{F\left(\hat{\gamma}_0 + \hat{\gamma}_1 W_{i1} + \hat{\gamma}_2 W_{i2} + \ldots\right)}$$

where f is the standard normal PDF and F is the standard normal CDF.

3. **Estimate the model $Y_i = \beta_0 + \beta_1 X_i + \beta_2 \hat{\lambda}_i + \varepsilon_i$ using the selected sample.**

Your selection equation (the part of the model that predicts truncation) should include all the independent variables used to explain variation in the value of the dependent variable plus some additional variables that only influence the chances of truncation and not the level of the dependent variable. In other words, the X variables should be a subset of the W variables.

Lucky for you, most econometric software can estimate Heckman models. Figure 14-7 shows STATA outputs that use data from a sample of females to estimate how age affects hourly wages (the natural log of hourly wages is the dependent variable). I obtained the results by using the "heckman" command in STATA. Note that the "select" option is required to define the selection equation. In order to obtain the alternative Heckit estimates, you can use the "twostep" option. The output shows you how many observations have unobserved values for the dependent variable and how each of the variables affects the selection process.

```
. * Heckman ML estimation

. heckman lnhrwage age, select (age ownchild)

Iteration 0:  log likelihood = -161675.88
Iteration 1:  log likelihood =  -159041.2
Iteration 2:  log likelihood = -156094.41
Iteration 3:  log likelihood = -155818.57
Iteration 4:  log likelihood = -155806.76
Iteration 5:  log likelihood = -155806.28
Iteration 6:  log likelihood = -155806.28

Heckman selection model                    Number of obs =  129009
(regression model with sample selection)    Wald chi2(1) =   55321
                                            Prob > chi2  =   73688

                                            Walk chi2(1) = 3469.78
Log likelihood = -155806.3                  Prob > chi2  =  0.0000
```

lnhrwage	Coef.	Std. Err.	z	P>|t|	[95% Conf. Interval]	
lhrwage						
age	.0106172	.0001802	58.90	0.000	.0102639	.0109705
_cons	2.305555	.0114167	201.95	0.000	2.283178	2.327931
select						
age	-.0035006	.0002683	-13.05	0.000	-.0040265	-.0029747
ownchild	-.543048	.0033788	-16.07	0.000	-.060927	-.0476825
_cons	.3618933	.0123487	29.31	0.000	.3376903	.3860962
/athrho	.0937429	.0224953	4.17	0.000	.049653	.1378328
/lnsigma	-.4952532	.0028987	-170.85	0.000	-.5009346	-.4895718
rho	.0934693	.0222987			.0496123	.1369665
sigma	.6094166	.0017665			.6059641	.6128888
lambda	.0569617	.0136625			.0301838	.0837397

```
. estat sum

Estimation sample regress          Number of obs = 73688
```

Variable	Mean	Std. Dev.	Min	Max
lnhrwage	2.780857	.6224905	-8.69951	7.1309
age	41.08797	12.53627	18	64

```
. * Heckman two step (Heckit) estimation

. heckman lnhrwage age, select (age ownchild) twostep
note: two-step estimate of rho = 1.0005352 is truncated to 1

Heckman selection model - two-step estimates   Number of obs =  129009
(regression model with sample selection)        Censored obs  =   55321
                                                Uncensored obs =  73688

                                                Wald chi2(1) = 1098.62
                                                Prob > chi2  =  0.0000
```

lnhrwage	Coef.	Std. Err.	z	P>|t|	[95% Conf. Interval]	
lhrwage						
age	.0091651	.0002765	33.15	0.000	.0086231	.009707
_cons	1.749355	.0597074	29.30	0.000	1.632331	1.86638
select						
age	-.0034798	.0002687	-12.95	0.000	-.0040065	-.0029531
ownchild	-.0522367	.0033522	-15.58	0.000	-.0588068	-.0456666
_cons	.3596791	.0123605	29.10	0.000	.335453	.3839052
mills						
lambda	.9549106	.0946793	10.09	0.000	.7693427	1.148479
rho	1.00000					
sigma	.95491059					

Figure 14-7: STATA output from estimating a Heckman selection model.

Again, you can interpret the resulting coefficients from the estimation of a Heckman selection model the same way as traditional marginal effects from OLS. In Figure 14-7, an additional year of age is associated with a 1.06 percent increase in the hourly wage, on average (keep in mind that this interpretation uses the fact that the dependent variable is measured in logs). Estimation of a Heckman selection model also produces a chi-squared statistic, which is similar to the *F*-statistic in OLS and tests the null hypothesis that estimated model doesn't produce a higher likelihood than a model with only a constant term.

In a selection model, the direction of bias from using OLS depends on the nature of the selection process. In Figure 14-8, I estimate the same model from Figure 14-7, but I use OLS instead of the Heckman technique. In this particular example, the selection doesn't produce a large bias in the coefficients. The Heckman results suggest that an additional year of age increases hourly earnings, on average, by 1.06 percent while the OLS results imply a 1.07 percent increase.

Figure 14-8:
STATA
output
using OLS
to estimate
a model
that should
use the
Heckman
technique.

```
. * OLS with self selected sample

. regress lnhrwage age
```

Source	SS	df	MS		Number of obs =	73688
					F (1,73686) =	3595.23
Model	1328.33962	1	1328.33962		Prob > F =	0.0000
Residual	27224.9639	73686	.369472681		R-squared =	0.0465
					Adj R-squared =	0.0465
Total	28553.3036	73687	.38749445		Root MSE =	.60784

cenhrs	Coef.	Std. Err.	t	P>|t|	[95% Conf. Interval]	
age	.01071	.0001786	59.96	0.000	.0103599	.0110601
_cons	2.340804	.0076731	305.07	0.000	2.325764	2.355843

Part VI
Extending the Basic Econometric Model

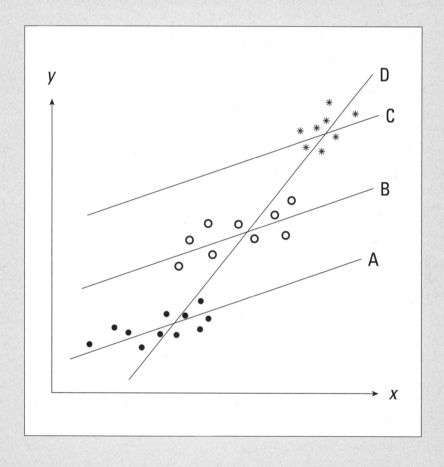

If you're interested in discovering econometric methods of forecasting, you'll love the free bonus chapter I provide at www.dummies.com/extras/econometrics.

In this part . . .

✔ Use time-series data for *static models* (where the dependent variable reacts instantaneously to changes in the independent variable) and *dynamic models* (where the dependent variable doesn't react fully to a change in the independent variable during the period in which the change occurs).

✔ Modify traditional econometric estimation techniques to handle *pooled cross-sectional data* (data that has been collected over time) and discover how analyzing pooled cross-sections can be useful in evaluating policy changes that occur at a specific point in time.

✔ Analyze important economic questions that can't be addressed using data that are exclusively cross sectional or time series by turning to *panel data* (data that features identical cross-sectional units included in each time period that data are collected).

Chapter 15

Static and Dynamic Models

In This Chapter

▶ Recognizing the difference between static and dynamic models

▶ Identifying and eliminating time trends

▶ Spotting seasonal patterns in data

*W*ith time-series data, you obtain measurements on one or more variables captured over time in a given space (a specific country, state, and so on). In some cases, this leads to econometric models with unique characteristics. In this chapter, I provide some examples of regression models using time-series data, and I discuss models that are similar to those used with cross-sectional data (static models) and others that are unique to time-series applications (dynamic models). I also show you how time-series models can be used to estimate trends and seasonality.

Using Contemporaneous and Lagged Variables in Regression Analysis

When you're using time-series data, you can assume that the independent variables have a contemporaneous (static) or lagged (dynamic) effect on your dependent variable. It depends on how your econometric model assumes that the dependent variable will react:

✔ If it reacts instantaneously to changes in the independent variable(s), then your model is *static* and will estimate a *contemporaneous* relationship at time *t*.

✔ If it doesn't react fully to a change in the independent variable(s) during the period in which the change occurs, then your model is *dynamic* and will estimate both a *contemporaneous* relationship at time *t* and *lagged* relationship at time *t* – 1.

You can specify a generic static model as $Y_t = \beta_0 + \beta_1 X_t + \varepsilon_t$, where the *t* subscripts denote the importance of the chronological ordering of observations.

A generic dynamic model is a *distributed lag model*. You can specify it as

$$Y_t = \alpha + \delta_0 X_t + \delta_1 X_{t-1} + \delta_2 X_{t-2} + \ldots + \delta_r X_{t-r} + \varepsilon_t$$

where the t subscripts denote the time period and r denotes the maximum number of lags (the maximum number of periods it takes for the dependent variable to fully absorb changes in the independent variables).

In the distributed lag model, $Y_t = \alpha + \delta_0 X_t + \delta_1 X_{t-1} + \delta_2 X_{t-2} + \ldots + \delta_r X_{t-r} + \varepsilon_t$, δ_0 captures the immediate impact of a one-unit increase in the independent variable. This term is known as the *impact multiplier*, or *short-run propensity*. The long-run increase in the dependent variable due to a one-time, permanent increase in the independent variable is $\delta_0 + \delta_1 + \delta_2 + \ldots + \delta_r$. It's called the *long-run propensity*.

The following sections zero in on the dynamic model to show you some of the inherent problems in the model and how you can test and correct for autocorrelation in the model.

Examining problems with dynamic models

In practice, distributed lag models can be plagued by estimation problems. The two most common issues are high multicollinearity and the loss of degrees of freedom. You'd expect the lag coefficients to steadily decline as the change in the independent variables is gradually absorbed by the dependent variable, but high multicollinearity usually causes the coefficient estimates to display erratic behavior. Furthermore, losing degrees of freedom for each additional lag increases the standard errors and reduces the chances of finding statistically significant coefficients.

A common solution to the estimation issues associated with distributed lag models is to replace the lagged values of the independent variable with a lagged value of the dependent variable. This type of dynamic model is known as an autoregressive model.

A simple autoregressive model can be expressed as $Y_t = \alpha + \delta X_t + \gamma Y_{t-1} + \varepsilon_t$, where the dependent variable (Y_t) is assumed to be influenced by the contemporaneous (current) value of the independent variable (X_t) and the lagged (previous) value of the dependent variable (Y_{t-1}).

Using the assumption that the same model holds in previous periods, I can show that the autoregressive model is equivalent to the distributed lag model. My model in the current period is $Y_t = \alpha + \delta X_t + \gamma Y_{t-1} + \varepsilon_t$, so in the previous period my autoregressive model would be $Y_{t-1} = \alpha + \delta X_{t-1} + \gamma Y_{t-2} + \varepsilon_{t-1}$. I can now substitute for Y_{t-1} and get either

$$Y_t = \alpha + \delta X_t + \gamma(\alpha + \delta X_{t-1} + \gamma Y_{t-2} + \varepsilon_{t-1}) + \varepsilon_t$$

or

$$Y_t = (\alpha + \gamma\alpha) + \delta X_t + \gamma\delta X_{t-1} + \gamma^2 Y_{t-2} + (\gamma\varepsilon_{t-1} + \varepsilon_t)$$

Through recursive substitution, I end up with

$$Y_t = \alpha^* + \delta X_t + \gamma\delta X_{t-1} + \gamma^2\delta X_{t-2} + \gamma^3\delta X_{t-3} + \dots + \gamma^r\delta X_{t-r} + \varepsilon_t^*$$

which allows me to directly compare the coefficients in the distributed lag model to those of the autoregressive model. The resulting comparison is $\delta_1 = \gamma\delta$, $\delta_2 = \gamma^2\delta$, $\delta_3 = \gamma^3\delta$, ..., $\delta_r = \gamma^r\delta$. Consequently, any value for γ between 0 and 1 ensures a steadily declining effect for changes in the independent variable that occurred in the more distant past.

In Figure 15-1, I use STATA to estimate both an autoregressive model (15-1a) and a distributed lag model (Figure 15-1b) with the same dependent variable, Y_t, inventories. The data consists of yearly sales and inventory data from 1950 to 1991. Prior to performing any time-series operation, I have to specify which variable captures the time component using the "tsset" command. That command keeps the data internally organized and allows me to perform lag operations that rely on the order of the data.

```
. tsset Year
        time variable:  Year, 1950 to 1991
              delta:  1 unit
```

```
. regress Inventories Sales L1.Inventories
```

Source	SS	df	MS		
				Number of obs =	41
				F(2, 38) =28524.77	
Model	2.6865e+12	2	1.3432e+12	Prob > F =	0.0000
Residual	1.7894e+09	38	47090602.5	R-squared =	0.9993
				Adj R-squared =	0.9993
Total	2.6883e+12	40	6.7207e+10	Root MSE =	6862.3

Inventories	Coef.	Std. Err.	t	P>|t|	[95% Conf. Interval]	
Sales	1.28675	.0887745	14.49	0.000	1.107036	1.466465
Inventories						
L1.	.1794903	.0594496	3.02	0.005	.0591407	.2998398
_cons	2449.299	1717.869	1.43	0.162	-1028.344	5926.943

a

```
. regress Inventories Sales L1.Sales L2.Sales L3.Sales L4.Sales
```

Source	SS	df	MS		
				Number of obs =	38
				F(5, 32) = 8826.95	
Model	2.4922e+12	5	4.9845e+11	Prob > F =	0.0000
Residual	1.8070e+09	32	56468889	R-squared =	0.9993
				Adj R-squared =	0.9992
Total	2.4940e+12	37	6.7407e+10	Root MSE =	7514.6

Inventories	Coef.	Std. Err.	t	P>|t|	[95% Conf. Interval]	
Sales						
--.	1.271806	.1159413	10.97	0.000	1.035641	1.507971
L1.	.418248	.2171756	1.93	0.063	-.0241243	.8606203
L2.	-.2680389	.2339104	-1.15	0.260	-.7444987	.2084209
L3.	.3478805	.2262945	1.54	0.134	-.1130662	.8088273
L4.	-.2151242	.1438196	-1.50	0.145	-.5080751	.0778267
_cons	2501.72	2067.663	1.21	0.235	-1709.971	6713.412

b

Figure 15-1: STATA output of (a) autoregressive and (b) distributed lag models.

The results first show the estimates from the autoregressive model. Using those estimates, I can calculate the distributed lag coefficients and write the autoregressive results in distributed lag format as

$$\delta_1 = \gamma\delta = (0.18)(1.29) = 0.232$$
$$\delta_2 = \gamma^2\delta = (0.18)^2(1.29) = 0.042$$
$$\delta_3 = \gamma^3\delta = (0.18)^3(1.29) = 0.008$$
$$\delta_4 = \gamma^4\delta = (0.18)^4(1.29) = 0.001$$

Notice, however, that these results aren't consistent with the distributed lag estimates from STATA because, for example, $\delta_1 = 0.232$ in the autoregressive model while $\delta_1 = 0.418$ in the distributed lag model. The distributed lag estimates (Figure 15-1b) suffer from unpredictable shifts in the parameter estimates because they're plagued by high collinearity. Therefore, when estimating dynamic models, applied econometricians prefer the autoregressive model (Figure 15-1a) to the distributed lag model.

Testing and correcting for autocorrelation in dynamic models

Autocorrelation occurs when the error term is serially correlated, which means that the error term in one period is correlated with the error term in another period. (I provide a more precise definition of autocorrelation in Chapter 12).

Autocorrelation is a typical problem that arises with time-series data. In its presence, the standard errors are likely to be biased, and the resulting measures of statistical significance aren't reliable (I suggest some solutions to this issue in Chapter 12). However, in dynamic models of the form $Y_t = \alpha + \delta X_t + \gamma Y_{t-1} + \varepsilon_t$, the problem of autocorrelation is more common and more serious. Autocorrelation in a dynamic model causes the OLS coefficients to be biased.

I can show the source of bias in a dynamic model with autocorrelation $\varepsilon_t = \rho\varepsilon_{t-1} + u_t$ by substituting the autocorrelation process into the model, so $Y_t = \alpha + \delta X_t + \gamma Y_{t-1} + \rho\varepsilon_{t-1} + u_t$. If I lag the original model by one period, I have $Y_{t-1} = \alpha + \delta X_{t-1} + \gamma Y_{t-2} + \varepsilon_{t-1}$. Consequently, I find that a change in ε_{t-1} causes both ε_t and Y_{t-1} to change. Because Y_{t-1} is an independent variable in the original model, its relationship (correlation) with ε_t is problematic because it violates a classical linear regression model (CLRM) assumption that the value of the error term and independent variables isn't correlated.

Because econometricians view biased coefficients to be more problematic than biased standard errors, testing for autocorrelation is essential if you're estimating a dynamic model. Turn to the Breusch-Godfrey test in this scenario. (I provide step-by-step instructions for performing this test in Chapter 12.) If you find evidence of autocorrelation, you can perform the preferred method of autocorrelation correction with dynamic models: feasible generalized least squares (FGLS). You can find the details of this procedure in Chapter 12.

Avoid using the Durbin-Watson *d* statistic when you're estimating a dynamic time-series model. Although it's a common test for autocorrelation in static time-series models, if you try to use it in a dynamic time series model, you're more likely to find no evidence of autocorrelation even in its presence. In a dynamic model, the Durbin-Watson *d* statistic is biased toward 2 (that is, finding no autocorrelation).

Projecting Time Trends with OLS

Most economic time series grow over time, but sometimes time series actually decline over time. In either case, you're looking at a *time trend.*

The most common models capturing time trends are either *linear* or *exponential.* If the dependent variable has a relatively steady increase over time, your best bet is to model the relationship with a linear time trend. However, if the *growth rate* is fairly steady (while the rate at which the value of the dependent variable changes isn't constant), then you need to model the relationship with an exponential time trend.

- A linear time trend has the form $Y_t = \alpha_0 + \alpha_1 t + \varepsilon_t$, where *t* is the time trend variable (usually a sequential numbering of the time periods beginning with a value of 1) and α_1 is the time trend coefficient and represents the rate at which the *value* of the dependent variable changes, on average, in each subsequent time period. If α_1 is positive, then the dependent variable increases over time. If α_1 is negative, then the dependent variable decreases over time.

- You can express an exponential time trend as $\ln Y_t = \alpha_0 + \alpha_1 t + \varepsilon_t$, where *t* is the time trend variable and α_1 is the time trend coefficient and represents the rate at which the *growth* of the dependent variable changes, on average, in each subsequent time period. If α_1 is positive, then the dependent variable's growth rate is positive over time. If α_1 is negative, then the dependent variable's growth rate is negative over time. (I provide additional details about these types of exponential functions in Chapter 8.)

In Figure 15-2, I use STATA to graph yearly inventories from 1950 to 1991 and estimate a time trend model. Most datasets don't contain a time variable, so you can do as I do here and sort the data using the variable that captures the sequencing of observations *(year)* and create the time variable. Given the depiction of the time series in Figure 15-2, applying the exponential time trend model is most appropriate in this case. The estimated value of 0.07 for α_1 implies that, on average, inventories have grown at a rate of approximately 7 percent per year.

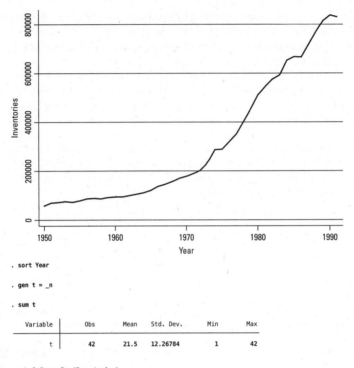

```
. sort Year

. gen t = _n

. sum t
```

Variable	Obs	Mean	Std. Dev.	Min	Max
t	42	21.5	12.26784	1	42

```
. gen lnInv = log(Inventories)

. regress lnInv t
```

Figure 15-2:
STATA
yearly
time-series
graph and
output from
estimating
a time trend
model.

Source	SS	df	MS			
Model	30.8147566	1	30.8147566			
Residual	.736217771	40	.018405444			
Total	31.5509744	41	.769535961			

```
Number of obs =      42
F(  1,    40) = 1674.22
Prob > F      =  0.0000
R-squared     =  0.9767
Adj R-squared =  0.9761
Root MSE      =  .13567
```

lnInv	Coef.	Std. Err.	t	P>|t|	[95% Conf.	Interval]
t	.0706674	.0017271	40.92	0.000	.0671768	.074158
_cons	10.76778	.0426266	252.61	0.000	10.68163	10.85394

In my example, creating the trend variable is a straightforward procedure because there's only one time variable. But in some cases, multiple time variables exist. For example, with monthly data that spans several years, the data is likely to contain a *year* and *month* variable. In that case, you'd want to sort by both year and month before you create the trend variable.

When dealing with observations measured over multiple time periods, the value of the trend variable should always represent the order of the observation in a chronological sequence.

If you'd like to avoid using a log transformation of your dependent variable (perhaps it doesn't seem appropriate with the other factors that you've included in the model as independent variables), then a quadratic time trend can also work well in situations where the time trend isn't linear. Although higher order polynomials could be used for your time trend, they aren't popular among applied econometricians because they're difficult to justify theoretically and typically consume additional degrees of freedom without significantly increasing the explanatory power.

In the following subsections, you extend your ability to use time trends in econometric models. Specifically, you see how time trends can be used to mitigate problems of spurious correlation and how trend coefficients can be used to detrend time-series data.

Spurious correlation and time series

The change/trend (positive or negative) of values over time isn't necessarily unique to your dependent variable. In general, all time-series variables (including your independent variables) are susceptible to this tendency. The consequence of failing to properly account for this common trend component is that you'll overstate the explanatory power of your independent variables.

If your regression model contains dependent and independent variables that are trending, then you end up with a *spurious correlation problem*. Using regression results when spurious correlation is present leads to erroneous conclusions about the causal effect of the independent variable(s).

Consider the model

$$Y_t = \beta_0 + \beta_1 X_{t1} + \beta_2 X_{t2} + \ldots + \beta_p X_{tp} + \varepsilon_t$$

where you believe that X directly causes Y. If, however, both X and Y exhibit an upward (or downward) trend for reasons unrelated to the relationship they have with each other, the results appear to show that X has a strong effect on Y.

If time significantly explains variation in the dependent variable and is also correlated with your independent variable, then you've excluded a relevant variable from your model and have introduced bias into your estimated coefficients.

Adding some form of time trend component (linear, quadratic, or exponential) to your regression takes care of the spurious correlation problem. The time trend now picks up the co-movement of your variables and allows you to make more convincing arguments about their causal relationship.

For example, if you have a situation where unobserved factors are causing your dependent and independent variables to increase (or decrease) over time, then you should estimate a model like this:

$$Y_t = \beta_0 + \beta_1 X_{t1} + \beta_2 X_{t2} + \ldots + \beta_p X_{tp} + \lambda t + \varepsilon_t$$

where X represents your independent variable and t is a trend variable (a sequential numbering of the time periods beginning with a value of 1). In this model, suppose I initially use U.S. GDP as the Y variable and my age as the only X variable. I find a positive relationship between my age and GDP, giving the appearance that my increasing age causes GDP growth. This occurs because both increase over time. If I include the time trend variable, t, then the explanatory power of my age disappears.

Including a trend variable doesn't always reduce the explanatory power of other independent variables. If your dependent variable trends in one direction and your independent variable trends in the other direction, then the inclusion of the trend variable may increase the significance of your independent variable.

Detrending time-series data

If you remove trending patterns from the data, that data is considered *trend-adjusted* or *detrended*. The main point of estimating a regression model with detrended data is to derive the explanatory power of the other independent variables.

If you want to obtain a goodness-of-fit measure that isolates the influence of your independent variables, you need to estimate your model with detrended values for both your dependent and independent variables.

Here's how to obtain the goodness-of-fit, or R-squared, net of trend effects:

1. **Regress your dependent variable on the trend variable to obtain the estimated function $Y_t = \hat{\alpha}_0 + \hat{\alpha}_1 t + \hat{\varepsilon}_{tY}$ and retain the residuals from this regression.**

2. **Regress each of your independent variables on the trend variable to obtain the estimated functions $X_{tk} = \hat{\alpha}_{0k} + \hat{\alpha}_{1k} t + \hat{\varepsilon}_{tX_k}$, where k represents a specific independent variable, and retain the residuals from all k of these regressions.**

3. **Regress the residuals obtained in Step 1 ($\hat{\varepsilon}_{tY}$) on the residuals obtained in Step 2 ($\hat{\varepsilon}_{tX_k}$) to estimate $\hat{\varepsilon}_{tY} = \beta_0 + \beta_1 \hat{\varepsilon}_{tX_k} + u_t$.**

   The R-squared from this regression provides a better of measure of fit when the time series exhibits extensive trending.

The traditional R-squared can be overinflated when the data contains significant trending. Under these circumstances, you can find an alternative R-squared value by estimating a regression with detrended data.

In Figure 15-3, I use STATA to estimate the impact of yearly sales on inventories from 1950 to 1991. First I estimate the model with the raw data. Then I estimate the model with detrended data. Detrending the data has a small effect on the results in Figure 15-3. As expected, the R-squared is smaller after the data is detrended (0.9936 compared to 0.9992), but the difference isn't large. In this case, the result implies that the independent variable's ability to explain variation in the dependent variable isn't being highly overstated by trending.

```
. sort Year

. gen t = _n

. regress Inventories Sales
```

Source	SS	df	MS				
Model	2.7511e+12	1	2.7511e+12		Number of obs =		42
Residual	2.2222e+09	40	55556036.6		F(1, 40) =49518.79		
					Prob > F = 0.0000		
					R-squared = 0.9992		
					Adj R-squared = 0.9992		
Total	2.7533e+12	41	6.7153e+10		Root MSE = 7453.6		

Inventories	Coef.	Std. Err.	t	P>|t|	[95% Conf.	Interval]
Sales	1.554329	.0069849	222.53	0.000	1.540213	1.568446
_cons	1668.669	1806.696	0.92	0.361	-1982.799	5320.138

```
. regress Inventories t
```

Source	SS	df	MS				
Model	2.4083e+12	1	2.4083e+12		Number of obs =		42
Residual	3.4503e+11	40	8.6257e+09		F(1, 40) = 279.20		
					Prob > F = 0.0000		
					R-squared = 0.8747		
					Adj R-squared = 0.8716		
Total	2.7533e+12	41	6.7153e+10		Root MSE = 92874		

Inventories	Coef.	Std. Err.	t	P>|t|	[95% Conf.	Interval]
t	19755.67	1182.323	16.71	0.000	17366.11	22145.24
_cons	-113021.6	29181.26	-3.87	0.000	-171999.1	-54044.07

```
. predict eInv, resid

. regress Sales t
```

Source	SS	df	MS				
Model	9.9480e+11	1	9.9480e+11		Number of obs =		42
Residual	1.4392e+11	40	3.5979e+09		F(1, 40) = 276.49		
					Prob > F = 0.0000		
					R-squared = 0.8736		
					Adj R-squared = 0.8705		
Total	1.1387e+12	41	2.7774e+10		Root MSE = 59983		

Sales	Coef.	Std. Err.	t	P>|t|	[95% Conf.	Interval]
t	12697.18	763.6001	16.63	0.000	11153.89	14240.47
_cons	-73509.99	18846.64	-3.90	0.000	-111600.5	-35419.51

```
. predict eSales, resid
. regress eInv eSales
```

Figure 15-3: STATA time-series output from estimating a detrended model.

Source	SS	df	MS				
Model	3.4282e+11	1	3.4282e+11		Number of obs =		42
Residual	2.2026e+09	40	55064350.8		F(1, 40) = 6225.88		
					Prob > F = 0.0000		
					R-squared = 0.9936		
					Adj R-squared = 0.9935		
Total	3.4503e+11	41	8.4153e+09		Root MSE = 7420.5		

eInv	Coef.	Std. Err.	t	P>|t|	[95% Conf.	Interval]
eSales	1.543403	.0195605	78.90	0.000	1.50387	1.582936
_cons	-.0003685	1145.014	-0.00	1.000	-2314.159	2314.158

In your primary econometric results, report the estimates from the model with the raw data and trend variable(s), not the detrended data.

Using OLS for Seasonal Adjustments

The higher the frequency of an economic time series, the more likely it is to display seasonal patterns. For example, retail sales figures often exhibit a significant increase around the winter holidays. When you're dealing with quarterly data, this increase is likely to be reflected with larger values in the fourth quarter of each year. However, with monthly data, the change is more evident with even sharper increases in sales during the months of November and December.

The most common models capturing seasonal patterns include dummy variables representing the frequency with which the data were collected (usually quarter or month dummies).

A typical seasonal pattern is modeled with the specification $Y_t = \alpha_0 + \alpha_1 S_1 + \alpha_2 S_2 + \ldots + \varepsilon_t$

where S variables are your season dummy variables (flip to Chapter 9 for more on dummy variables) and the various α are the season coefficients representing the impact of each season, on average, on the dependent variable. If an α is positive, then the dependent variable increases during that season. If an α is negative, then the dependent variable decreases during that season.

In Figure 15-4, I use STATA to graph the log of monthly souvenir sales from 1987 to 1993 and estimate a seasonal pattern model. The dummy variables capturing the month of each observation have already been created. Given the depiction of the time series here, I can deduce that December will have significantly larger sales figures in comparison to other months. Using January as the reference month, several months have significantly larger sales figures. In comparison to January, sales are 74 percent larger in March and increase by more than 200 percent, on average, in December.

In the following sections, I explain how you can estimate the effect of seasonal variation on your dependent variable and then tell you how to remove seasonal patterns from your time-series data.

Estimating seasonality effects

Seasonality effects can be correlated with both your dependent and independent variables. In order to avoid confounding the seasonality effects with those of your independent variables, you need to explicitly control for the season in which the measurement is observed.

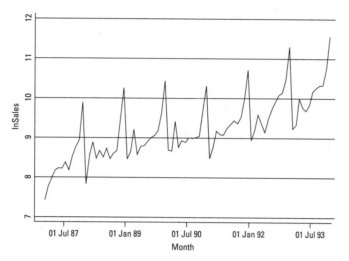

```
. regress lnSales Feb Mar Apr May Jun Jul Aug Sep Oct Nov Dec
```

Source	SS	df	MS		
Model	25.10103	11	2.28191182	Number of obs =	84
Residual	26.7134703	72	.37102042	F(11, 72) =	6.15
				Prob > F =	0.0000
				R-squared =	0.4844
Total	51.8145002	83	.624271087	Adj R-squared =	0.4057
				Root MSE =	.60911

Figure 15-4: STATA monthly time-series graph and output from estimating a seasonal pattern model.

lnSales	Coef.	Std. Err.	t	P>|t|	[95% Conf.	Interval]
Feb	.2734365	.3255854	0.84	0.404	-.375606	.9224791
Mar	.7399923	.3255854	2.27	0.026	.0909498	1.389035
Apr	.4501129	.3255854	1.38	0.171	-.1989297	1.099155
May	.4975664	.3255854	1.53	0.131	-.1514762	1.146609
Jun	.5589275	.3255854	1.72	0.090	-.090115	1.20797
Jul	.7425735	.3255854	2.28	0.026	.0935309	1.391616
Aug	.7421033	.3255854	2.28	0.026	.0930607	1.391146
Sep	.8454884	.3255854	2.60	0.011	.1964458	1.494531
Oct	.9455705	.3255854	2.90	0.005	.296528	1.594613
Nov	1.426946	.3255854	4.38	0.000	.7779037	2.075989
Dec	2.204459	.3255854	6.77	0.000	1.555417	2.853502
_cons	8.434401	.2302236	36.64	0.000	7.975458	8.893343

If you include dummy variables for seasons along with the other relevant independent variables, you can simultaneously obtain better estimates of both seasonality and the effects of the other independent variables.

Consider the model $Y_t = \beta_0 + \beta_1 X_{t1} + \beta_2 X_{t2} + \ldots + \beta_p X_{tp} + \varepsilon_t$ for a situation in which you believe that X directly causes Y. If, however, both X and Y are affected by seasonal trends for reasons unrelated to the relationship they have with each other, then X appears to have a strong effect on Y.

If seasonality significantly explains variation in the dependent variable and is also correlated with your independent variable, then you've excluded relevant variables from your model and have introduced bias into your estimated coefficients.

Adding season dummy variables to your regression allows you to pick up the seasonal co-movement of your variables and therefore make more convincing arguments about the causal relationship between your independent variables (Xs) and dependent variable (Y).

If you have a situation where seasonal effects are likely, then you should estimate a model like

$$Y_t = \beta_0 + \beta_1 X_{t1} + \beta_2 X_{t2} + \dots + \beta_p X_{tp} + \lambda_1 S_1 + \lambda_2 S_2 + \dots + \varepsilon_t$$

where X represents your independent variable and S is your season dummy variable.

Deseasonalizing time-series data

In many cases, seasonal patterns are removed from time-series data when they're released on public databases. Data that has been stripped of its seasonal patterns is referred to as *seasonally adjusted* or *deseasonalized* data.

In order to obtain a goodness-of-fit measure that isolates the influence of your independent variables, you must estimate your model with deseasonalized values for both your dependent and independent variables. Here's how to do just that:

1. **Regress your dependent variable on the seasonal dummy variables to obtain the estimated function $Y_t = \hat{\alpha}_0 + \hat{\alpha}_1 S_1 + \hat{\alpha}_2 S_2 + \dots + \hat{\varepsilon}_{tY}$ and retain the residuals from this regression.**

2. **Regress each of your independent variables on the seasonal dummy variables to obtain the estimated functions $X_{tk} = \hat{\alpha}_{0k} + \hat{\alpha}_{1k} S_1 + \hat{\alpha}_{2k} S_2 + \dots + \hat{\varepsilon}_{tX_k}$, where k represents a specific independent variable, and retain the residuals from all k of these regressions.**

3. **Regress the residuals obtained in Step 1 ($\hat{\varepsilon}_{tY}$) on the residuals obtained in Step 2 ($\hat{\varepsilon}_{tX_k}$) to estimate $\hat{\varepsilon}_{tY} = \beta_0 + \beta_1 \hat{\varepsilon}_{tX_k} + u_t$.**

   The R-squared from this regression provides a better measure of fit when the time series exhibits considerable seasonality.

The traditional R-squared can be overinflated when the data contains significant seasonal patterns. If you encounter this situation, simply estimate a regression with deseasonalized data to find an alternative R-squared value.

Figure 15-5 uses STATA to estimate the impact of log monthly unemployment and a time trend on the log of souvenir sales between 1987 and 1993. I first estimate the model with the raw data, and then I estimate the model with deseasonalized data. I exclude the output for the intermediate steps to save space. As expected, the R-squared is smaller after the data is deseasonalized (0.9106 compared to 0.9539), but the difference isn't big. The coefficient estimates for the unemployment and trend variables are similar in both regressions, so the results imply that the role of the independent variables isn't affected by seasonal patterns.

```
. regress lnSales lnUnemp trend Feb Mar Apr May Jun Jul Aug Sep Oct Nov Dec
```

Source	SS	df	MS			Number of obs =	84
Model	49.4253891	13	3.801953			F(13, 70) =	111.40
Residual	2.38911119	70	.03413016			Prob > F =	0.0000
						R-squared =	0.9539
						Adj R-squared =	0.9453
Total	51.8145002	83	.624271087			Root MSE =	.18474

lnSales	Coef.	Std. Err.	t	P>|t|	[95% Conf.	Interval]
lnUnemp	-.1875467	.1386878	-1.35	0.181	-.4641508	.0890575
trend	.0238746	.0013805	17.29	0.000	.0211213	.0266279
Feb	.2563634	.0988315	2.59	0.012	.0592503	.4534766
Mar	.6924055	.0987856	7.01	0.000	.4953839	.8894271
Apr	.3722607	.0990965	3.76	0.000	.174619	.5699025
May	.3927384	.0994487	3.95	0.000	.1943943	.5910825
Jun	.423019	.1004122	4.21	0.000	.2227532	.6232848
Jul	.5832443	.1005876	5.80	0.000	.3826287	.7838598
Aug	.5598828	.1007014	5.56	0.000	.3590402	.7607255
Sep	.6465078	.100059	6.46	0.000	.4469465	.8460691
Oct	.7127969	.1016965	7.01	0.000	.5099696	.9156242
Nov	1.168791	.1022867	11.43	0.000	.9647869	1.372796
Dec	1.941815	.0999125	19.44	0.000	1.742546	2.141084
_cons	10.08174	1.83247	5.50	0.000	6.426995	13.73649

```
. regress lnSales Feb Mar Apr May Jun Jul Aug Sep Oct Nov Dec

. predict elnSales, resid

. regress lnUnemp Feb Mar Apr May Jun Jul Aug Sep Oct Nov Dec

. predict elnUnemp, resid

. regress trend Feb Mar Apr May Jun Jul Aug Sep Oct Nov Dec

. predict etrend, resid

. regress elnSales elnUnemp etrend
```

Source	SS	df	MS			Number of obs =	84
Model	24.324359	2	12.1621795			F(2, 81) =	412.34
Residual	2.3891112	81	.0294952			Prob > F =	0.0000
						R-squared =	0.9106
						Adj R-squared =	0.9084
Total	26.7134702	83	.321849039			Root MSE =	.17174

elnSales	Coef.	Std. Err.	t	P>|t|	[95% Conf.	Interval]
elnUnemp	-.1875467	.1289273	-1.45	0.150	-.4440715	.0689782
etrend	.0238746	.0012834	18.60	0.000	.0213211	.0264281
_cons	1.09e-09	.0187386	0.00	1.000	-.0372838	.0372838

Figure 15-5: STATA time-series output from estimating a deseasonalized model.

Econometricians mainly estimate the regression model with deseasonalized data to derive the explanatory power of the other independent variables. Your primary econometric results, however, should report the estimates from the model with the raw data and season dummy variables.

Chapter 16

Diving into Pooled Cross-Section Analysis

. . . .

In This Chapter

▶ Understanding the nature of pooled cross-sectional data

▶ Revealing the flexibility of pooled cross-section econometric analysis

▶ Estimating treatment or policy effects using the difference-in-difference estimator

. . . .

A pooled cross section combines independent cross-sectional data that has been collected over time. For example, the Current Population Survey collects independent cross-sectional data by surveying 60,000 randomly selected households in the United States each month. Combining or merging CPS data collected over many years into one dataset gives you a pooled cross section.

The advantage of pooled cross-sectional data is that more observations tend to improve the accuracy of econometric estimates, and the added time element allows you to explore dynamic adjustment (how your outcome of interest, or Y variable, responds to factors as they change over time). In this chapter, I show you how you can modify traditional econometric estimation techniques to handle pooled cross-sectional data and how this type of analysis can be particularly useful in examining changing relationships between variables and evaluating policy changes that occur at a specific point in time.

Adding a Dynamic Time Element to the Mix

Unlike typical cross-section analysis, which imposes a static nature to your models, a pooled cross section allows you to incorporate a dynamic time element. You can do this with a pooled cross section because cross-sectional units are observed in two or more periods.

Typically, pooled cross sections contain many more cross-sectional observations than the number of time periods being pooled. Consequently, the models usually resemble cross-sectional analysis with possible heteroskedasticity corrections (I cover heteroskedasticity in Chapter 11). Because the time gap between the collection of cross-sectional units is usually large (anywhere from one year to several years apart), autocorrelation and other time-series issues tend to be ignored (for details on autocorrelation, see Chapter 12).

It's not uncommon to confuse a pooled cross section with a panel dataset. Both contain cross-sectional measurements in multiple periods, but in a panel dataset the same cross-sectional units are included in each time period rather than being randomly selected in each period.

In the following sections, you see how pooled cross-sectional data can allow you to identify more complex relationships between your dependent and independent variables. In addition, I show you how to construct and estimate models that allow you to fully exploit the richness of pooled cross-sectional data.

Examining intercepts and/or slopes that change over time

With pooled cross-sectional data, the population distribution from which the random samples are drawn may change over time.

If you use a pooled cross section, you'll want to examine potential time effects. If you ignore these time effects, you may obtain biased estimates of your regression coefficients.

One possibility is that a changing population distribution results in different intercepts and/or slopes over time. In Figure 16-1, I illustrate how accounting for a changing intercept may be important with pooled cross-sectional data. If you don't account for time effects, you obtain the sample regression line 1A (with a biased estimate of the intercept). However, accounting for time allows you to identify lines 1B and 1C.

Time can also influence the impact of your independent variable on the dependent variable by altering the magnitude of the slope, as I show in Figure 16-2. If you ignore time effects, you'll end up with line 2A. Regression line 2A has heteroskedasticity (a topic I discuss in Chapter 11) and, more importantly, a biased estimate of the slope (impact of the independent variable). By accounting for time effects, you can identify lines 2B and 2C, which appropriately estimate the slope.

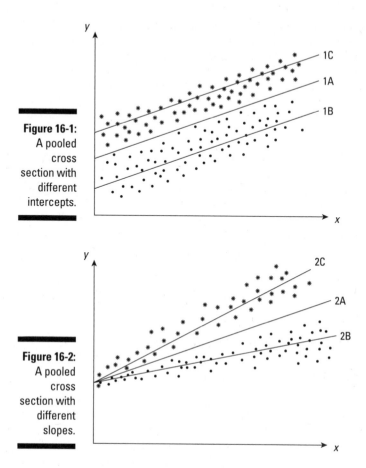

Figure 16-1: A pooled cross section with different intercepts.

Figure 16-2: A pooled cross section with different slopes.

Incorporating time dummy variables

You can account for a changing distribution of the population over time by using time-period dummy variables. Specifically, you can say that these variables take on a value of 1 for a given time period and 0 otherwise. (For the scoop on regular dummy variables, turn to Chapter 9.) Including dummy variables in your model for each time period, except the *reference period* (usually the first or last period of the pooled cross sections), allows you to identify changing parameter values.

TIP

You can tell whether the population distribution has changed by observing different intercepts and/or slopes.

The basic model utilizing pooled cross-sectional data is specified as

$$Y_i = \beta_0 + \beta_1 X_{i1} + \beta_2 X_{i2} + \ldots + \delta_1 R_{i1} + \delta_2 R_{i2} + \ldots + \varepsilon_i$$

where R represents the time period (1,2, ...) from which the cross-sectional observation was drawn. By examining the statistical significance of the estimated δ (or $\hat{\delta}$) terms, you can identify any shifts (whether up or down) in the relationship for a given period.

Adding time-period dummy variables interacted with the other independent variables allows you to identify both changing intercepts and slopes. If you have cross sections for two time periods — a quite common scenario — your model with dummies and interactions would be specified as

$$Y_i = \beta_0 + \beta_1 X_{i1} + \beta_2 X_{i2} + \ldots + \delta_0 R_i + \delta_1 (X_1 \cdot R)_i + \delta_2 (X_2 \cdot R)_i + \ldots + \varepsilon_i$$

where $(X_k \cdot R)$ represents the interaction of the independent X variable with the time period dummy variable. If you find that $\hat{\delta}_0$ is statistically significant, you have evidence that the function has shifted from one time period to the next. If any of the $\hat{\delta}_1$, $\hat{\delta}_2$, and so on are statistically significant, then the relationship between a particular X variable and the dependent variable changes over time.

If you're interested in any distributional change that may have occurred in your population of interest between time periods, you can perform an F-test of joint significance for all the δ (δ_0, δ_1, δ_2, ...) parameters (I discuss tests of joint significance in Chapter 7). Essentially, this test identifies whether the time period has a collective influence on the intercept and/or impact of the independent variables. It's equivalent to performing a Chow test for structural stability (I cover the Chow test in Chapter 8).

In Figure 16-3, I illustrate how you can create a pooled cross section in STATA. The data is compiled using two random samples of workers from the Current Population Survey (CPS) in 2010 and 2011. After you collect multiple cross sections with the same variables, especially one that captures the time period from which the cross section was drawn, you can use the "append" command in STATA to pool the cross sections. For males between the ages of 16 and 25, I'm interested in the impact of age on labor force participation. I use STATA to estimate a model using a time period dummy variable and its interaction with the age variable.

For ease of interpretation, I estimate a linear probability model (flip to Chapter 13 for full details on this type of model). The results suggest that young males were about 40 percent more likely to be in the labor force in 2011 compared to 2010. This has shifted the labor force participation rate up. In addition, the interaction coefficient implies that the relationship between age and labor-force participation has changed; an additional year of age is associated with 0.07 probability (7 percent) increase of labor force participation in 2010, but a 0.05 (0.07 – 0.02) probability (5 percent) increase in 2011. The *F*-test of joint significance for the time dummy variable and its interaction with the age variable is equivalent to a Chow test. In this case, the result rejects the null hypothesis of structural stability ($F = 70.47$, *p*-value < 0.01), so the relationship between the dependent and independent variables changed significantly over the time span covered by the data.

```
. use "/Research/Econometrics for Dummies/ExampleData/morg10-ch17.dta"

. append using "/Research/Econometrics for Dummies/ExampleData/morg11-ch17.dta"

. tab year

        year │      Freq.     Percent        Cum.
   ──────────┼───────────────────────────────────
        2010 │    321,277       56.19       56.19
        2011 │    250,447       43.81      100.00
   ──────────┼───────────────────────────────────
       Total │    571,724      100.00

. gen yr2011=year==2011

. keep if male==1 & (age>=16 & age<=25)
(525448 observations deleted)

. gen ageXyr2011=age*yr2011

. regress inlabforce age yr2011 ageXyr2011

      Source │       SS           df       MS            Number of obs =    46276
   ──────────┼──────────────────────────────          F(  3, 46272) =  2715.13
       Model │  1611.52886        3   537.176287          Prob > F      =   0.0000
    Residual │  9154.70027    46272   .197845355          R-squared     =   0.1497
   ──────────┼──────────────────────────────          Adj R-squared =   0.1496
       Total │  10766.2291    46275   .232657572          Root MSE      =    .4448

  inlabforce │      Coef.   Std. Err.      t    P>|t|     [95% Conf. Interval]
   ──────────┼────────────────────────────────────────────────────────────
         age │   .0729431   .0009406    77.55   0.000     .0710996    .0747867
      yr2011 │   .3998289   .0351295    11.38   0.000     .3309746    .4686832
  ageXyr2011 │  -.0180107   .0016542   -10.89   0.000    -.0212529   -.0147685
       _cons │  -.8923129   .0193273   -46.17   0.000    -.9301947   -.8544312

. test yr2011 ageXyr2011

 ( 1)  yr2011 = 0
 ( 2)  ageXyr2011 = 0

       F(  2, 46272) =   70.47
            Prob > F =   0.0000
```

Figure 16-3: A STATA regression output with pooled cross-sectional data and time-period controls.

Using Experiments to Estimate Policy Effects with Pooled Cross Sections

Empirical researchers in the areas of labor, health, development, and other fields of economics are increasingly relying on pooled cross-sectional data for their analyses. Generally, if your interests are in any area of economics where policy evaluation is important, you'll probably want to introduce a time element into your analysis.

Measuring variables over a period of time and from a randomly selected group of observations enables you to quantify before and after outcomes. Then you can estimate the impact of policies that were implemented at some point in between the first period and the last period you observe the variables.

Experiments allow researchers to observe the impact of specific conditions by manipulating an independent variable. Because economists are often interested in how policies affect economic outcomes, experiments can be useful mechanisms to quantify *policy* (or *treatment*) *effects*. Two types of experiments exist: true experiments and natural (also known as quasi) experiments. The next sections tell you more about each type.

Benefitting from random assignment: A true experiment

In a *true experiment*, subjects are randomly assigned to two (or more) groups. One group from your population of interest is randomly assigned to the control group, and the remainder is assigned to the treatment group(s). With random assignment, you can estimate the policy (treatment) effect by calculating the average difference between the treatment and control groups, holding other independent influences constant.

The econometric specification to identify a treatment effect in a true experiment is

$$Y_i = \beta_0 + \beta_1 X_i + \beta_2 G_i + \varepsilon_i$$

where X captures the influence of factors unrelated to being in the treatment group and G is a dummy variable equal to 1 if the observation was subject to a specific policy (or treatment) and 0 otherwise. Consequently, $\hat{\beta}_2$ would estimate the average treatment (policy) effect on outcome Y.

In the model $Y_i = \beta_0 + \beta_1 X_i + \beta_2 G_i + \varepsilon_i$, the expected value of the treatment is as follows:

$$E(Y|G=1) - E(Y|G=0)$$
$$\left[\beta_0 + \beta_1 E(X|G=1) + \beta_2\right] - \left[\beta_0 + \beta_1 E(X|G=0)\right]$$

Note: In a true experiment, the $E(X)$ isn't affected by selection into the treatment group because subjects are randomly assigned, so $E(Y|G=1) - E(Y|G=0) = \beta_2$.

If conditions of a true experiment are present, you can estimate policy effects by adding a dummy variable to your econometric model that identifies the group who is subject to the new policy. If you're using a pooled cross section and a new policy was implemented in between the time the two cross sections were obtained, then a time period dummy can be used to identify the groups.

Working with predetermined subject groups: A natural (or quasi) experiment

In a *natural* (or *quasi*) *experiment,* subjects aren't randomly assigned to treatment and control groups. Instead, membership of subjects into their respective groups is determined by conditions outside your control. If placement into a treatment group isn't random, the estimation of policy (treatment) effects requires that you control for systematic differences between subjects in the control group and those in the treatment group.

In Figure 16-4, I illustrate a plausible scenario differentiating subjects from the control and treatment groups.

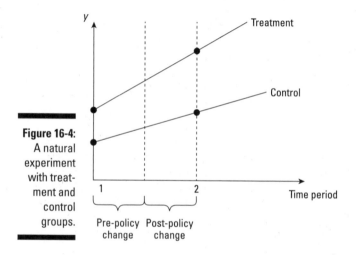

Figure 16-4: A natural experiment with treatment and control groups.

Subjects are usually observed at specific points in time (Period 1 and Period 2) with the first observation period occurring before the policy change and the subsequent observation period occurring after the policy change.

Some of the difference between the treatment and control groups post-policy change is preexisting. Without the randomization of a true experiment, subjects with certain characteristics may be more likely to belong to the treatment or control group. Additionally, another component of the post-policy change difference between the groups is a general trend.

In order to properly identify the policy effect, you need to difference out both preexisting differences between the groups and time-period effects. Consequently, the commonly accepted identification of policy effects is known as *difference-in-difference* (D-in-D).

In Figure 16-5, I decompose the difference between the treatment and control groups to illustrate the policy effect. Note that the policy effect must account for differences in the control and treatment groups as well as the impact of time itself.

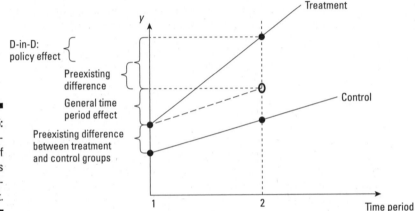

Figure 16-5: A decomposition of differences to find policy effect.

You can estimate the policy effect directly with pooled cross-sectional data and an econometric model specified as

$$Y_i = \beta_0 + \beta_1 G_i + \beta_2 R_i + \beta_3 (G \cdot R)_i + \varepsilon_i$$

where G equals 1 if the subject is in the control group and 0 if it isn't, R equals 1 if the subject was observed in the second period and 0 otherwise, and $(G \cdot R)$ is the interaction between G and R (I fill you in on interaction terms in Chapter 9). In this model, β_3 is the D-in-D parameter capturing the policy effect.

In Table 16-1, I use the parameters from the model $Y_i = \beta_0 + \beta_1 G_i + \beta_2 R_i + \beta_3 (G \cdot R)_i + \varepsilon_i$ to show how this specification identifies the policy (D-in-D) effect.

Table 16-1 Difference-in-Difference Econometric Model

	Before (Period 1)	After (Period 2)	After – Before (Period 2 – Period 1)
Control Group	β_0	$\beta_0 + \beta_2$	β_2
Treatment Group	$\beta_0 + \beta_1$	$\beta_0 + \beta_1 + \beta_2 + \beta_3$	$\beta_2 + \beta_3$
Treatment – Control	β_1	$\beta_1 + \beta_3$	β_3

If you want to measure a policy effect, you can do so by estimating one econometric model and focusing on one coefficient $(\hat{\beta}_3)$.

In applied settings, you can modify the basic D-in-D econometric model to control for other characteristics that may vary systematically across subjects. In a typical scenario, your D-in-D model will have the form $Y_i = \beta_0 + \beta_1 G_i + \beta_2 R_i + \beta_3 (G \cdot R)_i + \beta_4 X_i + \ldots + \varepsilon_i$, where X represents additional control variables that augment the basic D-in-D model.

In Figure 16-6, I illustrate how you can create a pooled cross section in STATA and estimate a D-in-D model. You collect multiple cross sections with the same variables, especially ones that capture the time period from which the cross section was drawn. Then you can use the "append" command in STATA to pool the cross sections. In this example, I look at the impact of increasing the minimum wage on labor-force participation for males between the ages of 16 and 25. Using a pooled cross section of the Current Population Survey (CPS) from 2010 and 2011, I can identify a control group where there was no change in the minimum wage (the state of Indiana) and a treatment group where there was a change in the minimum wage (the state of Illinois).

I estimate a linear probability model so the results are easy to interpret. (Check out Chapter 13 for info on these models.) The results suggest that young males in Illinois and Indiana were about 6 percent more likely to be in the labor force in 2011 compared to 2010, holding other factors constant. The labor-force participation rate shifted up. In addition, for every additional year of age, young males in these states increase their probability of labor force participation by 0.08 (8 percent). Finally, the D-in-D estimator of –0.09 implies that the policy change (increased minimum wage in Illinois) was associated with a decrease in labor force participation among young men.

```
. use "/Research/Econometrics for Dummies/ExampleData/morg10-ch17.dta"

. append using "/Research/Econometrics for Dummies/ExampleData/morg11-ch17.dta"

. tab year

    year |     Freq.    Percent      Cum.
---------+---------------------------------
    2010 |   321,277      56.19     56.19
    2011 |   250,447      43.81    100.00
---------+---------------------------------
   Total |   571,724     100.00

. gen yr2011=year==2011

. keep if male==1 & (age>=16 & age<=25)
(525448 observations deleted)

. keep if state==32 | state==33
(44135 observations deleted)

. gen treatment=state==33

. gen treatXyr2011=treatment*yr2011

. regress inlabforce age yr2011 treatment treatXyr2011
```

Source	SS	df	MS
Model	94.4617072	4	23.6154268
Residual	417.665336	2136	.195536206
Total	512.127043	2140	.239311703

Number of obs = 2141
F(4, 2136) = 120.77
Prob > F = 0.0000
R-squared = 0.1844
Adj R-squared = 0.1829
Root MSE = .44219

inlabforce	Coef.	Std. Err.	t	P>|t|	[95% Conf.	Interval]
age	.0776738	.0036316	21.39	0.000	.0705519	.0847956
yr2011	.0606339	.0353527	1.72	0.086	-.0086954	.1299632
treatment	.011574	.02775	0.42	0.677	-.0428458	.0659939
treatXyr2011	-.09384	.0420265	-2.23	0.026	-.1762571	-.0114229
_cons	-1.012548	.0756678	-13.38	0.000	-1.160939	-.8641581

Figure 16-6: STATA output of a difference-in-difference model.

Although the model in Figure 16-6 controls for age, the model could be expanded to control for other factors that may differ systematically between the years, including education, marital status, and many other potential characteristics. However, that expansion wouldn't change how you estimate the D-in-D (policy effect) or interpret the results.

Chapter 17

Panel Econometrics

• •

In This Chapter

▶ Reducing bias by using panel data

▶ Understanding the difference between fixed effects and random effects estimation

▶ Using the Hausman test results to choose the appropriate panel model

• •

*L*ike pooled cross-sectional data (which I cover in Chapter 16), *panel (or longitudinal) data* also includes both cross-sectional and time-series dimensions. The fundamental difference is that the identical cross-sectional units (individuals, firms, cities, countries, and so on) are included in each time period during which data are collected rather than randomly selecting a cross-sectional group in each time period. Examples of well-known panel datasets include the National Longitudinal Surveys (NLS), the Panel Study of Income Dynamics (PSID), and the Survey of Income and Program Participation (SIPP).

In this chapter, you discover how panel econometric analysis helps you deal with the elusive omitted variable problem that can be present in both cross-sectional and time-series regression analysis. You also see how software can be used to implement these procedures and appropriately deal with the special challenges that arise with panel-data analysis.

Estimating the Uniqueness of Each Individual Unit

One of the strengths of panel data is that it permits analysis of important economic questions that can't be addressed using data that are exclusively cross sectional or time series. By utilizing repeated information on the individual entities being investigated, you can control for the effects of some missing or unobserved variables. The things you don't observe can be important factors determining your outcome of interest, so dealing with this form of omitted variable bias can be a huge benefit of panel data.

An *observable variable* can be something like age, education, or anything that's typically identified in surveys. An *unobservable variable* can be an individual's work ethic, natural ability, or any information that's not easily obtained when data is collected.

Suppose the model that explains your outcome of interest is

$$Y_{it} = \beta_0 + \beta_1 X_{it} + \beta_2 w_{it} + \varepsilon_{it}$$

where $i = 1,\ldots, n$ represents the cross-sectional unit beginning with the first individual unit (1) and proceeding to the last (n), $t = 1,\ldots, T$ captures the time period in which the subject is observed beginning with the first time period (1) and proceeding to the last (T), X is an observable independent variable, and w is an unobservable independent variable.

The danger with combining panel data and OLS estimation is that you may end up with results containing *heterogeneity bias*. This bias occurs if you ignore characteristics that are unique to your cross-sectional units (relegate those things to the error term) and they're correlated with any of your independent variables (see Chapter 8 for a deeper look at omitted variable bias). The direction of the bias can be difficult to predict and is usually revealed only after you've appropriately handled systematic differences between your cross-sectional units (individual heterogeneity).

In Figures 17-1, 17-2, and 17-3, I illustrate some examples of heterogeneity bias resulting from ignoring individual fixed effects. In each of the figures, the slopes of lines A, B, and C represent the estimated impact of X on Y. However, in order to properly identify these lines, you need to account for the individual units that are represented in the panel data. If the panel is treated like a pooled cross section and you don't take measures to control for individual fixed effects, you run the risk of obtaining biased estimates of the relationship between X and Y. The lines labeled with a D identify the pooled (and biased) OLS estimates.

- ✔ In Figure 17-1, the pooled OLS estimate (line D) results in an overestimate of the impact of X on Y, as illustrated by the parallel lines A, B, and C.

- ✔ In Figure 17-2, the pooled OLS estimate (line D) results in an underestimate of the impact of X on Y, as illustrated by the parallel lines A, B, and C.

- ✔ In Figure 17-3, the pooled OLS results (line D) generate a negative estimated impact of X on Y when, as illustrated by the parallel lines A, B, and C, the effect is actually positive.

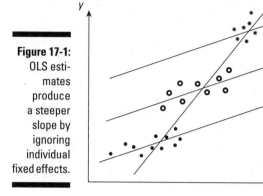

Figure 17-1:
OLS esti-
mates
produce
a steeper
slope by
ignoring
individual
fixed effects.

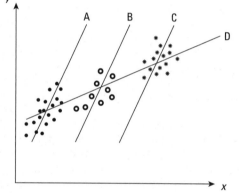

Figure 17-2:
OLS esti-
mates
produce a
flatter slope
by ignoring
individual
fixed effects.

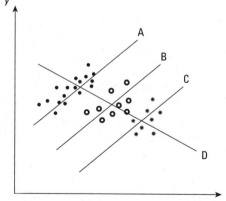

Figure 17-3:
OLS esti-
mates are in
the wrong
direction
because
individual
fixed effects
are ignored.

The existence of unobservable factors that consistently impact your outcome of interest (Y variable) is likely with panel data, which means you need to consider using one of three estimation methods (I tell you about each one in the following sections):

- ✔ First difference (FD) transformation
- ✔ Dummy variable (DV) regression
- ✔ The fixed effects (FE) estimator (the method most commonly used by applied econometricians)

First difference (FD) transformation

With panel data, you can deal with unobservable variables by applying a first difference (FD) to the data. To transform the data into an FD, you subtract the previous value of a variable from the current value of that variable for a particular cross-sectional unit and repeat the process for all variables in the analysis.

After you perform an FD transformation, you can estimate the model using OLS with all the first-differenced data. Doing so eliminates (differences out) any fixed effects associated with the cross-sectional units, even if those characteristics aren't observable. Repeated observations for the same entities allow you to get rid of the effect of unobservable factors only if those characteristics are constant over time for each entity.

In order to use the FD approach, I rely on a couple of assumptions. First, I assume that the values for the unobserved variable remain constant through time for a given subject, but vary across subjects; $w_{it} = w_i\ \forall t$, which means that w_{it} is equal to w_i for all values of t. Second, I assume that the model doesn't change over time; $Y_{it} = \beta_0 + \beta_1 X_{it} + \beta_2 w_{it} + \varepsilon_{it}$ and $Y_{it-1} = \delta_0 + \beta_1 X_{it-1} + \beta_2 w_{it-1} + \varepsilon_{it-1}$. After I establish these two assumptions, I can take the first difference (FD) of individual observations over time and obtain

$$(Y_{it} - Y_{it-1}) = (\beta_0 - \delta_0) + \beta_1(X_{it} - X_{it-1}) + \beta_2(w_{it} - w_{it-1}) + (\varepsilon_{it} - \varepsilon_{it-1})$$

$$\Delta Y_i = \alpha_0 + \beta_1 \Delta X_i + \Delta \varepsilon_i$$

where Δ denotes change and the unobserved variable (w) has been differenced away.

Dummy variable (DV) regression

If you have panel data, the simplest approach in estimating your model is to pool all the years of data and apply ordinary least squares (OLS) so that you're essentially ignoring the panel nature of the data. (I explain model estimation with pooled cross-sectional data in Chapter 16.) In that case, your model would look something like

$$Y_{it} = \beta_0 + \beta_1 X_{it} + v_{it}$$

where $v_{it} = w_i + \varepsilon_{it}$. The v_{it} term is known as the *composite error* because it contains individual fixed effects and an idiosyncratic error. The *individual fixed effects* are unobservable factors associated with the individual subjects, whereas the *idiosyncratic error* represents a truly random element associated with a particular subject at a specific point in time.

One way to account for individual fixed effects is by using the *dummy variable* (DV) regression. You apply this approach by including dummy variables in your model for each cross-sectional unit, making it a straightforward extension to the basic use of dummy variables that I cover in Chapter 9.

Panel data is a necessary prerequisite for estimating a DV model. With cross-sectional data, this approach leads you to defining a dummy variable for every observation. Consequently, you exhaust all your degrees of freedom and end up with meaningless results.

A model that explicitly accounts for individual fixed effects can be specified as $Y_{it} = \alpha_{i0} + \beta X_{it} + \varepsilon_{it}$, where α_{i0} is a unique intercept for each individual (the *i*th cross-sectional unit). More generally, a DV model can be represented as

$$Y_{it} = \sum_{i=1}^{n} \alpha_{i0} A_i + \sum_{k=1}^{p} \beta_k X_{it,k} + \varepsilon_{it}$$

where $A = 1$ for any observation that pertains to individual i and 0 otherwise.

If your data contains a large number of individuals (cross-sectional units), which is quite common with panel data, then the DV approach can be computationally burdensome (even for a computer) and impractical. A better alternative to this approach is the fixed effects (FE) estimator, which I describe in the next section.

Fixed effects (FE) estimator

The most common method of dealing with fixed effects of cross-sectional units is known as the *fixed effects (FE) estimator*. FE estimation is applied by *time demeaning* the data. In other words, you calculate the average value of a variable over time for each cross-sectional unit and subtract this mean from all observed values of a given cross-sectional unit, repeating the procedure for all the cross-sectional units. Demeaning deals with unobservable factors because it takes out any component that is constant over time. By assumption, that would be the entire amount of the unobservable variable.

Because the FE estimator is the most common method for dealing with individual fixed effects among applied econometricians, most econometrics software packages have a specific command that automatically performs the demeaning transformation of the data, properly calculates the degrees of freedom, and appropriately adjusts the standard errors.

For FE estimation, you must first specify the model as

$$\left(Y_{it} - \bar{Y}_i\right) = \beta_1\left(X_{it} - \bar{X}_i\right) + \beta_2\left(w_{it} - \bar{w}_i\right) + \left(\varepsilon_{it} - \bar{\varepsilon}_i\right)$$

$$\tilde{Y}_{it} = \beta_1 \tilde{X}_{it} + \tilde{\varepsilon}_{it}$$

where

$$\bar{Y}_i = \frac{\sum_{t=1}^{T} Y_{it}}{T}$$

$$\bar{X}_i = \frac{\sum_{t=1}^{T} X_{it}}{T}$$

$$\bar{w}_i = \frac{\sum_{t=1}^{T} w_{it}}{T}$$

and β_1 is known as the *fixed effects estimator* (or *within estimator*). The unobservable variable (w) has been demeaned away because the values are assumed constant over time. Finally, I place the ~ above the other variables to note they've been transformed into their time-demeaned versions (also called the *within transformation*).

You may be tempted to calculate the degrees of freedom with FE estimation using the traditional (OLS) calculation (total number of observations minus the number of estimated parameters), but be careful! First, notice that you don't have an intercept to work with. And remember that you lose one degree of freedom for each cross-sectional observation from demeaning. Consequently, the correct formula for calculating the degrees of freedom is $nT - n - p$, where n is the number of cross-sectional units, T is the number of time periods, and p is the number of independent variables.

Typically, FE models also include *time effect* controls. You can add them by adding dummy variables for each time period in which cross-sectional observations were obtained. With time effects, you capture anything that may affect all cross-sectional units equally, on average, at a specific point in time.

In Figure 17-4, I illustrate how you estimate an FE model in STATA. The data consists of a sample of workers from the 1997 National Longitudinal Survey of Youth (NLSY). The same individuals are observed for ten years (1997–2006), but I use only those who were between 18 and 25 years of age at the time of the first interview (1997). In order to utilize STATA's panel econometrics tools, I first use the "xtset" command to declare the data as panel and tag the variables that identify cross-sectional units and time periods. After I execute the "xtset" command, STATA can make any calculations relevant for estimation, including the time demeaning necessary for FE. For my subsample of workers, I'm interested in the impact of education on the natural log of wages. I use STATA to estimate OLS and FE models. For the FE model, I have to use the "xtreg" command and specify the "fe" option rather than use the standard "regress" or "reg" commands.

```
. xtset id year
       panel variable:  id (unbalanced)
        time variable:  year, 1997 to 2006, but with gaps
               delta:  1 unit

. regress lnhrwage yrseduc
```

Source	SS	df	MS
Model	283.011204	1	283.011204
Residual	16518.6761	43728	.377759698
Total	16801.6873	43729	.384222993

Number of obs = 43730
F(1, 43728) = 749.18
Prob > F   = 0.0000
R-squared   = 0.0168
Adj R-squared = 0.0168
Root MSE   = .61462

lnhrwage	Coef.	Std. Err.	t	P>|t|	[95% Conf.	Interval]
yrseduc	.039993	.0014611	27.37	0.000	.0371291	.0428568
_cons	1.601599	.0191661	83.56	0.000	1.564033	1.639165

```
. xtreg lnhrwage yrseduc, fe
```

Fixed-effects (within) regression
Group variable: **id**

Number of obs   = 43730
Number of groups = 8518

R-sq: within = 0.0370
       between = 0.0142
       overall = 0.0168

Obs per group: min = 1
                avg = 5.1
                max = 9

corr(u_i, Xb) = -0.2373

F(1,35211)   = 1351.68
Prob > F   = 0.0000

lnhrwage	Coef.	Std. Err.	t	P>|t|	[95% Conf.	Interval]
yrseduc	.0870681	.0023682	36.77	0.000	.0824263	.0917099
_cons	.9914059	.0308022	32.19	0.000	.9310326	1.051779
sigma_u	.4251403					
sigma_e	.53154302					
rho	.39013856	(fraction of variance due to u_i)				

F test that all u_i=0:   F(8517, 35211) =   2.73   Prob > F = 0.0000

Figure 17-4:
Using panel data to estimate an OLS and FE model in STATA.

As you can see in Figure 17-4, the impact of education is larger with FE than with OLS. An additional year of education increases wages by 4 percent with the OLS estimates and increases wages by 8.7 percent with the FE estimates (I discuss the interpretation of coefficients with the log-linear specification in Chapter 8). Consequently, the OLS results underestimate the impact of education by ignoring unobserved individual heterogeneity.

Increasing the Efficiency of Estimation with Random Effects

If you have panel data, your econometric model can explicitly estimate the unobserved effects associated with your cross-sectional unit using the fixed effects (FE) model: $Y_{it} = \beta_0 + \beta_1 X_{it} + \beta_2 w_{it} + \varepsilon_{it}$, where $w_{it} = w_i$ are unobserved characteristics for each cross-sectional unit that don't vary over time. (I explain how to estimate this model in the preceding section.) On the other hand, your econometric model can allow all unobserved effects to be relegated to the error term by specifying the model as

$$Y_{it} = \beta_0 + \beta_1 X_{it} + v_{it}$$

where $v_{it} = w_i + \varepsilon_{it}$. This approach is known as the *random effects (RE) model* and is the focus of this section.

With panel data, the advantage of the RE model over the FE model is more efficient estimates of the regression parameters. The RE technique doesn't estimate the fixed effects separately for each cross-sectional unit, so you get fewer estimated parameters, increased degrees of freedom, and smaller standard errors.

The composite error term and assumptions of random effects model

As with other types of estimation methods, the legitimacy of using the RE technique to estimate your model $Y_{it} = \beta_0 + \beta_1 X_{it} + v_{it}$ rests on the characteristics of its error term $v_{it} = w_i + \varepsilon_{it}$. The error term in a RE model is known as the *composite error term* because it combines two components. This term was also used in the previous section (where you learn about the fixed effects model), but the random effects model requires that you pay more attention to the specific components of the error term:

> ✔ The unobserved effects associated with each particular cross-sectional unit (w_i)
>
> ✔ A completely random element that isn't associated with the cross-sectional units (ε_{it})

A critical assumption of the RE model is that the unobserved individual effect (w_i) isn't correlated with the independent variable(s); $Cov(X_{it}, w_i) = 0$. If the individual effect is correlated with the independent variable(s), then the RE estimate is biased.

The assumption that the individual effects aren't correlated with the independent variable(s) doesn't imply that the individual effects are identical for every observation. Rather, it implies that their values are random (some negative and some positive) with no association with the observed values of the independent variable(s). Therefore, the individual effects are appropriately captured by the intercept term; $E(w_i \mid X_i) = \beta_0$. In addition, for the homoskedasticity assumption to hold, you must also impose a constant variance on the individual effects; $Var(w_i \mid X_i) = \sigma_w^2$ (I cover the homoskedasticity assumption in detail in Chapter 11).

The random effects (RE) estimator

If you have panel data and believe that variable Y depends on variable X, then you may be tempted to estimate the model $Y_{it} = \beta_0 + \beta_1 X_{it} + v_{it}$ using OLS. However, your results would be flawed because OLS ignores the unique nature of the error term. The composite error term (v_{it}) is $v_{it} = w_i + \varepsilon_{it}$. Although ε_{it} satisfies the classical linear regression model (CLRM) assumptions, the inclusion of w_i in the composite error results in a CLRM assumption violation. (For a refresher on the CLRM assumptions, see Chapters 6 and 7.)

If you relegate the individual effects (w_i) to the error term, you create positive serial correlation in the composite error. It occurs because individual cross-sectional units with positive errors in one period are also likely to have positive errors in other periods, and vice versa. As a result, RE estimation requires feasible generalized least squares (FGLS) rather than OLS to appropriately eliminate serial correlation in the error term and to produce the correct standard errors and test statistics. (To find out more about FGLS, turn to Chapter 12.)

The serial correlation in the composite error of a RE model is

$$Corr(v_{it}, v_{is}) = \frac{\sigma_w^2}{\sigma_w^2 + \sigma_\varepsilon^2}$$

where $\sigma_w^2 = Var(w_i)$ and $\sigma_\varepsilon^2 = Var(\varepsilon_{it})$. The generalized least squares (GLS) transformation is performed by first defining the parameter

$$\lambda = 1 - \sqrt{\frac{\sigma_\varepsilon^2}{\sigma_\varepsilon^2 + T\sigma_w^2}}$$

where T is the number of time periods in the panel and $0 \le \lambda \le 1$. Then λ is used to produce the GLS transformation

$$Y_{it} - \lambda\bar{Y}_i = \beta_0(1-\lambda) + \beta_1(X_{it} - \lambda\bar{X}_i) + (v_{it} - \lambda\bar{v}_i)$$

where

$$\bar{Y}_i = \frac{\sum_{t=1}^{T}Y_{it}}{T}$$

$$\bar{X}_i = \frac{\sum_{t=1}^{T}X_{it}}{T}$$

$$\bar{v}_i = \frac{\sum_{t=1}^{T}v_{it}}{T}$$

The transformed error term no longer contains serial correlation.

In practice, the value of λ isn't known, so the transformation relies on its estimate ($\hat{\lambda}$). Replacing λ with $\hat{\lambda}$ results in the FGLS random effects estimator. Econometric software usually supports RE estimation by internally calculating $\hat{\lambda}$ and automatically producing the estimated β terms.

In an RE model, your independent variables can include individual characteristics that don't vary over time (such as gender and race) because they won't be differenced away as they are in the FE model. In addition, RE models are also likely to include *time-effect controls* — added dummy variables for each time period in which cross-sectional observations were obtained. With time effects, you capture anything that may affect all cross-sectional units equally, on average, at a specific point in time.

In Figure 17-5, I illustrate how you estimate an RE model in STATA using data on a sample of workers from the 1997 National Longitudinal Survey of Youth (NLSY). Specifically, I'm focusing on those individuals who were between 18 and 25 years of age at the time of the first interview. To make sure I can use the STATA panel econometrics tools, I first use the "xtset" command to declare the data as panel and tag the variables that identify cross-sectional units and time periods. I execute the "xtset" command, and then STATA can internally perform any calculations relevant for estimation, including adjustments for serial correlation necessary for RE. For my subsample of workers, I want to know the impact of education on the natural log of wages. I use STATA to estimate OLS and RE models. For the RE model, I must use the "xtreg" command and specify the "re" option instead of using the standard "regress" or "reg" commands.

```
. xtset id year
       panel variable:  id (unbalanced)
        time variable:  year, 1997 to 2006, but with gaps
                delta:  1 unit

. regress lnhrwage yrseduc
```

Source	SS	df	MS				Number of obs =	43730
							F(1, 43728) =	749.18
Model	283.011204	1	283.011204				Prob > F =	0.0000
Residual	16518.6761	43728	.377759698				R-squared =	0.0168
							Adj R-squared =	0.0168
Total	16801.6873	43729	.384222993				Root MSE =	.61462

lnhrwage	Coef.	Std. Err.	t	P>|t|	[95% Conf.	Interval]
yrseduc	.039993	.0014611	27.37	0.000	.0371291	.0428568
_cons	1.601599	.0191661	83.56	0.000	1.564033	1.639165

```
. xtreg lnhrwage yrseduc, re
```

Random-effects GLS regression			Number of obs =	43730
Group variable: **id**			Number of groups =	8518

R-sq: within = 0.0370			Obs per group: min =	1
between = 0.0142			avg =	5.1
overall = 0.0168			max =	9

			Wald chi2(1) =	1114.54
corr(u_i, X) = 0 (assumed)			Prob > chi2 =	0.0000

lnhrwage	Coef.	Std. Err.	z	P>|z|	[95% Conf.	Interval]
yrseduc	.0579394	.0017355	33.38	0.000	.0545379	.0613409
_cons	1.363473	.0227878	59.83	0.000	1.31881	1.408136
sigma_u	.31219387					
sigma_e	.53154302					
rho	.25648485	(fraction of variance due to u_i)				

Figure 17-5: Using panel data to estimate an OLS and RE model in STATA.

Figure 17-5 clearly shows that the impact of education is larger with RE than with OLS. An additional year of education increases wages by 4 percent with the OLS estimates but increases wages by 5.7 percent with the RE estimates (I discuss the interpretation of coefficients with the log-linear specification in Chapter 8). Consequently, the OLS results underestimate the impact of education by ignoring serial correlation in the error term.

Testing Efficiency against Consistency with the Hausman Test

In practice, data can always surprise you with a failure of what appear to be even the most rational assumptions. Additionally, you may not even be able to make a strong case for the sensibility of an assumption. A particularly good example of this is assuming the individual fixed effects in an RE model aren't correlated with the independent variable(s). For example, in a wage model, you may include an individual's education as an independent variable along with other measurable human capital and specific job traits while relegating the unobserved individual characteristics to the error term. This approach may be sensible, but it's also possible that natural ability, work ethic, and other individual fixed effects are correlated with occupational choices and the tendency to acquire human capital.

The RE model produces more efficient estimates than the FE model. However, if individual fixed effects are correlated with the independent variable(s), then the RE estimates will be biased. In that case, the FE estimates would be preferred. The Hausman test checks the RE assumptions and helps you decide between RE and FE estimation.

A *Hausman test* examines differences in the estimated parameters, and the result is used to determine whether the RE and FE estimates are significantly different. The null hypothesis of the Hausman test is that if the assumptions of the RE model hold, then the RE model produces the same estimated parameters as the FE model but they're better (meaning they have more efficiency or smaller standard errors). If the RE assumptions don't hold, then the estimated parameters are significantly different and the RE estimates contain bias. This result is the alternative hypothesis of the Hausman test. If you fail to reject the null hypothesis in a Hausman test, you use the RE estimates. On the other hand, if you reject the null hypothesis in a Hausman test, using the FE estimates as the alternative hypothesis implies that the FE estimates are consistent.

If heteroskedasticity is present, the Hausman test results could be misleading. The solution involves estimating an auxiliary regression that includes all the variables from your original model with an additional set of variables (defined as time averages of all your time-varying independent variables). After estimating this auxiliary regression, you perform a joint test of significance on the coefficients of those additional variables (I cover joint hypothesis tests for subsets of independent variables in Chapter 7). If you fail to reject the null hypothesis that the coefficients are simultaneously zero, then you use the RE estimates. If you reject the null hypothesis, you use the FE estimates.

In a model with one independent variable, the Hausman test statistic is defined as

$$H = \frac{\left(\hat{\beta}_{1(FE)} - \hat{\beta}_{1(RE)}\right)^2}{\sigma^2_{\hat{\beta}_{1(FE)}} - \sigma^2_{\hat{\beta}_{1(RE)}}} \sim \chi^2_1$$

where $\hat{\beta}_1$ is the estimated coefficient for the independent variable, $\sigma^2_{\hat{\beta}_1}$ is the estimated variance of the coefficient, and *FE* and *RE* subscripts denote the values were obtained, respectively, by fixed effects and random effects estimation. The distribution of the test statistic is chi-squared with 1 degree of freedom. The general idea can be extended to models with more than one independent variable (*p* degrees of freedom), but that requires matrix algebra. Fortunately, STATA (and some other econometric software) allows you to perform a Hausman test without any manual calculations or matrix operations.

To see a Hausman test run on real data, check out Figure 17-6. In this case, I took data from the 1997 National Longitudinal Survey of Youth (NLSY) and used STATA's "xtset" command in order to classify the data as panel and tag the variables identifying cross-sectional units and time periods. Now I can use STATA to estimate FE and RE models to better gauge the impact of education on the natural log of wages. As you can see in Figure 17-6, the impact of education is larger with FE than with RE. A difference in the estimated coefficients, however, isn't enough to ensure that I should rely on the FE estimates. I also need to take into account the standard errors of the estimates. The Hausman test accounts for both differences in the estimated parameters and their standard errors. In this case, it confirms that I should reject the assumptions of the RE model (with a large chi-squared value and low *p*-value) and use the FE estimates.

```
. xtset id year
       panel variable:  id (unbalanced)
        time variable:  year, 1997 to 2006, but with gaps
                delta:  1 unit

. xtreg lnhrwage yrseduc, fe

Fixed-effects (within) regression              Number of obs      =      43730
Group variable: id                             Number of groups   =       8518

R-sq:  within  = 0.0370                         Obs per group: min =          1
       between = 0.0142                                        avg =        5.1
       overall = 0.0168                                        max =          9

                                                F(1,35211)         =    1351.68
corr(u_i, Xb)  = -0.2373                         Prob > F           =     0.0000
```

lnhrwage	Coef.	Std. Err.	t	P>|t|	[95% Conf.	Interval]
yrseduc	.0870681	.0023682	36.77	0.000	.0824263	.0917099
_cons	.9914059	.0308022	32.19	0.000	.9310326	1.051779
sigma_u	.4251403					
sigma_e	.53154302					
rho	.39013856	(fraction of variance due to u_i)				

```
F test that all u_i=0:     F(8517, 35211) =     2.73                Prob > F = 0.0000

. estimates store fixedeffects

. xtreg lnhrwage yrseduc, re

Random-effects GLS regression                  Number of obs      =      43730
Group variable: id                             Number of groups   =       8518

R-sq:  within  = 0.0370                         Obs per group: min =          1
       between = 0.0142                                        avg =        5.1
       overall = 0.0168                                        max =          9

                                                Wald chi2(1)       =    1114.54
corr(u_i, X)   = 0 (assumed)                     Prob > chi2        =     0.0000
```

lnhrwage	Coef.	Std. Err.	z	P>|z|	[95% Conf.	Interval]
yrseduc	.0579394	.0017355	33.38	0.000	.0545379	.0613409
_cons	1.363473	.0227878	59.83	0.000	1.31881	1.408136
sigma_u	.31219387					
sigma_e	.53154302					
rho	.25648485	(fraction of variance due to u_i)				

```
. hausman fixedeffects
```

Figure 17-6:
Using
STATA to
perform a
Hausman
test after
estimating
FE and RE
models.

	Coefficients			sqrt(diag(V_b-V_B))
	(b) fixedeffects	(B) .	(b-B) Difference	S.E.
yrseduc	.0870681	.0579394	.0291287	.0016114

```
                                    b = consistent under Ho and Ha; obtained from xtreg
                                    B = inconsistent under Ha, efficient under Ho; obtained from xtreg

                      Test:  Ho:  difference in coefficients not systematic

                             chi2(1) = (b-B)'[(V_b-V_B)^(-1)](b-B)
                                     =      326.78
                          Prob>chi2 =      0.0000
```

Part VII
The Part of Tens

the
part of
tens

Visit www.dummies.com/extras/econometrics to discover ten practical applications of what you're spending so much time studying. You may be intrigued — and even motivated — by what you see.

In this part . . .

- Understand the core components of an econometrics project, whether that project is a 15- to 30-page paper, a presentation, or a combination of a paper and a presentation.

- Keep the basic elements of sound econometric analysis in mind so you can avoid committing the most common mistakes in applied econometrics.

Chapter 18

Ten Components of a Good Econometrics Research Project

*I*n some econometrics courses, a research project may consist of writing a paper that's anywhere from 15 to 30 pages in length (including references, tables, and graphs). In other cases, your econometrics professor may expect you to give a presentation on a research topic in combination with (or instead of) writing a paper. No matter what the specifics of your class assignment, you'll probably be expected to come up with a topic, collect data, use econometrics software to complete the analysis, and interpret your findings. That sounds like a lot, but this chapter breaks down the ten components you need to include in any econometrics research project.

Introducing Your Topic and Posing the Primary Question of Interest

The first paragraphs of your research paper should provide an interesting description of your topic. This section is important because it either captures your readers' attention or bores them right from the start.

Econometrics uses models and data for the purpose of shedding light on economic puzzles. When you choose a topic and write an explanation of it, make sure you're clear about the purpose of your study and how it's important beyond the exhibition of your quantitative skills.

The introductory section of your research project should include the following two components, in this order:

- ✔ **Explanation of the topic:** Provide some interesting background information about your topic and then describe the question that's addressed by the research.

- ✔ **Description of your approach:** Provide a clear description of your population of interest and how it's represented in your sample data. Also, describe how you analyze the data and why you chose the approach you describe. Keep this description brief, because you discuss the details of the empirical approach and specific data issues in subsequent sections of the research project.

Discussing the Relevance and Importance of Your Topic

The introductory section of the paper should also motivate the subject so that readers appreciate the importance of the topic and your findings.

The first paragraph of your introductory section should provide a basic explanation of your research question to spark the reader's interest (see the preceding section), and you should follow it up in the second paragraph with a more profound argument for the importance and relevance of the topic. For example, does your work challenge a long-held belief in economics and is, therefore, grounded in theory? Is the research question new, based on your interests, and empirically driven? Do the results have potential policy implications? If you can't answer "yes" to at least one of these questions, then you'll need to carefully explain why the use of econometrics is essential to addressing your research question. This section of your research is important because it gets readers to understand the importance of the topic and care about your results.

Reviewing the Existing Literature

Other researchers are likely to have examined the topic of your paper (or something closely related), so one section of your paper should review other research on the topic. The length of this section depends on the amount of previous research that's been completed on your topic, but you should plan on about two to four pages of literature review. This section should be placed immediately after introducing the topic and briefly describing your contribution in the introduction, but before you begin getting into the details of your model and data.

In your literature-review section, focus on summarizing, highlighting the strengths, and pointing out the weaknesses of prior research. Unless the goal of your work is to replicate or update an existing study with new data, you probably want to focus on one of the weaknesses in the prior literature that you intend your own econometric work to address.

In your literature review, refrain from using Internet, newspaper, or magazine sources. Instead, keep the focus of your reading and review of papers to those published in scholarly journals. Save the popular press sources, such as newspaper and magazine articles, for motivating the topic (in the introductory section) or providing closure (in the concluding section).

Here are some sources for finding other econometricians' work you can reference:

- ✔ Google Scholar (scholar.google.com) lets you search by keyword.

- ✔ Social Science Research Network (www.ssrn.com) contains a repository of working papers with the latest research findings.

- ✔ Websites of economics journals that are likely to have published papers on your topic may offer free articles.

- ✔ Economic Journals on the web (http://www.oswego.edu/~economic/journals.htm) provides a list of economic journals.

- ✔ EconLit (www.aeaweb.org/econlit/) lists sources of economic research and is available through most electronic resources of university libraries.

Describing the Conceptual or Theoretical Framework

One of the characteristics that differentiates applied research in econometrics from other applications of statistical analysis is a theoretical structure supporting the empirical work. In other words, the theoretical structure from your knowledge of economics is emphasized in econometrics (and should justify the connection between your dependent and independent variables) rather than focus only on the statistical fit between variables.

By tapping into your vast stores of common sense and using solid economic theory, you can come to methodical conclusions about which variables are independent and can be used to explain your outcome of interest. When explaining the theoretical structure of your analysis, be sure to clearly explain the rationale behind the variables you use.

Using a theoretical framework before estimating models (the mathematical functions representing the relationship between your variables) means that you should think carefully about the process generating your outcome of interest. In particular, you should provide justification for the variables that you're including in the analysis. Models that provide this rationale are considered to be well specified (you can learn more about model specification by turning to Chapter 8).

Explaining Your Econometric Model

After you develop the theoretical structure of your model, you need to connect that with your empirical approach (that is, your method of statistical analysis and observation), which is formally known as your *econometric model*.

Economic theory guides your choice of dependent and independent variables. At this point, however, you should explain and justify any specification characteristics of the econometric model (logs, quadratic functions, qualitative dependent variables, and so on) that aren't directly addressed by the conceptual framework. This can be achieved with intuition, scatter plots, and/ or conventions derived by researchers in previously published work. Also, be sure to explain any notation that may not be familiar to readers and define the elements of the model (specific variables and any transformations).

You can help your readers follow your analysis if you highlight the components of the model that specifically address your research question. If there are contesting theories (economists may have different views about which variables should be included in the analysis and/or how they're related to each other), then you should explain whether this implies that you could end up with different estimates of the relationship between the variables in one model or if you should estimate more than one model.

Discussing the Estimation Method(s)

Because estimation usually assumes that certain statistical conditions hold, going from your econometric model to estimation may not be entirely straightforward.

Estimation problems arising from a failure of one (or more) of the classical linear regression model (CLRM) assumptions are common in applied econometric research. (I introduce you to these assumptions in Chapter 6.) If the empirical model has potential problems — such as multicollinearity or heteroskedasticity — you should describe the source, discuss how your results may be affected, and explain how you'll address the complications.

Most estimation problems have universally accepted solutions (for example, using maximum likelihood to estimate a probit model with a qualitative dependent variable), but you should plan on devoting at least one paragraph and up to a page to a discussion of the specific estimation methods used in your paper.

It's usually a good idea to estimate your model using OLS to obtain baseline results, even if you ultimately decide to use a different estimation technique. You may find that the results are similar and OLS is the easiest to interpret.

Providing a Detailed Description of Your Data

Your econometric results are only as good the data used to estimate your model(s).

Give a thorough description of the data you use. Address these issues:

- ✔ How the dataset was acquired and its source(s)
- ✔ The nature of the data (cross sectional, time series, or panel)
- ✔ The time span covered by the data
- ✔ How and with what frequency the data was collected
- ✔ The number of observations present
- ✔ Whether any observations were thrown out and why
- ✔ Summary statistics (means, standard deviations, and so on) for any variables used in your econometric model(s)

Approximately one paragraph of your research paper should describe the content of the data and convince readers that its use is sensible for your research question. In an additional paragraph or two, use quantitative summary statistics to persuade readers that the data is reliable and of high quality.

If this section of your research project adequately addresses these questions, readers will feel more comfortable about any subsequent conclusions that result from the econometric analysis.

You can also use an appendix table (placed after your references) to list variable names, define variables, and list your data sources. This can save space in the body of your paper.

Constructing Tables and Graphs to Display Your Results

Most econometric research projects involve estimating numerous variations of related models. After you choose which results are most important and relevant to addressing your research question, you need to organize them in a concise manner.

A useful table typically contains estimates from several different yet related models. It can help convince readers that your results are robust, or it can lead into a discussion about why they're sensitive to changes in specification (you can learn all about robustness and sensitivity analysis in Chapter 8). Although concise tables of the model estimates are no substitute for a good discussion of the results in the text, they allow readers to see all the variables and variations of your model while quickly assessing the results. Many of the papers that you use in your literature review contain good examples for structuring your tables.

Never report your econometric results with a display of the output from your econometrics software. Instead, summarize your results in organized tables and/or graphs. A number of table-generating commands are available in STATA, including "estout," "tabout," and "outreg2." The programs to execute these functions can be downloaded into your version of STATA by typing "findit *command name*" or "help *command name*" on the command line.

Interpreting the Reported Results

Readers may lose track of details regarding the specification of your econometric model, the scale of the variables, and other aspects that influence how your results should be interpreted.

Reporting your econometric results is not enough; you also need to decipher the results for your readers. The most important element in the discussion of your results is the evaluation of statistical significance and magnitude for the primary variables of interest (the ones most important in addressing the research question). Some of your variables may be more difficult to understand (because, for example, they're measured in logs, or the model is nonlinear), so you need to provide an interpretation of the coefficient estimates for your readers. This discussion should include an explanation of magnitude, directionality (positive/negative effects), statistical significance, and the relationship with the research question and theoretical hypotheses posed earlier in your paper.

If you faced any additional issues when estimating your econometric model, you should also discuss these problems. Try to be specific about how your results may be affected and why you weren't able to address these issues with your econometric methodology.

Summarizing What You Learned

The conclusion of your research project should synthesize your results and explain how they're connected to your primary question.

When you summarize your work, begin by explaining what you did in your analysis. Then discuss what you discovered and the implications of those discoveries. Finally, express some limitations of your research (without being too critical) and make some suggestions for future research on the topic.

Be sure to avoid these common mistakes when drawing your conclusions:

- **Focusing on variables with coefficients that are statistically significant even when the magnitude of their effect on the dependent variable is negligible (nearly no effect):** After you establish that a variable is statistically significant, focus your attention on the coefficient. A variable's impact is important if it is both statistically significant and associated with a significant magnitude. Sometimes variables have coefficients that are highly statistically significant, but there's no economic significance associated with the result because, in an economic sense, the magnitude is close to zero or has no discernible impact.

- **Ignoring variables with statistically insignificant coefficients:** Sometimes the most important finding in a research project is that a variable doesn't have a statistically significant coefficient. In some cases, economic theory or the prevailing wisdom has suggested that a specific relationship (positive or negative) would exist between your independent and dependent variables. If you discover that two variables have no statistically significant relationship, that finding itself is potentially important. It could suggest that the existing theory is flawed or that there are limitations with the empirical analysis of the research question. Either way, these results shouldn't be immediately dismissed.

Chapter 19

Ten Common Mistakes in Applied Econometrics

*I*t's no coincidence that you have to take introductory economics, intermediate economic theory, and statistics courses before taking econometrics courses. Avoiding mistakes when you do econometric analysis depends on your ability to apply knowledge you acquired before and during your econometrics class. However, when you're focusing on the technical skills that you have to master to use econometrics, you may lose sight of some of the basic elements that characterize sound econometric analysis. You can use this chapter's rundown of common pitfalls to help you improve your application of econometric analysis.

Failing to Use Your Common Sense and Knowledge of Economic Theory

One of the characteristics that differentiate applied research in econometrics from other applications of statistical analysis is the use of economic theory and common sense to motivate the connection between the independent and dependent variables.

In econometrics, you should be able to make a strong case for the independent variables (Xs) causing changes in the dependent variable (Y). You need sound theory and good common sense to justify your approach. Doing so allows you to provide a sensible interpretation of your results in addition to the typical measures of statistical significance and fit.

If the relationship between your dependent and independent variables isn't obvious, you need to explain the causal assumptions of your model.

Asking the Wrong Questions First

Getting obsessed with the technical details of estimating econometric models can be easy. However, you should always take a step back and ask yourself why you're doing what you're doing. Why will others find my topic interesting and important? Is the value of my dependent variable likely to be influenced by my independent variables in the same period, or should I be using lagged values for the independent variables? Can I explain why some variables are linear, others are in logs, and some are polynomials? You should ask yourself these types of questions before you estimate an econometric model, let alone before you deal with complications such as heteroskedasticity and autocorrelation.

Conceptual questions are more important to ask than technical ones.

Ignoring the Work and Contributions of Others

Failing to connect your work with that of others who have examined your research question or something closely related to it is a serious mistake. Understanding how others have dealt with similar issues can help you figure out which model to use, may yield refinements in your work, and allows readers to better understand the relevance of your topic.

In your literature review, focus on papers or segments of papers that are directly related to your work. Summarize the approach, data, and findings of other researchers. Finally, be clear about how your work fits in with what's already been done by others, what's been improved, and/or how new dimensions of the topic have been explored (I provide more details about this component of your work in Chapter 18).

Failing to Familiarize Yourself with the Data

Students often assume that the data they're working with is complete for all variables and that the reported information is accurate. You can reduce your chances of getting unwelcome surprises in your results by doing some exploratory work that includes descriptive statistics, line charts (for time-series data), frequency distributions, and even listings of some individual data values.

A number of undesirable outcomes can result from failing to get familiar with your analysis data. These three examples are perhaps the most common:

- **Variables you thought were measured continuously are actually in categories or groups.** For example, in some surveys, respondents are asked about their education level. When the data is made available to researchers, this information may be converted into years of education or codes may be used to place individuals into education categories (high school graduate, two-year college degree, and so on). If it's the latter, you need to create dummy variables before proceeding with estimation (you can learn how to deal with categorical data and create dummy variables in Chapter 9).

- **Measurements that you believed were real values are actually missing values.** In some datasets, missing values are given a code rather than left blank. For example, if a variable is measuring a respondent's age, you may see *998* or *999* for some observations. In that case, *998* may indicate the respondent didn't know the answer, and *999* may indicate that he or she refused to answer the question; you'd need to read the data codebook to find the precise meaning of such values (if the codebook isn't readily available, you may need to contact the data provider directly). In either case, the value should be treated as missing and recoded as such before you perform any estimation.

- **Data values that appear perfectly legitimate are actually censored values.** In some surveys, respondent confidentiality is maintained by limiting the value of certain variables. Respondent income, for example, may be "top-coded" at some value. If the respondent's income is above the limiting value, then the response is simply assigned the limiting value (you can find out how to deal with this type of data in your econometric analysis by reading Chapter 14).

Making It Too Complicated

The art of econometrics lies in finding the appropriate specification or functional form to model your particular outcome of interest. In many cases, however, theory can be vague about the specific elements of a model's specification.

Given the uncertainty of choosing the "perfect" specification, many applied econometricians make the mistake of overspecifying their models (meaning they include numerous irrelevant variables) or favor complicated estimation methods over more straightforward techniques. It can result in undesirable estimator properties and difficulty interpreting the meaning of the results.

Overspecification by including too many irrelevant variables in a regression model increases the standard errors of your coefficients and reduces the chances you'll find statistical significance. If theory and common sense aren't fairly conclusive about the hypothesized effect of a variable, it's probably best to refrain from including it. Overspecification can also manifest itself with complicated functional forms that aren't necessary to deal with theoretical concerns or data issues. Some functions may be more difficult to interpret and distract readers from the main point of the econometric analysis. Consequently, additional sophistication in your model should be introduced as necessary and not simply to exhibit your econometric skills. (I provide more details about overspecification in Chapter 8.)

Being Inflexible to Real-World Complications

The solutions or predictions derived by using economic theories use logical deduction and/or mathematical proof that usually rely on the *ceteris paribus* (all else constant) assumption. The data you use to test economic hypotheses, however, are derived from a world where agents (individuals, firms, or what have you) are engaged with their surrounding environment in ways that aren't likely to satisfy the *ceteris paribus* assumption because many of the variables defining their specific circumstances vary considerably from one observation to another.

Don't give up on a research question or a dataset because you can't obtain data for all the variables that you think are required to test a hypothesis. If you apply that criterion, no research question is ever appropriate and no dataset is ever good enough. In all likelihood, you'll need to use some *proxies* (variables that approximately measure what you'd ideally like to capture) and use econometric techniques to deal with any estimation issues (you can obtain some tips on how to describe your data in Chapter 19).

Typically, the data you acquire won't contain all the information structured in a way proposed by the theoretical model. Use proxies that seem appropriate and that others would find acceptable. Also, avoid forcing a particular dataset into estimation that isn't appropriate for the research question — for example, using aggregate, state-level data when the theory applies to individuals or using cross-sectional data when a time element is part of your story.

Looking the Other Way When You See Bizarre Results

Most econometric research projects contain estimation results for numerous variations of related models. You want to focus on your primary variables of interest (core variables), but make sure you examine all of your results. That means don't ignore unreasonable results (mostly insignificant estimates, coefficients with the wrong sign, and magnitudes that are too large) and proceed to reporting and interpretation. If some results don't pass a common-sense test, then the statistical tests are likely to be meaningless and may even indicate that you've made a mistake with your variables, the estimation technique, or both.

Address any estimation problems that lead to perverse results before you draw conclusions about your results. You should check the accuracy of your data, the completeness of the information, the construction of your variables, and the specification of your model (you can turn to Chapter 8 for more on specification issues). Correcting for estimation issues that are adversely affecting other estimates can drastically change your conclusions.

Obsessing over Measures of Fit and Statistical Significance

After you estimate an econometric model, focus your attention and guide the reader (if you're writing a research paper) to the results that are most relevant in addressing your research question.

The importance of your results shouldn't be determined on the basis of fit (R-squared values) or statistical significance alone. Sure, statistically insignificant coefficients suggest that your independent variable isn't likely to affect your dependent variable. However, if the lack of a relationship is new or unexpected, this finding may be significant! The importance of such a finding is that it may suggest that standard economic theory doesn't hold.

The primary finding in many of the best papers using econometrics involves findings of statistical insignificance. For example, some researchers find that increases in the minimum wage aren't related to changes in employment, despite the fact that many microeconomics textbooks use minimum wages as an example of a price floor that causes reductions in employment. In another area, some papers suggest that immigration doesn't have a significant effect on wages of native-born workers, even though the theoretical examples in labor economics textbooks usually suggest that wages would fall.

Forgetting about Economic Significance

You can use measures of statistical significance to determine which variables aren't likely to have an effect on the dependent variable, but you can't use them to determine which variables have a relevant effect.

After you've established that a variable is statistically significant, don't forget to focus your attention on the coefficient. Sometimes variables can have coefficients that are highly statistically significant even though no economic significance is associated with the result.

The most important element in the discussion of your results is the evaluation of statistical significance *and* magnitude for the primary variables of interest. If a variable has a statistically significant coefficient but the magnitude is too small to be of any importance, then you should be clear about its lack of economic significance.

Assuming Your Results Are Robust

In most cases, economic theory allows for a considerable amount of flexibility in determining the exact specification of the econometric model. You'll want to see if minor adjustments change your results.

Don't assume that only one econometric model can apply to your research question and that the results won't change with reasonable modifications to your specification. You want to perform robustness (or sensitivity) analysis to show that your model estimates aren't sensitive (are robust) to slight variations in specification.

The validity of your data, variable selection, and model specification are all enhanced with successful robustness checks. If you're not able to show any proof of this, readers will have doubts about your results and conclusions.

Appendix

Statistical Tables

• •

*T*his appendix includes tables that are commonly used for various hypothesis tests in econometric analysis. Hypothesis test results rely on a comparison of an appropriate test statistic with the critical value from a statistical table.

The Standard Normal Distribution

The standard normal table shows the right-tail probability (density) at various points along the standard normal distribution.

Table A-1			The Standard Normal Distribution						
z	*0.00*	*0.01*	*0.02*	*0.03*	*0.04*	*0.05*	*0.06*	*0.07*	*0.08*	*0.09*
0.0	0.5000	0.4960	0.4920	0.4880	0.4840	0.4801	0.4761	0.4721	0.4681	0.4641
0.1	0.4602	0.4562	0.4522	0.4483	0.4443	0.4404	0.4364	0.4325	0.4286	0.4247
0.2	0.4207	0.4168	0.4129	0.4090	0.4052	0.4013	0.3974	0.3936	0.3897	0.3859
0.3	0.3821	0.3783	0.3745	0.3707	0.3669	0.3632	0.3594	0.3557	0.3520	0.3483
0.4	0.3446	0.3409	0.3372	0.3336	0.3300	0.3264	0.3228	0.3192	0.3156	0.3121
0.5	0.3085	0.3050	0.3015	0.2981	0.2946	0.2912	0.2877	0.2843	0.2810	0.2776
0.6	0.2743	0.2709	0.2676	0.2643	0.2611	0.2578	0.2546	0.2514	0.2483	0.2451
0.7	0.2420	0.2389	0.2358	0.2327	0.2296	0.2266	0.2236	0.2206	0.2177	0.2148
0.8	0.2119	0.2090	0.2061	0.2033	0.2005	0.1977	0.1949	0.1922	0.1894	0.1867
0.9	0.1841	0.1814	0.1788	0.1762	0.1736	0.1711	0.1685	0.1660	0.1635	0.1611
1.0	0.1587	0.1562	0.1539	0.1515	0.1492	0.1469	0.1446	0.1423	0.1401	0.1379
1.1	0.1357	0.1335	0.1314	0.1292	0.1271	0.1251	0.1230	0.1210	0.1190	0.1170
1.2	0.1151	0.1131	0.1112	0.1093	0.1075	0.1056	0.1038	0.1020	0.1003	0.0985
1.3	0.0968	0.0951	0.0934	0.0918	0.0901	0.0885	0.0869	0.0853	0.0838	0.0823
1.4	0.0808	0.0793	0.0778	0.0764	0.0749	0.0735	0.0721	0.0708	0.0694	0.0681
1.5	0.0668	0.0655	0.0643	0.0630	0.0618	0.0606	0.0594	0.0582	0.0571	0.0559
1.6	0.0548	0.0537	0.0526	0.0516	0.0505	0.0495	0.0485	0.0475	0.0465	0.0455

(continued)

Table A-1 *(continued)*

z	0.00	0.01	0.02	0.03	0.04	0.05	0.06	0.07	0.08	0.09
1.7	0.0446	0.0436	0.0427	0.0418	0.0409	0.0401	0.0392	0.0384	0.0375	0.0367
1.8	0.0359	0.0351	0.0344	0.0336	0.0329	0.0322	0.0314	0.0307	0.0301	0.0294
1.9	0.0287	0.0281	0.0274	0.0268	0.0262	0.0256	0.0250	0.0244	0.0239	0.0233
2.0	0.0228	0.0222	0.0217	0.0212	0.0207	0.0202	0.0197	0.0192	0.0188	0.0183
2.1	0.0179	0.0174	0.0170	0.0166	0.0162	0.0158	0.0154	0.0150	0.0146	0.0143
2.2	0.0139	0.0136	0.0132	0.0129	0.0125	0.0122	0.0119	0.0116	0.0113	0.0110
2.3	0.0107	0.0104	0.0102	0.0099	0.0096	0.0094	0.0091	0.0089	0.0087	0.0084
2.4	0.0082	0.0080	0.0078	0.0075	0.0073	0.0071	0.0069	0.0068	0.0066	0.0064
2.5	0.0062	0.0060	0.0059	0.0057	0.0055	0.0054	0.0052	0.0051	0.0049	0.0048
2.6	0.0047	0.0045	0.0044	0.0043	0.0041	0.0040	0.0039	0.0038	0.0037	0.0036
2.7	0.0035	0.0034	0.0033	0.0032	0.0031	0.0030	0.0029	0.0028	0.0027	0.0026
2.8	0.0026	0.0025	0.0024	0.0023	0.0023	0.0022	0.0021	0.0021	0.0020	0.0019
2.9	0.0019	0.0018	0.0018	0.0017	0.0016	0.0016	0.0015	0.0015	0.0014	0.0014
3.0	0.0013	0.0013	0.0013	0.0012	0.0012	0.0011	0.0011	0.0011	0.0010	0.0010

t-Distribution

The t table shows the value associated with each one-tail and two-tail probability (α) for various degrees of freedom (df).

Table A-2   The *t*-Distribution

df \ α	0.10	0.05	0.025	0.01	0.005
	0.20	0.10	0.05	0.02	0.01
1	3.08	6.31	12.71	31.82	63.66
2	1.89	2.92	4.30	6.96	9.92
3	1.64	2.35	3.18	4.54	5.84
4	1.53	2.13	2.78	3.75	4.60
5	1.48	2.02	2.57	3.36	4.03
6	1.44	1.94	2.45	3.14	3.71
7	1.41	1.89	2.36	3.00	3.50
8	1.40	1.86	2.31	2.90	3.36

df\α	0.10	0.05	0.025	0.01	0.005
	0.20	0.10	0.05	0.02	0.01
9	1.38	1.83	2.26	2.82	3.25
10	1.37	1.81	2.23	2.76	3.17
11	1.36	1.80	2.20	2.72	3.11
12	1.36	1.78	2.18	2.68	3.05
13	1.35	1.77	2.16	2.65	3.01
14	1.35	1.76	2.14	2.62	2.98
15	1.34	1.75	2.13	2.60	2.95
16	1.34	1.75	2.12	2.58	2.92
17	1.33	1.74	2.11	2.57	2.90
18	1.33	1.73	2.10	2.55	2.88
19	1.33	1.73	2.09	2.54	2.86
20	1.33	1.72	2.09	2.53	2.85
21	1.32	1.72	2.08	2.52	2.83
22	1.32	1.72	2.07	2.51	2.82
23	1.32	1.71	2.07	2.50	2.81
24	1.32	1.71	2.06	2.49	2.80
25	1.32	1.71	2.06	2.49	2.79
26	1.31	1.71	2.06	2.48	2.78
27	1.31	1.70	2.05	2.47	2.77
28	1.31	1.70	2.05	2.47	2.76
29	1.31	1.70	2.05	2.46	2.76
30	1.31	1.70	2.04	2.46	2.75
40	1.30	1.68	2.02	2.42	2.70
60	1.30	1.67	2.00	2.39	2.66
120	1.29	1.66	1.98	2.36	2.62
∞	1.28	1.64	1.96	2.33	2.58

Chi-Squared Distribution

The chi-squared table shows the value associated with each right-tail probability (α) for various degrees of freedom (df).

Table A-3		The Chi-Squared Distribution			
df \ α	0.10	0.05	0.025	0.01	0.005
1	2.706	3.841	5.024	6.635	7.879
2	4.605	5.991	7.378	9.21	10.597
3	6.251	7.815	9.348	11.345	12.838
4	7.779	9.488	11.143	13.277	14.86
5	9.236	11.07	12.833	15.086	16.75
6	10.645	12.592	14.449	16.812	18.548
7	12.017	14.067	16.013	18.475	20.278
8	13.362	15.507	17.535	20.09	21.955
9	14.684	16.919	19.023	21.666	23.589
10	15.987	18.307	20.483	23.209	25.188
11	17.275	19.675	21.92	24.725	26.757
12	18.549	21.026	23.337	26.217	28.3
13	19.812	22.362	24.736	27.688	29.819
14	21.064	23.685	26.119	29.141	31.319
15	22.307	24.996	27.488	30.578	32.801
16	23.542	26.296	28.845	32	34.267
17	24.769	27.587	30.191	33.409	35.718
18	25.989	28.869	31.526	34.805	37.156
19	27.204	30.144	32.852	36.191	38.582
20	28.412	31.41	34.17	37.566	39.997
21	29.615	32.671	35.479	38.932	41.401
22	30.813	33.924	36.781	40.289	42.796
23	32.007	35.172	38.076	41.638	44.181
24	33.196	36.415	39.364	42.98	45.559
25	34.382	37.652	40.646	44.314	46.928
30	40.256	43.773	46.979	50.892	53.672
40	51.805	55.758	59.342	63.691	66.766
50	63.167	67.505	71.42	76.154	79.49
60	74.397	79.082	83.298	88.379	91.952
70	85.527	90.531	95.023	100.425	104.215
80	96.578	101.879	106.629	112.329	116.321
90	107.565	113.145	118.136	124.116	128.299
100	118.498	124.342	129.561	135.807	140.169

F-Distribution

The *F* table shows the right-tail critical *F*-values at the 5 percent level of significance for a specific number of degrees of freedom in the numerator (df_n) and denominator (df_d). **Note:** This table is a highly abridged version of an *F* table; your econometrics textbook should have a more complete version.

Table A-4			The *F*-Distribution ($\alpha = 0.05$)				
$df_d \backslash df_n$	**10**	**20**	**30**	**40**	**60**	**120**	**∞**
10	2.98	2.77	2.70	2.66	2.62	2.58	2.54
20	2.35	2.12	2.04	1.99	1.95	1.90	1.84
30	2.16	1.93	1.84	1.79	1.74	1.68	1.62
40	2.08	1.84	1.74	1.69	1.64	1.58	1.51
60	1.99	1.75	1.65	1.59	1.53	1.47	1.39
120	1.91	1.66	1.55	1.50	1.43	1.35	1.25
∞	1.83	1.57	1.46	1.39	1.32	1.22	1.00

Durbin-Watson d-Statistic

The Durbin-Watson *d* table shows the lower and upper bound values at the 5 percent level of significance for a specific number of estimated coefficients (independent variables plus the intercept, $p + 1$) and time periods (observations, *T*) in the data.

Table A-5			Durbin-Watson *d*-Statistic ($\alpha = 0.05$)				
$p + 1$	**2**		**3**		**4**		**5**	
T	d_l	d_u	d_l	d_u	d_l	d_u	d_l	d_u
25	1.2879	1.4537	1.2063	1.5495	1.1228	1.6540	1.0381	1.7666
26	1.3022	1.4614	1.2236	1.5528	1.1432	1.6523	1.0616	1.7591
27	1.3157	1.4688	1.2399	1.5562	1.1624	1.6510	1.0836	1.7527
28	1.3284	1.4759	1.2553	1.5596	1.1805	1.6503	1.1044	1.7473
29	1.3405	1.4828	1.2699	1.5631	1.1976	1.6499	1.1241	1.7426
30	1.3520	1.4894	1.2837	1.5666	1.2138	1.6498	1.1426	1.7386

(continued)

Table A-5 *(continued)*

p + 1	2		3		4		5	
T	d_l	d_u	d_l	d_u	d_l	d_u	d_l	d_u
31	1.3630	1.4957	1.2969	1.5701	1.2292	1.6500	1.1602	1.7352
32	1.3734	1.5019	1.3093	1.5736	1.2437	1.6505	1.1769	1.7323
33	1.3834	1.5078	1.3212	1.5770	1.2576	1.6511	1.1927	1.7298
34	1.3929	1.5136	1.3325	1.5805	1.2707	1.6519	1.2078	1.7277
35	1.4019	1.5191	1.3433	1.5838	1.2833	1.6528	1.2221	1.7259
36	1.4107	1.5245	1.3537	1.5872	1.2953	1.6539	1.2358	1.7245
37	1.4190	1.5297	1.3635	1.5904	1.3068	1.6550	1.2489	1.7233
38	1.4270	1.5348	1.3730	1.5937	1.3177	1.6563	1.2614	1.7223
39	1.4347	1.5396	1.3821	1.5969	1.3283	1.6575	1.2734	1.7215
40	1.4421	1.5444	1.3908	1.6000	1.3384	1.6589	1.2848	1.7209
41	1.4493	1.5490	1.3992	1.6031	1.3480	1.6603	1.2958	1.7205
42	1.4562	1.5534	1.4073	1.6061	1.3573	1.6617	1.3064	1.7202
43	1.4628	1.5577	1.4151	1.6091	1.3663	1.6632	1.3166	1.7200
44	1.4692	1.5619	1.4226	1.6120	1.3749	1.6647	1.3263	1.7200
45	1.4754	1.5660	1.4298	1.6148	1.3832	1.6662	1.3357	1.7200
46	1.4814	1.5700	1.4368	1.6176	1.3912	1.6677	1.3448	1.7201
47	1.4872	1.5739	1.4435	1.6204	1.3989	1.6692	1.3535	1.7203
48	1.4928	1.5776	1.4500	1.6231	1.4064	1.6708	1.3619	1.7206
49	1.4982	1.5813	1.4564	1.6257	1.4136	1.6723	1.3701	1.7210
50	1.5035	1.5849	1.4625	1.6283	1.4206	1.6739	1.3779	1.7214

Index

• •

• *S* •

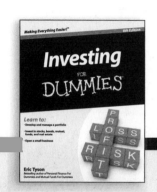
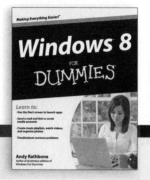

Math & Science

Algebra I For Dummies,
2nd Edition
978-0-470-55964-2

Anatomy and Physiology
For Dummies,
2nd Edition
978-0-470-92326-9

Astronomy For Dummies,
3rd Edition
978-1-118-37697-3

Biology For Dummies,
2nd Edition
978-0-470-59875-7

Chemistry For Dummies,
2nd Edition
978-1-1180-0730-3

Pre-Algebra Essentials
For Dummies
978-0-470-61838-7

Microsoft Office

Excel 2013 For Dummies
978-1-118-51012-4

Office 2013 All-in-One
For Dummies
978-1-118-51636-2

PowerPoint 2013
For Dummies
978-1-118-50253-2

Word 2013 For Dummies
978-1-118-49123-2

Music

Blues Harmonica
For Dummies
978-1-118-25269-7

Guitar For Dummies,
3rd Edition
978-1-118-11554-1

iPod & iTunes
For Dummies,
10th Edition
978-1-118-50864-0

Programming

Android Application
Development For
Dummies, 2nd Edition
978-1-118-38710-8

iOS 6 Application
Development For Dummies
978-1-118-50880-0

Java For Dummies,
5th Edition
978-0-470-37173-2

Religion & Inspiration

The Bible For Dummies
978-0-7645-5296-0

Buddhism For Dummies,
2nd Edition
978-1-118-02379-2

Catholicism For Dummies,
2nd Edition
978-1-118-07778-8

Self-Help & Relationships

Bipolar Disorder
For Dummies,
2nd Edition
978-1-118-33882-7

Meditation For Dummies,
3rd Edition
978-1-118-29144-3

Seniors

Computers For Seniors
For Dummies,
3rd Edition
978-1-118-11553-4

iPad For Seniors
For Dummies,
5th Edition
978-1-118-49708-1

Social Security
For Dummies
978-1-118-20573-0

Smartphones & Tablets

Android Phones
For Dummies
978-1-118-16952-0

Kindle Fire HD
For Dummies
978-1-118-42223-6

NOOK HD For Dummies,
Portable Edition
978-1-118-39498-4

Surface For Dummies
978-1-118-49634-3

Test Prep

ACT For Dummies,
5th Edition
978-1-118-01259-8

ASVAB For Dummies,
3rd Edition
978-0-470-63760-9

GRE For Dummies,
7th Edition
978-0-470-88921-3

Officer Candidate Tests,
For Dummies
978-0-470-59876-4

Physician's Assistant Exa
For Dummies
978-1-118-11556-5

Series 7 Exam
For Dummies
978-0-470-09932-2

Windows 8

Windows 8 For Dummies
978-1-118-13461-0

Windows 8 For Dummies,
Book + DVD Bundle
978-1-118-27167-4

Windows 8 All-in-One
For Dummies
978-1-118-11920-4

ⓔ Available in print and e-book formats.

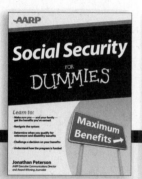